PENGUIN BOOKS

Healing Our History

Robert Consedine was raised in an Irish Catholic 'community' in the working-class Christchurch suburb of Addington. From his involvement with the civil-rights movement in the United States to international relief aid visiting of Third World countries, Robert has witnessed the struggle for human dignity in some of the most marginalised environments in the world. Jailed for two weeks for his involvement with the anti-Springbok tour protests of 1981, Robert was deeply affected by stories from Maori prisoners, stories reflecting every kind of dispossession: disconnection from family, land, language, culture, unemployment, abuse, violence, low self-esteem, and personal and institutional racism.

Subsequently, Robert and Trish Consedine with the support of a network of Maori and Pakeha were inspired to set up Waitangi Associates—an organisation that uses a combination of innovative educational strategies to assist the people of New Zealand in learning about and creatively confronting our colonial history.

Joanna Consedine grew up in an environment where she was aware from a young age about what constituted fairness and justice in the world. Her background inspired her to choose courses at university that deepened these values. Since completing her Bachelor of Arts with Honours (First class) (Major: Education) in 1995, she has worked as tutor of a work-based training programme, facilitating the unemployed and school leavers with no formal qualifications into further training and employment opportunities. Returning home to New Zealand after her OE, Joanna then undertook contract work for Waitangi Associates and is currently employed as a career consultant for Career Services *rapuara*.

What people said about the first edition

'Robert and Joanna Consedine have managed to be thoughtfully provocative . . . challenging and inclusive . . . using our history in all its shades and variety as a means of understanding where we are now and why'.

John Campbell, Radio New Zealand

'There have been many Treaty books adding fuel to the debate – this one adds light, not heat'.

Chris Bourke, *North and South*

'. . . this new book about the Treaty of Waitangi will offer many New Zealanders their first true understanding of the topic . . . it is a wonderful book. It is a very good read . . . it is well written'.

Prime Minister Helen Clark

'This book provides some genuinely important and much needed insight to advance justice, reconciliation and healing between Pakeha and Maori'.

Mike Riddell, *Tui Motu InterIslands*

'I hope . . . many more New Zealanders will read [this book] carefully and . . . come to an awareness of the history we have been denied'.

Emeritus Professor Ivan Snook

'Should more New Zealanders read this book [the authors] will have made a big contribution to the shaping of our future'.

Terry Hearn, *Otago Daily Times*

Healing Our History

The Challenge of
The Treaty of Waitangi

Robert Consedine &
Joanna Consedine

PENGUIN BOOKS

PENGUIN BOOKS

Published by the Penguin Group

Penguin Group (NZ), cnr Airborne and Rosedale Roads, Albany,
Auckland 1310, New Zealand (a division of Pearson New Zealand Ltd)
Penguin Group (USA) Inc., 375 Hudson Street,
New York, New York 10014, USA
Penguin Group (Canada), 10 Alcorn Avenue, Toronto,
Ontario, Canada M4V 3B2 (a division of Pearson Penguin Canada Inc.)
Penguin Books Ltd, 80 Strand, London, WC2R 0RL, England
Penguin Ireland, 25 St Stephen's Green,
Dublin 2, Ireland (a division of Penguin Books Ltd)
Penguin Group (Australia), 250 Camberwell Road, Camberwell,
Victoria 3124, Australia (a division of Pearson Australia Group Pty Ltd)
Penguin Books India Pvt Ltd, 11, Community Centre,
Panchsheel Park, New Delhi - 110 017, India
Penguin Books (South Africa) (Pty) Ltd, 24 Sturdee Avenue,
Rosebank, Johannesburg 2196, South Africa

Penguin Books Ltd, Registered Offices: 80 Strand, London,
WC2R 0RL, England

First published by Penguin Group (NZ), 2001
This edition published 2005
1 3 5 7 9 10 8 6 4 2

Designed by Mary Egan
Typeset by Egan-Reid Ltd
Printed in Australia by McPherson's Printing Group

ISBN 0 14 301986 4
A catalogue record for this book is available
from the National Library of New Zealand.

www.penguin.co.nz

In memory of a much-loved daughter, sister and friend
Suzanne Elizabeth Consedine
(1970–1993)
and

in memory of a loved friend, colleague and mentor
Dr Irihapeti Merenia Ramsden, NZOM
Ngai Tahu/Rangitane
(1946–2003)
and

in honour of
our Irish ancestors and indigenous peoples in their
centuries of struggle for justice

'Robert Consedine is an Irish Catholic from Christchurch keenly aware of the situation of Maori, ravaged by the impact of colonisation which brought Robert's forebears to New Zealand. We are all heirs to our histories and the challenge is whether we can learn from them and be reconciled and united.

'Robert has long been involved in Treaty of Waitangi workshops. He speaks of forgiveness, healing, acknowledging the pain of history, reparation and the restoration of right relationships. None is an easy option, but each is a necessary step towards a better New Zealand for all of us. This is a good book.'

Sir Paul Reeves

'I remember singing background vocals on the Australian Aboriginal group Yothu Yindi's song "Treaty". I felt proud at the time that at least New Zealand had a treaty. After reading *Healing Our History* I am reminded that we have no reason to feel smug. The theme, for Pakeha, of personal responsibility, to learn and apply the lessons of history, comes through loud and clear. Robert and Joanna Consedine contextualise our own story with stories from other places, allowing a breath of air into the argument.

'Frank Sargeson out of print. Ronald Hugh Morrieson out of print. Literary and historical amnesia spring from the same culture of forgetting. *Healing Our History* reminds us that for all the stories of duplicity, cruelty and ignorance, there may still be one place where poetry and politics can meet.'

Tim Finn

CONTENTS

ACKNOWLEDGEMENTS

Many people have generously shared their time, knowledge and resources to contribute to the writing and updating of this book. In particular we recognise Trish Consedine for her love and care of us during the process. We deeply appreciate Trish's unwavering support in creating the space for us to write and her technical competence in managing the manuscript, completing the bibliography and checking the seemingly endless footnotes!

Our heartfelt thanks to our friend and colleague Frances Hancock whose generosity of spirit, mentoring, editing and writing skills have assisted us in the crafting of this book. We also acknowledge her research contribution and remain grateful to her committed involvement from the book's inception.

We acknowledge with gratitude Sister Pauline O'Regan for her willingness to write the foreword to this book and for the wisdom she has gifted throughout the writing process.

We particularly acknowledge Irihapeti Ramsden (Ngai Tahu/ Rangitane), who died in 2003 and who was an adviser and mentor to the Waitangi Associates team for more than 10 years. Irihapeti and Robert had worked in a parallel process and co-facilitated in a variety of settings throughout New Zealand. Our team will always remember and appreciate her willingness to share her profound insights, knowledge, wisdom and professional feedback in an ongoing evaluation of our work.

We would like to thank those who read our draft text and provided us with valuable feedback and/or relevant research material. These include: Bernadette, Michael, James, Noel and Marie Consedine; Ivan Snook; Joe, Bernadette and Dara O'Hagan; gkisedtanamoogk and family; Sisters Teresa O'Connor, Helen Goggin, Marie McCrea and Monica Stack (deceased); Reverend Maurice Gray; Louise Tankersley; Father John O'Connor; Paul Moon; Jim McAloon; Paul Dalziel; Moana Jackson; Colin McGeorge; Murray Fastier; Carol Mutch; Jan Millar; Katherine Peet; Warren Lidstone; Ruth Millar; and Adrienne Alton-Lee.

A special thanks to John Truesdale for his constant technological support at any hour and assistance in physically producing the manuscript. John's skilful support of our work over many years is deeply appreciated.

We also remember our friends and colleagues John L'Estrange and Margot Hamblett. John died suddenly on 3 August 2000. His ability to integrate complex historical and contemporary issues around the Treaty debate, and his willingness to share his knowledge, was strongly valued by our team. John had read early drafts of this book and gave us valuable feedback. We appreciate and remember his contribution. Margot, who died on Waitangi Day, 6 February 2001, had a long involvement with and commitment to Treaty education. We miss her gentle presence.

Our deep gratitude to our friends and colleagues Suzanne McNabb, Trish O'Donnell and John Faisandier for their commitment to Treaty education and for working alongside us. We also acknowledge the inspiration and commitment of the networks of Treaty educators throughout New Zealand, including Project Waitangi, Churches Programme on Racism, the Rowan Partnership and Network Waitangi.

Our thanks to the many people in different organisations and community groups who have supported Treaty education workshops provided by Waitangi Associates over the years. In particular we acknowledge Paul Fitzharris, Lesley McTurk, Bruce Ross, Helen Matthews, Darlene Sanderson and Ronnie Joy Leah for their support of Treaty education workshops. We are grateful for your contributions and your willingness to endorse this Treaty education process.

To all our family and friends who supported us throughout the writing of the first edition of this book, we continue to feel blessed and extremely fortunate to have you all in our lives.

Updating this edition has been a challenge, given the environment of rapid change where the Treaty discourse is wide-ranging, vigorous and often very polarised. We want to thank Suzanne McNabb for her superb management of this process. We value her time, patience, energy and sense of humour!

We also acknowledge the generosity and expertise of Jim McAloon, Father Kevin Burns, Dr Kathie Irwin, Ruth Millar, Myra Kunowski, Brendon Hokowhitu, David Williams, Hirini Matunga, Sean Brosnahan and Bernadette Consedine for their support in providing updated research, checking factual information and/or assisting in the writing process.

We acknowledge Geoff Walker, Publishing Director of Penguin Books (NZ), for originally recognising the potential of this book and offering positive and encouraging feedback throughout the writing of it and also his ongoing support. We thank Rebecca Lal and the team at Penguin for their support in publishing this updated edition and remain grateful to our editor, Rachel Scott, for her continued skill, advice and support in the editorial process.

FOREWORD

The title of this book is significant. This is essentially a critique of colonisation in all its aspects, with special emphasis on the colonisation of New Zealand and the place of the Treaty of Waitangi in that process. Why then the title *Healing Our History*? The authors are claiming, quite correctly in my view, that only by facing the facts of history and accepting what they reveal about colonisation can we know true reconciliation with Maori. Truth is a necessary pre-requisite for the healing of broken relationships wherever we find them. But the indigenous people of New Zealand, and indeed of every other colonised country, are not looking to see us grovel. They have little patience with guilt, and they are offended by senti-mentality and the superficial apology (the act of contrition without a firm purpose of amendment). They would simply like to hear us acknowledge that what happened in the past did in fact happen. If after that, we say the word *sorry* and this is followed by reparation and commitment to a new relationship, it would have real meaning.

All this is not to say that nothing has been done in this matter in New Zealand. We have made a beginning in our act of amendment, but there is a long way to go. Legislation for justice is one thing, forming a spirit of justice in our hearts is quite another. Saint Paul never tired of teaching that the spirit is above the law and the law without love is dead.

Colonisation has done great harm to members of the human family. Some of it stemmed from greed, some from arrogance, some from pure ignorance. This book refuses to excuse the worst excesses of colonisation on the grounds of the social and political climate in which they were done. Too often the environmental context has been a rationale for excusing things that are inherently immoral. The defence of the indefensible institution of slavery is but one example of this. Evil is evil in any age. Nor does this book allow institutions such as the church to hide behind the claim that the injustices done in its name were due entirely to the weakness of its individual members. The evils of colonisation, as this book shows, were most often the result of injustices incorporated within official policies of both the state and the church. The punches have been pulled for far too long. The authors of this book show no inclination to pull them further!

Robert and Joanna Consedine are a father/daughter team to be reckoned with. They have written with the most conscientious attention to the facts and they have grounded it in careful research. They are Pakeha writing primarily for a Pakeha readership. They are convinced that until Pakeha bridge the knowledge gap about the Treaty of Waitangi and come to terms with the facts surrounding it neither Maori nor Pakeha can fully heal their relationship with each other. May this book make a very real contribution to the attainment of that goal. As Hamlet once said: 'Tis a consummation devoutly to be wished.'

Sister Pauline O'Regan, CBE

PREFACE

At the start of 2004 the leader of the Opposition National Party made a dramatic speech attacking alleged 'Maori privileges'. The speech attracted considerable public support. The Labour government moved quickly to reverse what was called 'race-based' Maori policy, and although the publicity died quite quickly, the issues did not.[1] A debate had begun in which the major political parties indulged in a level of explicit anti-Maori rhetoric primarily to shore up their political ratings. White privilege and authority were reasserted. Neither party had the courage to explain the purpose of the 'affirmative action' policies. Both have failed to inform New Zealanders about Maori rights. Indian activist and Booker Prize-winning author Arundhati Roy has issued a warning that is relevant for New Zealand politicians as the political rhetoric escalates: '[T]hat manipulating these huge, raging human feelings for their own narrow purposes may yield instant results, but eventually and inexorably, they have disastrous consequences'.[2]

The question of alleged 'Maori privileges' raised a much deeper question. Why is it that Pakeha are so unconscious about the immense level of their own privilege, which they regard as 'normal'? Who were the primary beneficiaries of our colonial history? These questions have inspired a completely new chapter in this updated book (Chapter 10), which I have called 'White Privilege: The

Hidden Benefits'. What is clear is that unless policies designed to support Maori are seen in the context of a history that has conferred staggering benefits on European settlers, they will never be understood. As the late Michael King often said, 'Context is everything.'

With the detailed updating of this book two main themes emerge. The first is that of white privilege. The second is the dramatic growth in Treaty relationships that has occurred over the past twenty years. The changes are exciting and productive. The Treaty relationship is now firmly at the top of the political agenda. Although this means it is more controversial than ever, this is to be celebrated. Despite the polarisation there is a depth of maturity in many areas of the debate. There is also an immense amount of visionary activity on the ground. In cities and small towns, community groups and large institutions, thousands of New Zealanders, Pakeha and Maori together, are developing new, holistic and very rich relationships. They are discovering each other and the results are enriching the entire country.

While my daughter Joanna has worked alongside me on the first and second editions of this book, any 'first-person' text in the narrative is my own, reflecting my experience. I also have sole authorship of Chapters 2–5 and Chapter 10. This book is a culmination of the knowledge, analysis and reflections of more than 40 years' involvement in a variety of social justice situations. It is a response to many of the questions people ask when they find out what I do, and the positive response to the Treaty education work in which I am involved.

This book is not a handbook for Treaty education workshop leaders. Like any professional educators, Treaty workshop leaders require a variety of specialist skills and knowledge. This book is not about Maori culture, nor am I presenting a Maori perspective. It has been written to promote the importance of Treaty education and is inspired by the ongoing level of support I have received from networks of Maori and Pakeha, individually and in over 150 organisations and community groups at every level of the system.

The histories in this book are limited to the context and spirit in which the book is written. I have focused on those aspects of history that are connected to my personal journey. This models a central feature of the workshop process, which encourages participants to integrate their own personal story with the story of the country. Through leading workshops at every level of New Zealand society I have discovered that viewing New Zealand's colonial history as part of the historical, global process of colonisation enables participants to contextualise the New Zealand experience. In that process I have drawn on a variety of histories, many of which are listed in the bibliography. The authors see our contribution as complementary to these outstanding histories.

This book challenges all New Zealanders to accept responsibility for learning the colonial history of their country in order to become better informed, and support change that values all people, regardless of their cultural background. Proper recognition and understanding of what has happened to indigenous peoples is required for healing to begin. There are a multitude of ways people can respond to the challenge. I hope this book encourages readers to think, reflect and act on what they read. Also, that it invokes in people a desire to seek out more specialist information from the research that is now emerging, particularly from indigenous writers. In this new climate there are powerful reasons to hope for an integrated inclusive society.

Robert Consedine
Waitangi Associates Ltd
PO Box 35089
Christchurch
robert@waitangi.co.nz
www.waitangi.co.nz

INTRODUCTION

Christchurch, 1981

'Have you ever blown a safe?' a voice asked.

I looked across at the other bed where a young Maori man was lying, reading a newspaper. I felt shell-shocked as I prepared to spend my first night in a cell at Addington jail. It was not completely unfamiliar territory. As a child I had often visited prisoners with my father, who was an official prison visitor. But this had been an exhausting day. Getting into jail was not easy.

'Name's Gellie,' said the voice from the bed.

'Hi, Gellie,' I said, 'and no, I've never blown a safe.'

I was feeling scared; this was my first serious brush with the world of crime since I had stopped pinching bull's-eyes from the corner dairy opposite the convent school nearly 30 years earlier. I soon learned that Gellie was the best safe-breaker in the district. His trademark was gelignite.

'Heard about you guys,' said Gellie. 'Right on. Stick it to 'em, eh. You'll get used to it in here,' he continued with complete authority as he sat up. I could tell I was listening to the voice of experience. 'If you're gonna survive in here, you better learn some exercises and stay fit.'

'That would be great,' I said, 'but not tonight. I'm exhausted, I'm starving and I need some sleep.'

I couldn't believe what I had done. I was one of four anti-Springbok tour protesters who had been jailed that morning after two days of civil disobedience. A highly trained group of 21 people had embarked on a careful plan to send four of us to prison. We had engaged in a series of non-violent, peaceful protests, with the specific intention of being jailed and going on a publicity-attracting hunger strike. The plan had worked perfectly. After climbing the scaffolding outside the rugby union building in Christchurch and chaining ourselves to the scaffolding poles, we had proclaimed loudly to a gathering crowd that we intended to stop the racist all-white South African Springbok rugby tour of New Zealand, which was due to start within two weeks. We stood burning the South African and New Zealand flags.

Our Action Against the Tour back-up team was on the street, each with a role to play in this high-publicity political action. Some handled the media. Some made speeches. Others handed out leaflets and collected money. The organisation was superb. We even had a fire extinguisher on hand in case the wind changed during the flag-burning. It was not part of our agenda to burn the building down!

It wasn't long before the street was closed and 32 police officers swarmed the building with long batons and bolt-cutters. As the police climbed the scaffolding to arrest us we reached down to assist them. This was a non-violent protest and we were determined that no one would get hurt, including the police. Up on the scaffolding the police proceeded to arrest us for 'being in possession of a building'.

We were fingerprinted and photographed, then locked up in the central police station before being marched before a District Court judge who, as anticipated, granted us bail on our own recognisance. Our next plan was immediately put into action. We made our way to the National Party's Christchurch headquarters, where we sprayed the word 'Guilty' in our own blood on the walls of the building. The road was closed once more by the police and this time we were arrested for wilful damage.

At that moment I realised how difficult it was to go to jail in New Zealand—if you are a white, middle-class male. The police who came to arrest us simply did not want to lock us up, and once again we were remanded on $500 bail on our own recognisance. But this time we refused to sign the bail bond, leaving the police no option but to jail us.

The impact of being in jail was unexpected. The first thing I noticed was that the jail was overcrowded with Maori prisoners. As we settled into the dull routine of prison life on our hunger strike there was nothing to do but listen and learn. I began taking notes on their stories, and observing the behaviour of the Maori inmates and their interactions with the guards. I was staggered that so many of the stories reflected disconnection from family, unemployment, abuse, violence, low self-esteem, and personal and institutional racism. This was a side of New Zealand that I knew almost nothing about.

After two weeks in prison without food we were ordered to leave. Our hunger strike had been reported on the BBC in London and by some sections of the North American, South African and European news media, and we had received messages of support from all over the world, particularly from New Zealand, Australia, South Africa and Ireland. We concluded that our political action had been a success, and the following weeks saw tens of thousands of New Zealanders mobilise against the tour.

The impact of meeting so many Maori in prison stayed in my mind. Here I was protesting against racial oppression in South Africa, when it was clearly also happening in New Zealand. My awareness of Maori dissatisfaction had been growing since the emergence in the late 1960s of Nga Tamatoa, a university-based radical movement of young Maori. The great land march of 1975, led by Dame Whina Cooper, and the occupation of Bastion Point in suburban Auckland in 1978 had also raised my awareness.

Around the time of the tour and after it many Pakeha New Zealanders, including myself, accepted the challenge issued by Maori activists.[1] The challenge was threefold: first, learn your own history, cultural identity and cultural values; second, take responsibility for your own lack of awareness of New Zealand colonial history, particularly the implications of the Treaty of Waitangi; and third, create a process that begins to challenge the majority culture of which you are a member. The message was clear. Start by educating yourselves and your own people. If Maori were going to receive justice, Pakeha had to change. A number of Pakeha took this challenge seriously and began to relearn the history of New Zealand.

What I found out about New Zealand's colonial history shocked me profoundly. The colonial history of New Zealand since the signing of the Treaty of Waitangi in 1840 was a history of dishonoured promises, fraud, theft and violence against Maori by the government through a process of systematic colonisation. At every level of the political and economic system Maori had been marginalised. In that process Maori have continued to be divided, which undoubtedly has compounded the problem.

Although there have been many attempts throughout history by the state to assist Maori, many government policies have been paternalistic and assimilationist in nature. I discovered, further, that this history parallels that of many other colonised countries. I could see that it was a history that we needed to confront, understand, acknowledge and heal.

This knowledge challenged and transformed the way I viewed my country. I became part of a large network of Pakeha people who went on to create a process that would challenge the social conditioning many Pakeha (including myself) had received, in which the Pakeha way of doing things was assumed to be 'normal'. An emerging network of Pakeha Treaty of Waitangi educators, with strong accountability to Maori, began to experiment by trial and error with a variety of education programmes, with the focus on working with the majority Pakeha population. This process included continuing to educate ourselves.

By the late 1980s an educational programme had been refined to take the form of a highly interactive, accelerated two-day workshop. It was designed as a starting point for Pakeha to address the widespread lack of understanding of colonial history, culture, cultural heritage, racism, sovereignty and self-determination for indigenous peoples, and to contribute to informed and reasoned debate. This programme forms the basis of Treaty workshops today.

The workshop process is based on the premise that although indigenous peoples are driving the process of change, the role of the majority Pakeha culture is critical. Since the mid-1980s Treaty workshops have been delivered to tens of thousands of New Zealanders at all levels of New Zealand society. At minimum, the workshop dissipates a considerable amount of the fear that exists in Pakeha society in response to Maori demands. At best, the workshops politicise and empower people to honour the commitments made in Te Tiriti o Waitangi.

The workshop model is continually evolving and offers an holistic way of dealing with and creating change. Thousands of New Zealanders will affirm that it works. It is based on a personal journey for each participant and one of the main reasons for its success is that new information learned about colonial history is integrated into each person's own story. Engaging both the head and the heart is pivotal to the success of the workshop model.

In using the terms 'Pakeha' and 'Maori' throughout this book it is not my intention to exclude people from other cultures from the Treaty workshop process. It is simply that I recognise that the New Zealand European population is numerically the majority culture in New Zealand. The Treaty of Waitangi provides the basis for all other cultures to have a relationship with Maori, the first inhabitants of New Zealand. A multicultural society would be the outcome of 'right Treaty relationships'[2], and this framework could be considered in any country where treaties exist with indigenous peoples.

This book was written with the intention of raising the profile of Treaty education in New Zealand and stressing the need for it. I want to encourage all New Zealanders to learn their own country's colonial history and understand its implications for today. It is crucial to be informed about the issues in order to participate in meaningful debate about New Zealand's future.

The book is presented in two parts: *The History* and *The Healing*. In both sections I have incorporated stories from my own life. These experiences are not necessarily presented in chronological order but rather serve to illustrate the theme of each chapter.

The History
The first section of the book examines elements of my own personal history and aspects of the colonial history of Ireland, British

Columbia (Canada), Australia and New Zealand.

Chapter 1 looks at the shaping of my own identity as a Pakeha of Irish Catholic descent. My childhood values never left me; if anything, they have strengthened my commitment to 'walking the talk' in relation to the values I strongly hold.

My awareness of the effects of colonisation on indigenous peoples came about largely as a result of travelling through developing countries in the 1970s. In Chapter 2 I provide fragments of the colonial histories of Ireland, Canada and Australia to illustrate the global nature of colonisation. As increasing numbers of workshop participants are aware, Treaty relationships and issues of national identity are under discussion in many colonised countries.

Chapter 3 explores the role of Christian missionaries in the colonisation process and the impact of their actions on indigenous peoples. In Chapter 4 I briefly outline the colonial history of New Zealand and the fate of the Treaty relationship between Maori and the Crown. Against a backdrop of sustained political protest led by Maori, new government policies and court opinions have contributed to a fresh approach to the Crown–Maori relationship, and this changing direction in the Treaty relationship is discussed in Chapter 5. Chapter 6 looks at why many adult New Zealanders today are so ill-informed about this country's colonial history by examining the role of the education system and the information gap it has left.

The Healing
The second part of the book explores some of the steps that need to be taken at individual and collective societal levels to heal our history.

Chapter 7 begins with how I got involved in Treaty education and how I work as a Treaty educator. I will illustrate some of the strategies used to enable workshop participants to explore their own positions, draw their own conclusions and feel more confident about engaging in the Treaty debate. The importance of valuing our own story and making connections with how our identity is shaped is explored in Chapter 8. Chapter 9 examines why Treaty education is best done through 'parallel process', with Maori and Pakeha initially attending separate workshops.

Chapter 10 is a new chapter written especially for the updated edition of this book. It raises the challenging issue of 'white privilege' —the hidden benefits that generations of Pakeha have enjoyed through no effort of their own. Decades of government policies had the effect of destroying the Maori economic base as Maori land and resources were transferred to Pakeha ownership. Chapter 11 looks at the strengths and limitations of the process of acknowledgement, and forgiveness of pain and hurt, in order to pave the way for reconciliation. Examples from Australia, Canada and New Zealand show how the healing process is evolving in each of these countries.

The last chapter presents some of the issues facing this country in its future relationship with Maori. As these issues go to the core of our national identity, all New Zealanders need to become involved in the Treaty debate, for the issues will not go away. Indigenous peoples everywhere are insisting that countries cast off the shackles of colonial domination, and the continuing political activity by Maori in New Zealand is a constant reminder that their people have been deeply hurt and continue to suffer. Their pain expresses itself not just in political action reported in the media but also in appalling social statistics: poorer health, a higher crime rate, lower educational achievement and higher unemployment.

Indigenous survivors everywhere are demanding that majority cultures redress past injustices and honour treaties made with their ancestors. They are driving the political process and demanding that governments confront the illegalities underpinning colonial history. They are taking governments to court and using Crown laws to demand redress for the theft of land throughout colonial histories.

If these rights continue to be denied, in New Zealand as elsewhere, the seeds of future conflict will continue to germinate. This is the time and we are the generation who must respond to this enormous challenge. Successive governments in New Zealand have con-sistently failed to deliver Treaty education and this failure needs to be addressed if historical grievances are to be resolved and justice achieved for indigenous peoples and other citizens. Treaty education is essential to just and equitable social relationships.

PART ONE
The History

History, despite its wrenching pain,
Cannot be unlived, but if faced
With courage, need not be lived again.

Maya Angelou
ON THE PULSE OF THE MORNING

ONE

Faith, Spuds and Hospitality

Addington, Christchurch

I made my way in pitch darkness across the school playground, wet and fearful that I wouldn't arrive in time. My hands and face were bitterly cold. The lights were out as I walked quietly through the back door of the church. The red sanctuary lamp up ahead flickered across the pews, providing enough light for me to make my way up the aisle. I saw an outline of still, black forms, like a row of sentries guarding the 'real presence' of God. The nuns were always early, kneeling before Mary's larger-than-life statue, saying their morning prayers. An occasional cough or the clinking of rosary beads interrupted the eerie silence. This was Lourdes and Fatima recreated in Addington, a working-class suburb of Christchurch, New Zealand.

I was starting a normal day in the life of a 10-year-old altar boy in our local Catholic parish. I was up at six—summer and winter—and off on my bike to serve the priest as he offered the Mass, the ancient ceremony of the Catholic Church in Latin. I knew the Mass off by heart, word for word. As an eight-year-old I had learned all the Latin I needed to know from my friend Ivan Snook. Dressed in my surplice and soutane, lighting the candles on the altar, I felt at one with my surroundings.

When the priest finally arrived the Mass began *In nomine patris et filii spiritus sancti* and we entered into the exquisite ritual of the liturgy. Priest, altar boy and people: each knew their role perfectly, intoned the rituals prescribed by the Roman Catholic Church. I felt pride in the importance of my role. I was doing God's work.

To be a child in Addington in the 1940s and 1950s was both exciting and arduous. There was always something happening. Addington had to be one of the most interesting suburbs in the world in which to have a childhood. The suburb had two hotels, a psychiatric hospital, a remand jail, a racecourse, the showgrounds, a flour mill, army barracks, stockyards and the Addington railway workshops where many of the men, including my father, worked.

Within Addington during the last quarter of the nineteenth century was a Catholic ghetto, where Irish Catholic immigrants clustered.[1] Many were descendants of poor immigrants driven from Ireland by the aftermath of the penal laws and the potato famines. In Addington the Irish remained on the fringe of the English Protestant establishment that ruled Christchurch, a city founded on the British class system.

My father often talked, without rancour, about Addington being different from the rest of Christchurch. He spoke of the difficulty for 'us' in getting jobs. Irish Catholics were the outsiders: they knew they had to look after their own. Catholics did not expect to get good jobs and if they did, they did not expect to get promoted. My father was never promoted at the railway workshops. 'No Irish Need Apply', very much permeated this subculture of Christchurch. I accepted this: it was just the way life was.

Catholic institutions dominated our community life. The church, presbytery, hall, school and convent were located together in the centre of the parish. Nearby was the Mount Magdala home for 'fallen women', the St John of God home for intellectually handicapped children, two orphanages and a Carmelite monastery with a prayer life sustaining the whole community. Addington appeared to cater for every eventuality.

Identity for us Consedines revolved around large, strong families: Irish Catholic and working class. I am a fourth-generation Irish Pakeha. My great-grandfather arrived on the West Coast of the South Island in the early 1860s. There were seven in our immediate family—my parents Freda and Lang, and five kids: Michael, me, James, Noel and Marie. Life was simple, sometimes hard, yet we always knew God was looking out for us. When Noel got meningitis at the age of five my father went to the Carmelite monastery to ask the sisters to pray for him. We thought he'd die, but he didn't. 'Thank God for the prayers of the Carmelites,' said my father, with little credit to the two doctors who had stayed all night and looked after his son!

There was no sex in Addington—at least nothing overt. I never knew where my brothers and sister came from—they each just appeared one day. In fact, where all those large Irish Catholic, working-class families came from was a mystery to me. I decided the women went to a hospital in town called Lewisham to get their babies. I once questioned a priest, who told me that I would find out when I was older. He also cautioned me that 'certain activities' caused blindness. Kissing for more than 10 seconds at a time was also mortally sinful.

We lived in an environment ruled by the parish priest and the expectations were enormous. The pride in who you were and what you stood for was matched by the enforcement of endless written and unwritten rules about life. The Blessed Virgin Mary was the model. The Ten Commandments handed by God to Moses, the Sermon on the Mount, the Seven Deadly Sins, the Commandments of the church and those of the parish priest (embellished by the nuns) ruled every aspect of our lives. At school no stone was left unturned in the search for perfection. If there was any doubt, the easiest solution, a strap, hung menacingly close to the classroom door. The girls often cried when strapped, while the boys competed to see who could take the most. As each child strove to live up to the highest ideals, the threat of eternal damnation hovered over the whole parish.

The cultural rules were also rigid. The authorities were as tough on those who broke them as they were supportive of those who kept them. Everyone knew who were Catholics and who were not. Hospitality to non-Catholics was courteous; they were, after all, potential Catholics. A limited friendship with Protestants was acceptable but woe betide anyone who dated, let alone married one. To marry outside the Catholic Church or to send your child to a state school were serious acts of disloyalty.

But if you were part of the culture there were many benefits. Solidarity was strong and provision was made for all. If any parishioners were in trouble the parish would close ranks around them. This was a community that nurtured, loved and supported its children. Young and old alike could go to Catholic concerts, tennis, table tennis, soccer and the best dances in Christchurch.

In return there were no limits to the demands that the parish could make on families. Men were expected to do the manual work around the parish and much of their spare time was taken up with new projects to enhance its structure. My father spent most of his spare time working as a carpenter for the network of Catholic institutions in the Addington parish. He never expected, nor received, any payment. Parents and teachers worked long hours supporting the Catholic school in a multitude of ways, as education was considered to be a way out of hardship. Fundraising and donations financed the church, school and convent—not a penny was received from the state. A network of Catholic schools was built out of the pockets of working-class parents and the near slave labour of the missionary religious orders who taught in the schools.

The annual church fair was the fundraising highlight, with profits the only major source of income for the nuns each year. Women were expected to bake and sew. Men ran the stalls, auctioning chickens and hams by the cartload and whisky by the carton. A word of praise from the patriarchal parish priest was ample reward for months of hard work. The relationship was simple: when the parish priest was pleased, God was pleased.

Irish Catholic descendants had a very clear view of the role of the government. They knew from their ancestry that they would get nothing from the state and they responded accordingly. It seemed that every illegal fundraising activity ever invented sooner or later happened in our parish. Either by accident or design, the local policeman always appeared to be Catholic. Turning a blind eye was a critical part of their training and invariably they were elsewhere when these activities took place. Illegal fundraising and avoiding taxes were considered morally legitimate.

Hard physical work was normal for all the adults and children living around us. The women cooked, cleaned, clothed, baked, sewed, knitted, bottled, and made jam, soap and ginger beer. The men, mostly on low wages, worked for an employer during the day, then for their neighbours, family and church at night or on Saturdays. But never on Sundays! The children helped around the house or worked in the vegetable garden. We also picked potatoes for cash at every available opportunity to pay school fees. We had a market garden, which kept us busy.

The most exciting week of the year in Addington was Show and Cup Week. Each year we started Show Day by planting 3000 tomato plants in our family's one and a quarter acres of spare land. The hoeing, weeding, spraying, staking, watering and removing of laterals gave our family a taste for growing good vegetables, and gardening is a practice we have continued for most of our lives.

My parents worked incredibly hard. They shared an enormous sense of hospitality and a real concern for the needs of others. 'Other people are worse off than us,' my father often said. Even though he was a working-class man with very little money, he kept giving things away, at times to my mother's despair. He believed in 'living the Sermon on the Mount'. This meant he would often bring home people who had been in jail, in Sunnyside (the local psychiatric hospital) or who were living alone. My mother made the visitors welcome and would have a meal ready on the table. Hospitality was part of the culture of the neighbourhood. It didn't matter who you were or what you did for a living, you were accepted and made to feel welcome. For me, visiting the local jail and psychiatric hospital and burying indigent men with my father introduced me to poverty of a different kind at an early age.

Living in Christchurch we spent a lot of time with my father's side of the family. We often had family gatherings at home, singing around the piano and giving little concerts. My mother was a pianist and, believing that we were all capable of singing, she encouraged us all—in fact it was compulsory. Visitors would arrive and the order

was given. 'Robert, stand in the corner and sing "Bless This House".'
Singing on my own at home and taking lead roles in school concerts
gave me a sense of confidence. I loved being out front—it was great
fun and a wonderful legacy. Music and singing have sustained me all
my life.

My mother's family lived in Auckland. Every year 'railways
families' received a free return pass to travel by train anywhere in
the country and this free pass enabled our family to have magical
annual holidays in Auckland with our relations. There was always a
great sense of adventure about the trip. We caught the night-time
sailing on either the *Hinemoa* or the *Rangatira* from Lyttelton to
Wellington, then took the overnight limited rail express from
Wellington to Auckland. We even had railway pies at Taumarunui
on the main-trunk line! When we arrived in Auckland the five of us
were farmed out to stay with different branches of our large family,
for up to six weeks. I loved the sense of freedom and independence.
Auckland was a magic place for working-class kids from Addington.
Some relations had farms, others had yachts on the Manukau
and Waitemata harbours, and our uncle Jim had a car—a Ford V8.
Wow!

I always assumed that everybody living in Addington was the same
as my family. Take Jim Amos, for example. He lived over our back
fence, was at Mass on Sundays and worked with my father at the
railway workshops. Little did I understand the significance of the
fact that at the end of his day he went off to the Addington Showgrounds on Lincoln Road to coach the Marist Seniors and later the
New Zealand rugby league team. A former international player, he
became national coach for the 1952 New Zealand tour of Australia,
the home series the following year, and the 1954 inaugural World
Cup in France. Each great success notwithstanding, he returned
home to the railway workshops after every tour.

Around the corner lived Bob Stuart. On his way to work at the
Ministry of Agriculture he regularly picked up my mother at the tram
stop, taking her to town in his Citroën. His quiet sense of hospitality
assisted my mother, who struggled to feed five children on a low
income. For her, owning a car was a distant dream. In his spare time

Bob was the All Black captain. With a long history in first-class rugby to his credit, he was chosen at the age of 32 to captain the 1953–54 All Black tour of Great Britain and France. It has been said that Bob Stuart personally revived great captaincy in New Zealand rugby. His brother Kevin was an All Black. Another brother, John, played for Canterbury. The Stuart family were also at Mass on Sundays.

It seems amazing to me now that both these men were in France in 1954, Amos coaching the New Zealand league team and Stuart captaining the All Blacks. The interest in league and rugby in the local neighbourhood was immense. Just as we didn't know, as kids, that we were poor, we also didn't know that, outside Addington, Jim Amos and Bob Stuart were famous. Yet they lived around the corner from each other—and from us! They were just part of the parish and good neighbours, and were treated accordingly.

I felt on top of life by the time I went to secondary school. I was dux of Addington Convent, a top primary school soccer player and, with my part-time job at a poultry farm, I felt like one of the richest kids in the neighbourhood. I was confident at boxing, too. This was a strong tradition for boys in Addington. We were expected to become good boxers and every year there was an annual tournament in the parish hall. By the age of eight I had learned the art of boxing and was able to knock someone out. While I never did, boxing skills gave me a confidence in my own safety that has never left me. I knew some of my strengths, but was careful not to show off. Skiting was treated with disdain. I was optimistic and hopeful, with an identity that was strong. I had been taught to be proud of who I was.

St Bede's College, in the north of Christchurch, was the Catholic equivalent of the Anglican Christ's College in the central city. Defeating each other at sporting and academic pursuits was an obsession for both schools. We had to be better than the Protestants in every way, even beating them at their own game. St Bede's offered a route to the middle class and the key to the city.

I was expected to go to St Bede's College. My older brother Michael had won a scholarship to go there, but what a mistake this was for me. The children in Addington were primarily sons and daughters of tradesmen and the working class, whereas St Bede's appeared to cater for children from middle-class families. I felt a terrible sense of isolation and just could not relate to the culture around me. Suddenly I became aware of my working-class background and saw how it counted against me. For the first time in my life I experienced the feeling of not belonging. I learned what it was like to feel marginalised and excluded. I later saw that, just like Christ's College, St Bede's had a culture that reinforced the Christchurch class system and reflected the repressed, violent, narrow educational orthodoxy of the 1950s. I was easily bored and lived for my ongoing involvement in Addington.

Outside school, which tended to interrupt the important things in life, my adolescence was filled with endless days of summer. By day I worked at the local poultry farm, cutting and distributing acres of grass for the fowls, or collecting, washing and packing thousands of eggs. Then it was home for a meal—always waiting on the table— and later off to play tennis until dark. Life was just as full in winter. School and homework were wedged in between table tennis three times a week, soccer on Saturday afternoons and the famous Spencer Street dance on Saturday night. We formed our own Celtic tabletennis club, including Paul Ives, our best player, who went on to win the New Zealand under-age titles.

Leaving school was pure liberation. I knew I wanted to continue my life with the strength of identity that I had experienced growing up in Addington. My childhood had imbued me with a strong sense that whatever happened in my life I would be okay. This has sustained me throughout my life as I have explored and travelled the world. Yet other seeds had also been sown, making me curious to learn more about other people and cultures, and about what constituted fairness and justice in the world.

I joined the Catholic Youth Movement (CYM), led by my friend Neil Williamson, and was given the tools, focus and analysis to begin to understand the world in the light of the gospel values I had absorbed. The See—Judge—Act method on which the CYM was based shaped the way I viewed the world and introduced me to a cross-section of interdenominational youth movements. In the mid-1960s, after seven years in the CYM, I was sent as a representative to Rome and later Brussels, exposing me to a network of people from liberation movements. My philosophical and spiritual outlook was being strongly shaped.

The fun in my life continued with the Spencer Street dance. In the early 1960s, while the Beatles and the Rolling Stones ruled the world, the Downbeats, Dinah Lee, Phil Garland and the Playboys, Ray Columbus and the Invaders, Max Merritt and the Meteors, and Johnny and the Revellers ruled the dance headquarters of Christchurch, located in our parish hall. As Master of Ceremonies I called the dance brackets, sorted out disputes and kept up the patter while bands changed personnel every half-hour. Up to 1200 people would pack the hall—licensed for 350—on a Saturday night, dancing from eight until midnight. Although alcohol was illegal in or near a dance hall, some arrived the worse for wear and occasionally there were fights. Rarely was there an arrest, although the police were usually in attendance for the last hour. Dad was often on the door and the rest of my family crept in the back door or through a window to avoid paying!

I remember my childhood days as a source of strength. I felt valued, I belonged, I had a place. Addington was my patch. I was part of the strong sense of community that existed in the area. I could walk down many Addington streets and name the families—O'Neill, Harnett, Campbell, Noonan, Clarke, Daly, Kelly, Stewart, Scott, McCloy, Coakley, Carey, Fowke, Ives, McIllhatton, Gilmore, McCann, Worters, Leeming, Sloane, Horgan, Snook, Thompson, Cumming, O'Connor, McGrade, Owens, O'Grady, Cahill, Costello, Stuart, Mahoney, Amos, Brosnahan, Pullar, Warren, Sloan, McGuinniety, Dowdall, Glover, Moller, Mercer, Neill—a litany of saints and scholars. I often bumped into someone I knew and this familiarity increased my sense of security.

My happy childhood memories, however, go against the more commonly told story of violence and poverty associated with growing up in a working-class Irish Catholic family. In the internationally renowned book *Angela's Ashes* Frank McCourt tells his grim story of growing up in Ireland. My childhood was far different. I was not blind to the violence and poverty around me: we could all name the drunks; we all knew the parents who dished out hidings at home and the teachers who did likewise at school. But my personal experience of this sort of violence was very limited.

Looking back, I realise also that as a child I had almost no awareness of or contact with Maori people. There was one Maori man in the parish and I never thought of him as having a different culture. At primary school I was often sent to find Rangi and Terry, who were the only Maori children in my class and who kept running away. No one seemed to know why and I never found out. But when I now recall what we were taught and the cultural framework in which the school operated, the answer seems obvious. I had a lot to learn about the concept of identity in this country.

TWO

Fragments of History: Ireland, Canada and Australia

Robert Consedine

Bangladesh, 1973

The heat was intense and the stench almost overwhelming. We were stuck in the middle of masses of desperate, hungry, screaming people, their outstretched arms waving papers at us. The crowd was turning ugly and beginning to surge towards where we were standing. I felt tightness in the pit of my stomach and an escalating panic. How was I going to escape?

We had just emerged from a small prefabricated hut that constituted the Red Cross headquarters in a large refugee camp west of Rangpur, in the north of Bangladesh.[1] The Red Cross officials were cautiously pushing their way through the crowd to where we were standing. They shouted at us to stand still and do nothing to provoke the crowd, which believed we had come from the United Nations to rescue them from the camp and to issue them with passports enabling them to leave the country. They were not going to let us go and no amount of negotiation would change that.

It was a dangerous situation. The Red Cross officials advised us not to make any abrupt movements. After some discussion they suggested that we move towards a jeep parked in the middle of the compound. We were instructed to climb into the back of the jeep and sit still. The crowd blocked our exit from the camp.

The Red Cross driver started the jeep, which was facing the wrong way, and drove slowly into the crowd, which began to move back. 'Hold on tight and keep your heads down,' an official instructed as space opened up behind the jeep. Suddenly the driver slammed the jeep into reverse and went backwards at breakneck speed. The crowd, caught unawares, started to chase us but soon gave up. We departed the camp at high speed—still in reverse—out of the gate, swung around and headed for the airstrip and a six-seater plane that would take us to Dhaka. We would spend the night there before heading across the border to Calcutta the following day.[2]

We took off in a small single-engine Red Cross plane and headed back down the Ganges River towards Dhaka. It was a very humid, still day and we had the doors of the plane wide open on both sides, flying at about 3000 feet, our seatbelts tightly fastened across our laps. We were on the verge of the monsoon season and the floods were imminent.

Somewhat to our alarm, our experienced pilot noted the very black thunderous clouds ahead and indicated that he hoped to reach Dhaka before the tropical storm struck. That was not to be.

Suddenly the pilot shouted: 'Slam the doors, tighten your belts, put your heads down!' He then called a mayday, banked and dived straight towards the nearest piece of relatively solid land. Fighting to keep control of the plane, after a few terrifying moments through near hurricane conditions, he brought it to a bumpy landing and sudden halt. He yelled at us to get out and we seized the wings on either side and pinned the plane to the ground to prevent it from being smashed to pieces.

As we stood there, soaked, desperately holding down the wings of the plane in the middle of a huge paddock, there was a rumble in the distance. I looked up to see armoured cars and jeeps emerging from the trees. A jeep screeched to a halt and an Indian officer jumped out, saluted smartly and informed us that we had landed in the middle of a Bengali Army exercise. The officer ordered his men to physically hold the plane and we were offered army transport to Dhaka. We were taken to a hotel under heavy guard.

In Dhaka another shock awaited me. On reaching the hotel I was told that my mother had died suddenly back in New Zealand. This news was hard to absorb in a country where people die prematurely by the tens of thousands. My arrival in Calcutta the next day took on an added poignancy as I watched the beggars at the airport and began walking the streets in mind-numbing culture shock. We found our modest accommodation and when we later re-emerged we stepped over bodies, some dead, as we made our way to Mother Teresa's Home for the Dying. Death, it seemed, was all around me.

At Mother Teresa's home people were brought in off the streets each day to die with some level of dignity. In a huge warehouse hundreds of people lay in rows on low-level stretchers, being ministered to by teams of the Missionaries of Charity. Standing there, thinking about my mother's death, I thanked God for her full, loving and rich life, and reflected on the much lesser life forced on millions of people by poverty.

I was grateful to be able to attend a Catholic Mass, celebrated by my friend and colleague Father John Curnow at Mother Teresa's headquarters on the day my mother was buried in Christchurch. The Mass celebrating her life took place in a large concrete chapel in the presence of hundreds of Missionaries of Charity. There was no furniture in the building except for an altar, so we knelt on the concrete floor. The sense of privilege I felt at that moment was quite profound.

A Growing Awareness

My trip was a United Nations-sponsored visit. Prime Minister Norman Kirk had asked Father John Curnow and I to visit the refugee camps in the north of Bangladesh, to determine the best way for New Zealand to provide food and medical assistance. An estimated 75,000 Bihari refugees were holed up in a disused railway siding, living in or under railway wagons and a whole tapestry of makeshift shelters.

We had attended a United Nations training course, which started in Calcutta then moved to New Delhi, Bombay and finally Poona. The course introduced us to a profound change in thinking about the provision of development assistance. A new philosophy of self-determination focused on the need for people to be the authors of their own development, to determine their own future and not to have solutions imposed on them by an outside power. By the early 1970s it had become clear that international aid by way of donor countries imposing 'solutions' was not working. The decade of development announced by President John F. Kennedy in the early 1960s and aimed at the Third World had been a complete failure: the countries were poorer and the people worse off.

This experience had a profound and lasting impact on me, creating a new level of awareness about the impact of colonisation on indigenous peoples. The conventional wisdom was that colonisation benefited indigenous peoples by bringing progress, spreading civilisation and introducing modern systems of governance. Yet the evidence from these countries suggested that 'progress' had benefited only a minority of the people, who had gained and maintained wealth because they helped further the aims of the colonisers. The majority still lived in conditions of immense poverty and dependence.

This view was reinforced later as I travelled through and read the histories of Ireland, Canada and Australia. While these are not Third World countries, many of their indigenous peoples live in Third World conditions as a result of the devastating social and economic outcomes of colonisation. How had this come about? What gave rise to colonisation?

The Role of Colonisation

The colonial era began towards the end of the fifteenth century with the rise of European powers built on the spoils of conquest of America, Asia and Africa.[3] The exploitation of resources and the extraction of wealth from these continents paved the way for colonisation to progress, and capitalism developed as a world system. Says J.M. Blaut: 'Capitalism became concentrated in Europe because colonialism gave Europeans the power both to develop their own society and to prevent development from occurring elsewhere.'[4]

There were no regulations for acquiring territories already under the jurisdiction of a recognised sovereign, so European powers would stake their claims of sovereignty by whatever means they could, including 'assertions of discovery, symbolic acts of possession, papal bulls, signing of treaties with rival states or local chiefs and princes, establishing settlements, and outright conquest by force of arms'.[5]

The rise of the British Empire in the eighteenth century signalled the 'second phase' of colonisation. By the time India gained independence in 1947 the British Empire covered a quarter of the world and over 500 million people.[6]

The economic motivation behind colonisation was unchanged. Colonisation opened up abundant resources, new markets and trade opportunities. The colonies also offered a destination for surplus populations. Economic structures were put in place in the new colonies, such as Canada, Australia and New Zealand, to benefit the 'mother country', and cheap labour was utilised to develop the natural resources and complement the capital invested in the colonies. In the case of the British Empire the labour supply was largely drawn from the poor and working class of Britain. The settlers, even labouring ones, were sold the hope of doing better than was possible at home, and the newly emerging settler economies were developed by marginalising indigenous populations and taking their resources without permission.

Capitalism was not the only driving force, however. Colonisation was also inspired by a belief that European civilisation was genuinely superior and that progress resulted from its diffusion throughout the rest of the world. Conquest of indigenous peoples was accomplished by maintaining an ideology of 'white' racial superiority. Non-European countries inhabited by 'black' people were seen, as in the case of Australia, as 'barbarous or unsettled and without settled law'.[7]

While Ireland, Canada and Australia are all colonised countries, the process of colonisation has been different in each. The following case studies reflect fragments of Irish, Canadian (British Columbian) and Australian history. These are not intended as definitive summaries but rather provide a framework within which to begin to interpret the contemporary issues arising from the colonial past.

It can be seen that lessons learned in one colonial setting were often re-applied in another. Ireland has been called the 'cradle of colonisation'. And Maire and Conor Cruise O'Brien tell us that: 'The conquest of Ireland provided the psychological basis, as well as part of the material basis and training, for the colonisation of a great part of the world.'[8] For example, the Suppression of Rebellion Act, which suspended basic rights for those found to be in rebellion against the Crown, passed in New Zealand in 1863, came from Ireland where it was passed in 1797.

Ireland: 'The Parent Figures Lied to Us'[9]

A few years ago my family and I were invited to meet Joe and Bernadette O'Hagan. Now deceased, Joe was a former member of the Irish Republican Army, the military wing of Sinn Fein. He had spent his entire life either in jail or on the run.[10] He became internationally famous when the IRA engineered his spectacular exit from Mountjoy jail in Dublin on 31 October 1973. A helicopter hovered over the exercise yard and took off with three of the most significant IRA men in the country, in what was described as a sensational escape. Joe, Bernadette and their six children have collectively spent 59 years in prison for the cause. Dara, one of their children, is a former member of the new Northern Ireland Assembly and has a doctorate in politics. When we met, we reflected on 800 years of Irish resistance to English colonisation, interwoven with the personal stories of Joe and Bernadette and their accumulated family experience. The O'Hagans' passion for and commitment to social justice have resulted in lives of extraordinary risk-taking.

Colonisation and Rebellion

Ireland was settled more than 9000 years ago.[11] It was never invaded by the Romans, but was ruled by politically independent tribes of feuding Irish clans, kings, earls and chieftains. From about AD 800 Viking raids over a period of nearly 400 years resulted in the development of many Irish cities that became international trading centres.[12] Over time the Vikings either left or gradually integrated with the Irish. In 1172 an English pope, Adrian I, gave authority to an English king, Henry II, to rule Ireland. The Norman, later English, conquest continued erratically until Henry VIII proclaimed himself King of Ireland in 1541.

However, despite various royal proclamations, English rule was far from secure and rebellions and resistance were constant. Researcher Theodore W. Allen sums up: 'The history of England in Ireland for more than four centuries, from early in the thirteenth century to the initiation of the plantation of Ulster in 1609, is a history of the failure of three strategies of social control.'[13] The Ulster plantation was one of the most important strategies, designed to supplant Gaelic-speaking Irish citizens with English settlers. The plan was meant to finance the settlement of English tenants in Ireland in numbers sufficient to provide a self-supporting militia to guarantee the eventual subjugation of the entire country. It was proclaimed that: 'No member of the Celtic Irish owning or learned classes was to be admitted [to the plantation boundaries].'[14] In practice, Irish tenants were admitted into the plantations for economic reasons, and religious animosity between the Irish Catholic and English Protestant settlers was fuelled by constant disputes over land.

After one series of rebellions, beginning in 1530, the Irish were defeated, despite receiving help from Spain in 1601. An enduring pattern had now been established: 'Catholic Ireland dominated by the superior force of Protestant England. Religion hardened, sharpened and preserved national animosities. It was a vicious circle, with English insecurity producing strong measures, which further stirred up the Irish, producing stronger measures.'[15]

The Penal Laws

Epitomising the repression were a series of anti-Catholic statutes known as the Penal Laws, some of which were modified in the 1770s but which were not repealed in the British Parliament until 1829. These statutes operated on a principle devised by the British Chancellor and Chief Justice that, except for purposes of repression and punishment, 'the law does not suppose any such person to exist as an Irish Roman Catholic'.[16]

The Penal Laws regulated every aspect of Irish life: civil, domestic and spiritual.[17] They were not primarily concerned with Catholic religious belief, but aimed at preventing Catholics owning property or being employers in industry.[18] Catholics were not allowed to vote or become parliamentary representatives. They were banned from practising law or holding a position in the military or in the public service. They could not become teachers or go to university. Catholics could not 'buy, inherit or receive gifts of land from Protestants', and faced restrictions on how long they could lease land.[19] By the middle of the eighteenth century Irish Catholics held only 7 per cent of Irish land.[20]

Allen notes that the Protestant rules gave special attention to breaking the tie of parent and child in Catholic Irish families. The most outrageous penal law had to be the sexual property rights that Protestant landlords exercised over female tenants. Allen assures us that even in the early nineteenth century there were cases in which this ultimate form of negation of the Catholic Irish family was stipulated in the lease as a privilege of the landlord.[21]

The abortive uprising of 1798, led by Protestant Wolfe Tone, brought about repression, and the British Parliament claimed complete supremacy over Ireland. The fact that a Protestant led the uprising was significant. It demonstrated that the Irish struggle was against an English, mainly absentee, landowning ruling class, not against Protestants per se. A century later the struggle continued. Protestant nationalist leader Charles Stewart Parnell, founder of the Land League, urged Catholics and Protestants to unite regardless of creed against oppressive landlords.[22]

Meanwhile many of the emerging Catholic middle class had joined the colonisers as an outcome of a deliberate English strategy. After the brutal crushing of the 1798 uprising, the strategy eventually included the repeal of most of the penal laws by 1829 and the disestablishment of the Church of Ireland in 1869. This led to a policy shift by the British from racial oppression to national oppression as the Irish middle class became incorporated into the British system of social control. This policy was well entrenched by 1793, upheld in law by 1829 and defined in practice by 1843.[23]

The Act of Union

The Act of Union between Great Britain and Ireland in 1801 symbolised the final absorption of Ireland into the United Kingdom with a policy of assimilation aimed at developing 'a sense of allegiance, a bond of solidarity between the allegedly fractious Irish and the imperial motherland'.[24] A state-aided national school system was established in 1831 as the key agency in this policy, and textbooks emphasised the close relationship between Britain and Ireland as the nucleus of the British Empire.[25] Outside of schools, the Irish remained dispossessed and resistance continued in a climate of increasing racism.

Racism played a pivotal role in the colonisation of Ireland. The Irish were portrayed in newspapers as having ape-like features, being lazy, drunkards and less than human. They were seen as a race apart, inferior in every way. 'Where the English were portrayed as honest, the Irish were liars, where the English worked and prospered, the Irish idled in poverty . . . English industriousness . . . contrasted with Irish disorder . . . Manly Protestantism [confronted] a cowardly and corrupt Catholicism.'[26] Similar racial stereotypes were developed in countries such as Australia, Canada and New Zealand against the Irish as well as the indigenous peoples. This enabled the colonisers to justify taking control of the resources.

The Potato 'Famine' 1845–52

The famine, often described as the greatest watershed in Irish history, left a scar on the psyche of Irish culture that is still evident today. The immediate problem was the failure of successive potato crops, which was predictable, but because Ireland was organised to meet the needs of the Protestant ascendancy, the English government failed to respond.[27] 'England had little interest in developing the infrastructure of Ireland. By the 1830s Ireland was subsidising the industrial revolution by feeding 2 million of England's population and was being systematically underdeveloped.'[28] The English government maintained free-market economic policies in Ireland, allowing successive potato crop failures to become a famine.[29] While the initial response to the famine was slow, some relief eventually reached

Ireland but it was too late. The population of Ireland, already reduced, declined by more than one-third through famine, famine-induced disease and emigration.[30] The outcome was an estimated loss of 2.8 million people over 15 years.

The Creation of Northern Ireland

The decades that followed were turbulent for Ireland. A treaty between Ireland and Britain in 1921 set up an Irish Free State as a self-governing dominion of the British Empire, with the same constitutional status as Canada, Australia, New Zealand and South Africa. A representative of the Crown was to be appointed in the same way as a dominion governor-general, and the members of the Irish Parliament were to take an oath of allegiance to the constitution and the Irish Free State, which pledged them to 'be faithful to His Majesty King George V, his heirs and successors'. The free state was to assume responsibility for part of Britain's public debt, yield certain defence facilities to British forces and in time of war give whatever assurance might be required by the British. Furthermore, the treaty granted to Northern Ireland the right to withdraw from the jurisdiction of the Dublin Parliament.[31]

All of these provisions were anathema to republican aspirations.

The terms of the treaty divided the country and resulted in a bloody civil war. Eventually an artificial boundary between the north of Ireland and the Irish Free State was created, after Britain failed to keep the terms of the treaty, and a large number of Catholics were permanently locked into a Protestant state ruled from London.[32]

The division in Ireland today is a living model of what happens to a country when the democratic wishes of the people are denied. Had the terms of the Irish treaty been honoured it is unlikely that Northern Ireland would have been created. International law professor Anthony Carty argues that a critical clause of the treaty was 'to make the boundary conform as closely as possible to the wishes of the population'.[33] But the wishes of the people were ignored.[34] Northern Ireland was not created in response to an Irish desire for self-government, says Des Wilson, international peace-prize winner and West Belfast community worker.

No one in Ireland of any political persuasion welcomed or wanted it. Its creation was an expedient imposed on the country by a hard-pressed British cabinet . . . Once the British imperial government had secured its interests in Ireland by installing an unchangeable pro-British regime in the north-east, and a regime in the south that could not or would not threaten its interests, the strategic ports it held in the independent part of Ireland were no longer necessary and it withdrew from them in 1938.[35]

The Discrimination Continues

The discrimination against Catholics in the north led to the formation of a civil-rights movement in the early 1960s. While Catholics were one-third of the population in the 1920s and nearly half by the 1980s, they were excluded, by law and prejudice, from nearly all positions of responsibility.[36] By the 1960s housing, employment, voting and political appointments were inextricably tied. Gerrymandering, the regular redrawing of electoral boundaries to favour Protestants, meant that Catholics could never be elected even if they had two-thirds of the votes. In local government approximately 220,000 Catholic votes were rendered politically meaningless.[37]

Derry proved to be the tinder-box. In the early 1960s Catholics outnumbered Protestants by two to one but through gerrymandering the Protestants won an election by 12 seats to eight. Protestants took charge of allocating housing, favouring themselves and leaving Catholics un-housed. This pattern occurred in other areas, such as employment.[38] But inevitably it all blew up in the Protestants' faces. British troops were brought in to quell the unrest in 1969 and thus the contemporary Irish Troubles began.[39] In the ensuing 30 years of conflict nearly 4000 people have been killed.

An Economic Issue

On the surface the Irish Troubles are always presented as a religious issue but in fact they are an economic issue. Many Catholics and Protestants have long recognised their commonality in the struggle. Des Wilson believes that the British strategy has always been to prevent a fusion of interests developing between Catholic and Protestant middle classes. Some Protestants rebelled against English rule 'not because they were being persecuted, but because they believed they would become more prosperous without London hanging around their commercial, industrial and social necks'.[40]

The English Parliament made a point of not interfering in the ongoing discrimination against Catholics. In fact a Speaker's ruling in the English House of Commons in 1922 went so far as to direct that Northern Ireland matters could not be raised.[41] Even in the 1960s the North of Ireland was discussed for less than two hours in total per year.

English public opinion is intensively conditioned by the continuous voluntary and compulsory censorship exercised by the English media in reporting to the British public. In the print media and on BBC television many programmes have been banned since the current troubles, despite the efforts of a minority of courageous journalists. The constant pressure on the media by the British government to show the British troops in a favourable light, regardless of their police-state terrorism, torture and illegal killings, has managed to keep English public opinion hostile to Irish republican opinion. Tim Pat Coogan summarises the media policy as

> a reluctance to allow the screening of material which might tend to arouse support for the nationalist position . . . any information which placed the security forces [British troops] in a bad light and an abhorrence of anything which depicted the IRA in situations which indicated either the possession of a degree of community support or a human face.[42]

This process of censorship reached a peak on 19 October 1988, when the British Home Secretary announced a ban on direct statements by representatives of Sinn Fein, Republican Sinn Fein and the Ulster Defence Association.[43]

Historian Philip Ferguson is pessimistic about the future: 'Northern Ireland was built into the British State; Britain is not likely to let go of it. The British ruling class clings on to this part of Ireland because to withdraw altogether would be to unravel the British state itself.'[44] The recent creation of a Scottish Parliament must surely signal an unravelling of the British state. Perhaps Ferguson is correct, but today there is an apparent recognition by both sides that there is no military solution. Despite its limitations, 71 per cent of the voters in the north and 94 per cent in the Irish Republic support the current peace process.[45] This level of support presents a new turning point in the relationship, and hope for a new dawn.

British Columbia, Canada: Denial to Recognition

In 1997 I was a keynote speaker and guest workshop leader at the Aboriginal Education Conference, A Gathering of Nations, in Victoria, British Columbia. I was invited to share the New Zealand Treaty experience from a 'European settler perspective' and to discuss the notion of European responsibility for healing history. School superintendents, lecturers in Native studies, schoolteachers and others involved in education in relationship to indigenous peoples came from all over British Columbia to attend the conference, some from remote areas via canoes and seaplanes.

I remember one workshop well. The questions and issues raised by participants took me by surprise because they so closely resembled a typical list articulated at the start of a Treaty workshop in New Zealand. Questions focused on protest by indigenous peoples, land claims, language, culture, treaties, settler identity and lack of connection to countries of origin. Some participants expressed the view that in their experience many European Canadians, including themselves, had limited knowledge of their own history and the history of colonisation in Canada. Other participants knew more. I utilised the diversity of knowledge within the group, alongside my own information about the colonial histories of British Columbia and New Zealand, to highlight the similarities and differences between the two countries. This gave me a great opportunity to demonstrate the New Zealand Treaty workshop model, as well as to learn more about the history of British Columbia.

Aboriginal Life Before European Contact

People arrived in the part of Canada now known as British Columbia before 9000 BC. Over time more than 40 peoples defined themselves by language, shared history, culture, spirituality, time-tested laws, elaborate resource management systems, changing relationships and geography. Within this population were eight language families whose hundreds of dialects outnumbered those found in Europe at the time.[46]

Before contact with Europeans the most recent estimates put the aboriginal population in British Columbia at 300,000 to 400,000.[47] European contact had a disastrous effect on this population, reducing it by as much as 80 per cent within a century.[48] Anthropologist Wilson Duff records a low point in 1929 of 22,605.[49] 'The most terrible single calamity', he says, 'was the smallpox epidemic in 1862, which killed about one-third of the native population.'[50] The total Canadian population is nearly 32 million. The aboriginal population is nearly 1 million, of which 170,025 live in British Columbia.[51]

Early European Contact

When the Spanish and British arrived in Canada they saw 'a wilderness for the taking, they did not see these complex [indigenous] societies'.[52] Europeans generally classed the native populations as savages and denied their right to sovereignty and even property rights.[53]

A recurring pattern of colonialism soon began to develop. Traders, settlers, trappers, adventurers and hunters drifted into Canada, the home of First Nations (indigenous Canadian) peoples. Missionaries arrived to evangelise the 'natives' and service the needs of the increasing numbers of European settlers, bringing with them a Christian gospel infused with the values and assumptions of the Empire.

Relationships were relatively peaceful and some mutual benefits emerged between the new settlers and the indigenous peoples, such as the exchange of new ideas, technology and opportunities for trade. Yet new settlers and missionaries began to see that their own interests would be further secured by the intervention of the 'mother' country. They called for law and order, stable governance and medical assistance for the 'natives' as European diseases were fast affecting the functioning of indigenous systems.

Royal Proclamation

The Royal Proclamation of 1763 forged a short-lived basis for co-operation and cohabitation between indigenous peoples and settlers.

The proclamation confirmed France's cession of Canada and other territories to Britain, and sought to avoid a costly war with Indians by affirming but limiting aboriginal sovereignty and land title.[54] The proclamation stated:

> Whereas it is just and reasonable and essential to our Interests, and the Security of our Colonies, that the several Nations or Tribes of Indians, with whom We are connected, and who live under our Protection, should not be molested or disturbed in the Possession of such Parts of our Dominions and Territories as, not having been ceded or purchased by us, are reserved to them or any of them, as their Hunting Grounds.[55]

Vast tracts of land in the west were reserved as 'Indian country', off-limits to European settlers unless they had a special royal licence. The proclamation recognised that the land belonged to First Nations—and had not been ceded to the Crown—and confirmed that aboriginal peoples had rights to land that pre-existed the assertion of British title. It also stated that in settled areas only the Crown could acquire land that Indians wished to sell.[56] It was under this policy that colonisation in North America began.[57]

The proclamation, in accordance with 'our Royal Will and Pleasure', set forth arrangements 'for the present, and until our further Pleasure be known'. But while there was some recognition of Indian 'interest' in lands they had occupied for hundreds, even thousands of years, a pervading ambiguity and sense of paternalistic royal benevolence set a trend for reinterpretation of the proclamation in dealing with issues of aboriginal title during the following century.[58] Within a decade there was a major policy shift. The emphasis shifted from securing Indian allegiance and mutual protection to actively assimilating Indians and orchestrating their removal to provide for increasing European settlement. This new emphasis shaped the policy of settler governments for well over the next hundred years.

Colonial Policy in British Columbia

The policies of the first two governors of British Columbia began undermining aboriginal title while paving the way for European settlement. Governor Douglas negotiated 14 treaties with specific

Indian groups between 1850 and 1854, relating to relatively small pockets of land on the south and east coast of Vancouver Island.[59] Known as the Douglas Treaties, these agreements recognised but effectively sought to extinguish aboriginal title.[60] Modelled on New Zealand precedents, they provided that the Salish and Kwakwaka'wakw signatories would retain their village sites and enclosed fields, the right to hunt over unoccupied land, and 'their fisheries as formerly'. Otherwise, they ceded their traditional territories 'to white people for ever'.[61] Douglas's policies left aboriginals with 'fewer rights, less land and less protection than the rest of their counterparts in Canada'.[62]

Douglas's replacement, Governor Trutch, was far more aggressive. He saw Indians as bestial, not human,[63] and he believed they had no future in colonial society and should make way for European settlers.[64] Trutch denied aboriginal rights, explicitly asserting that British Columbia Indians had never owned the land. He 'falsified the records of Douglas's dealing with the Indians over land and instituted a process of cutting down reserves . . . Indians also lost the option of pre-empting land'.[65] Trutch's policies were erroneous, dishonourable and illegal, but his influence was long-lasting and ensured that no further treaties were ever signed in British Columbia.[66] When the province later entered the confederation in 1871 it advocated policies ignoring aboriginal title and avoiding any requirement to make treaties.[67]

The Impact of Federal Government

When British Columbia joined Canada in 1871 the confederation extended its existing legislation over the territory. The 1860s had been an era of coercion, segregation and active assimilation and the British North America Act 1867, which established the Confederation of Colonies—Canadian federal state with a federal government, provinces and territories—also allocated 'jurisdiction over Indians and lands reserved for Indians' to that government. The Act of Gradual Enfranchisement of Indians and Better Management of Indian Affairs 1869 required most Indian tribes to register for enfranchisement (essentially Canadian citizenship) but the right to vote federally was confined to those who agreed to relinquish Indian status. Many Indians naturally resisted registration and were therefore disenfranchised. The Act granted the government powers over Indians (collectively known as bands) on reserves as though they were state wards.[68]

In 1876 the federal government passed the first comprehensive Indian Act designed to consolidate existing laws affecting Indians. This Act gave increasingly wide-ranging discretionary powers to the government-appointed Superintendent General of Indian Affairs. In the decades that followed these powers were used to repress Indian culture, prevent competitive trading, control the use of Indian monies and erode the Indian reserve land base. A provision was added to the Act in 1911, permitting 'the removal of reserves near urban areas without band consent'. Perhaps the most notorious example was the compulsory 'cutting off' of more than 19,000 hectares of valuable reserve land in British Columbia.[69]

The Oppression Intensifies

The impact of such legislation on First Nations was devastating. The resulting significant loss of their land base eroded their wealth, resources and traditional ways of life. It also contributed to the undermining of aboriginal culture and spirituality, and the dismantling of social and political structures, which collectively threatened their health and well-being as distinct peoples. Third World living conditions developed on many Indian reserves.

In 1927 the Indian Act was amended to make it illegal for First Nations to 'raise money or retain a lawyer to advance land claims'.[70] They were thus effectively unable to litigate claims or seek redress through the courts until further changes were made to the Indian Act in 1951. They were also shut out of Parliament during that time, blocking any meaningful political action. First Nations peoples in British Columbia were not given the vote until 1951.

The right to vote and the restoration of the right to take legal action kick-started aboriginal initiatives on the ground and in the courts aimed at pursuing land claims and self-government.[71] The Nisga'a group in British Columbia was the first to establish a tribal council, in 1955, to resume the campaign for land rights that had begun in the 1880s. The result was the precedent-setting case *Calder v. Attorney General of British Columbia 1973*, in which the Supreme Court declared that 'the concept of aboriginal title was part of Canadian law, whether such a title had been recognised by the government or not'.[72] In the mid-1970s the federal government responded with a land-claims policy and in 1982 it passed the Constitution Act, guaranteeing certain aboriginal, treaty and land-claims settlement rights.[73] At last progress was beginning to be made.

In 1991 the British Columbia Claims Task Force and a Treaty Claims Process were established. The government of British Columbia has since recognised the inherent right to self-government of aboriginal peoples, which may include managing their own affairs, exercising authority within their own jurisdiction, administering taxes, passing laws in negotiated areas, managing land and natural resources, and negotiating with other governments. Authority may include health, education and welfare programmes.[74] In 1997 the decision of the British Columbia Court of Appeal in *Delgamuukw v. British Columbia* affirmed that aboriginal claims to native title had never been extinguished.[75]

But the damage had been done. According to the Aboriginal Poverty Law Manual 2002, aboriginal people, half of whom live on reserves, represent about 5.4 per cent of the population. However:

- They make up 19 per cent of provincial prison inmates and 17 per cent of federal prison inmates (based on appearance only).

- They are eight times more likely than non-aboriginal people to become victims of homicide.

- They are 10 times more likely to commit homicide.

- Aboriginal women and children (under the age of 15) suffer the highest rates of abuse.

- Suicide rates are three to four times higher, with rates among young age groups being five to six times higher.

- The socio-economic conditions faced by Indians are low when compared to non-native Canadians. Social and economic conditions on most reserves in Canada are difficult.[76]

In addition, 45 per cent of all status Indians living on reserves are illiterate.[77]

These are the statistics of people who were dispossessed of their homeland and made wards of the state. They paint a sobering picture. Despite potential gains through land-claim settlements, none has yet been settled (see Chapter 11). There is much left to achieve in securing the survival of aboriginal people in Canada.

Australia: Terra Nullius to Amnesia to Awakening

In 1994 I attended the Mabo Conference in Sydney as part of the Ngai Tahu delegation from Christchurch.[78] The conference was a joint New Zealand and Australian gathering designed to reflect on the implications of the landmark Mabo decision which recognised the existence of Aboriginal title for the first time in Australian history. During two days of tense debate, various views on native title and mining issues were expressed appropriately. However, during the official conference dinner I encountered attitudes that were vastly different. I sat with a group of Australian mining company owners whose comments on Aboriginal peoples were appalling and unprintable. The traditional clash between the interests of miners and Aboriginal peoples was never more dire. But this continuing conflict is an inevitable outcome of Australia's colonial history.

Conquest by Declaration of *Terra Nullius*

The fiction of *terra nullius*, adopted in 1788, was based on the notion that Australia belonged to no one. It was 'empty land'. European powers reasoned that legitimate possession could be taken of any country that did not have political organisation and recognisable systems of authority.[79] When convicts and jailers arrived as part of the First Fleet on 7 February 1788 at Sydney Cove, officials raised the British flag, declaring sovereignty over New South Wales and ownership of the over two million square kilometres in the territory.[80] This declaration of sovereignty was extended over additional areas of Australia as settlement progressed.

As the colony began to grow, convicts became a key source of cheap labour. A large number of the English, Irish and Scottish poor convicted of minor offences were sent to Australia as convicts to work. Other poor from Britain enlisted in the army and navy to accompany the convicts as transport and occupation forces. The deportation of this potentially troublesome population, surplus to requirements in Britain, helped avert rebellion in the home countries.

20,000 Aborigines Killed in Frontier Conflict

As settlement increased, the demand for land increased rapidly and it was granted to settlers without any agreement with the Aboriginal occupants.[81] Close to 500,000 Aboriginal people, living in several hundred tribal groupings, lost ownership of land that had been occupied for 40,000 years—for 1600 generations or more.[82] Australian historian Henry Reynolds makes an informed guess that 20,000 Aborigines were killed in the violence of frontier conflict as their land was taken.[83] Those who resisted were driven inland and shot. In comparison, about 2500 settlers were killed by Aborigines at the time of invasion and settlement of Australia.[84]

The settlers justified their confiscation of Aboriginal land on the grounds that Aboriginal peoples held no title to land ownership and were not farmers because they did not use European farming methods such as fencing and cultivating land. They were judged by this standard to be not using the land productively. In Britain, of course, large sections of land were unoccupied and unfenced but the justification for this was that the land was 'all owned—or open to ownership. Title to wasteland in Britain was as secure as title to the best farmland. There was no obligation to cultivate'.[85] In fact Aborigines did recognise property rights and operated sophisticated systems of land usage.[86] Following European contact, however, they were increasingly left without land, socially dislocated and continually marginalised in all areas.

Survivors Marginalised

As colonial social, economic and political systems became established, the values of the majority culture began to permeate all aspects of institutional life. The education system was used not only to assimilate Aboriginal peoples into 'white' Australia, but also to endorse a particular way for 'white' Australians to view Aboriginal peoples:

> In school texts and in society at large at the turn of the [nineteenth] century, aborigines were seen as members of a race intellectually and socially far inferior to people of European descent: the only question was whether they were to be pitied or despised. At the ideological level, the effect of depicting Aborigines in this way was to justify the British occupation of the continent.[87]

A sanitised version of Australia's colonial history developed in 'white' Australia; an amnesia about the devastating impact colonisation had on Aboriginal peoples.

While Aboriginal peoples featured prominently in Australian historical records during the 1800s, Reynolds notes that between 1900 and the 1960s 'the Aborigines were virtually written out of Australian history'.[88] Aboriginal people had come to be seen as 'non-people', and were not even granted citizenship until 1967.

Genocide

Some 123 years after settlement, in 1911, the Aboriginal population of Australia had been reduced to 31,000.[89] Conquest of land, disease and social dislocation had all taken their toll. It is increasingly recognised, however, that a deliberate policy of genocide was also at work. At some stages in some states 'extermination' was unofficially condoned, and in all states the complete destruction of Aboriginal cultures was the aim.[90] The language said it all: politicians spoke of 'breeding them out', of 'the children of the bleaching', and of 'civilising' and 'Christianising' Aboriginal peoples.

Historian Dr Colin Tatz at the Centre for Comparative Genocide studies at Macquarie University in Sydney comments that historians tend to avoid using the word genocide. Instead, when writing Aboriginal history, they use words such as 'pacifying, killing, cleansing, excluding, exterminating, starving, poisoning, shooting, beheading, sterilising, exiling and removing'.[91]

Tatz argues that under the United Nations 1948 definition of genocide:

> Australia is guilty of at least three, possibly four, acts of genocide: first, the essentially private genocide, the physical killing committed by settlers and rogue police officers in the nineteenth century, while the state, in the form of colonial authorities stood silently by (for the most part); second, the twentieth century official state policy and practice of forcibly transferring children from one group to another with the express intention that *they cease being Aboriginal*; third, the twentieth century attempts to achieve the biological disappearance of those deemed 'half-caste' Aborigines; fourth, a *prima facie* case that Australia's actions to protect Aborigines in fact caused them serious bodily or mental harm . . . [for example] in sterilising Aboriginal women without consent.[92]

In a keynote address at the Mabo Conference Hal Wootten QC, head of the Royal Commission into Aboriginal Deaths in Custody, told delegates that in 1800 the average Aborigine was probably as well off as the average European. In fact, he said, Aboriginal peoples lived in more comfort than nine-tenths of the people in Eastern Europe.[93] Two hundred years later Aboriginal peoples are an underclass on the margins of a European society as an inevitable outcome of the destruction of their society under colonisation.

Australian historian Colin Tatz sums up the contemporary consequences:

> Even though the 2001 census indicated a tenfold increase in the Aboriginal population on that appalling figure of 1911 (from 31,000 to 410,003, this latter reflecting 2.2 per cent of the total population), Aborigines ended the twentieth century at the very top, or bottom, of every social indicator available: top of the medical statistics for diseases they didn't exhibit as recently as thirty years ago—coronary disease, cancer, diabetes, respiratory infections; bottom of the life expectancy table, at 50–55 years or less for males and around 55 years for females; with much greater rates of unemployment, much lower home ownership and considerably lower annual *per capita* income; an arrest and imprisonment rate grossly out of proportion to their numbers; the highest rate of suspension from schools; the highest rate of institutionalisation; with crimes now prevalent which were rare

as recently as the 1960s, namely, homicide, rape, child molestation, burglary, physical assaults, drug-peddling and drug-taking; and, sadly, youth suicide, no longer a criminal act, at a rate amongst the highest on this planet.[94]

Looking to the Future

Today there is no longer any justification for 'not knowing'. Two recent events have confronted white Australians with the facts of their own history. The first, in 1992, was the historic Mabo decision[95] and the second was the *Stolen Generations* report in 1997, which detailed the forced removal of 20,000–100,000 Aboriginal children from their parents over a 200-year period.[96] To ignore the challenge to understand and heal that history arising from these events would be to compound and collude with the devastation that has nearly destroyed 40,000 years of civilisation.

Conclusion

The impact of colonisation on indigenous peoples cannot be underestimated. Indigenous peoples had no resistance to the numerous European diseases that entered their countries. Biological warfare was inflicted on Native Americans by the British through the use of smallpox in the late eighteenth century and by the US Army in the early nineteenth century.[97] Some estimates put at 70 million the number of Native Americans killed in the last 500 years 'through a range of policies which collectively add up to genocide'.[98] The outcome in some colonies was, at worst, the systemic extermination of indigenous peoples.

Indigenous social, economic and political systems were dismantled as colonisation progressed and loss of land and authority became the norm. Historian Linda Tuhiwai Smith concludes that:

> Once initial invasions were accomplished any promises made to indigenous people were disregarded. Policies were implemented which denied the validity of indigenous peoples' claim to existence, to land and territories, to the right of self-determination, to the survival of language and forms of cultural knowledge, to natural resources and systems for living within their own cultural environments.[99]

The outcome of colonisation today for indigenous peoples is evident in the social statistics as in many countries they continue to suffer poorer health, die younger, and maintain lower employment rates and scholastic achievement. Disproportionate numbers of indigenous people are either in jail, homeless or living in poverty.

Many indigenous cultures survived colonisation. Yet, inevitably, the damage inflicted on their social, economic and political systems prevented many from developing modern structures. Now, in the twenty-first century, indigenous peoples in their ceaseless struggle against historical and contemporary injustices are confronting governments with demands that they honour treaty promises, recognise indigenous common-law rights and uphold the right of self-determination.

These legitimate demands need to be addressed. To fail to do so is to invite eruptions of violence such as those recently in Fiji, the Solomon Islands, Bougainville, the Marshall Islands, Te Ao Maohi/French Polynesia, Belau (Palau), East Timor, West Papua/Irian Jaya, Rongelap and Hawaii, to name a few.[100]

No country benefits from having a permanently marginalised population. The hope is that ultimately majority populations will act in solidarity with indigenous peoples to redress the injustices of colonial history.

THREE

Missionary Conquest: Christianity and Colonisation

Robert Consedine

Burnt Church Indian Reservation, 1992

It was silent when I woke and still dark outside. Soon I heard a stir of movement from somewhere in the cabin. 'Time to rise, Robert.' The gentle voice of my friend and colleague Frances Hancock called me to the 'first light' ceremony to greet the dawn and offer thanksgiving for the gifts of creation. I got up, dressed hurriedly and went outside.

Gkisedtanamoogk, a member of the Wampanoag Nation, was lighting a fire near the teepee behind the cabin. Soon we were joined by his wife and our host Miigam'agan, a member of the Micmac Nation. Gkisedtanamoogk began the ceremony by burning sweetgrass in the fire. Each of us then blessed ourselves with the sweetgrass. The beautiful chant came in waves, and as the sun emerged through the surrounding woods the fire warmed our chilled extremities. By the middle of the day, when the ceremony was well over and the sun directly overhead, we ate light refreshments. When the sun went down we went to bed.

It was autumn when I visited Esgenoopotitj, also known as the

Burnt Church Reservation. It was part of the ancestral home of the Micmac Nation, which is one of five tribes of the Wabanaki Confederacy, and was located in New Brunswick, on the edge of the Gulf of St Lawrence in Canada. I had been invited there as part of my study tour through North America in 1992. My purpose was to network with First Nation and African American peoples, discussing with them their histories, treaties, colonisation, genocide and survival, and also discussing racism and the human journey.

As well as visiting Miigam'agan, gkisedtanamoogk and other members of their family and community at Esgenoopotitj, I also visited a Passamaquaddy and a Penobscot reservation just across the border in the United States.

My time among Wabanaki peoples introduced me quite simply to another way of being. Theirs is a way of life intimately connected to the natural rhythms of the earth, one that constantly acknowledges the Creator in every process. My hosts talked of a living relationship with the land and all its creatures, with the seasons and the time of day. I learned that some children are named after particular birds or animals, and that the presence of certain animals around the house carries particular meaning. Bears, for example, are considered to be full of wisdom. If a bear arrives then there is likely to be a purpose to the visit. Great significance is also attributed to an eagle flying overhead at a particular time. An eagle feather is sacred to the Wabanaki.

At Esgenoopotitj I found myself among people who believe that the western world does not live according to the cycle of creation and that as a result we are always at odds with nature. It is from this that problems emerge. Gkisedtanamoogk spoke of the historical struggle of the Wabanaki peoples, who have for so long occupied the lands and regions currently known as and usurped by the nation states of Canada and the United States. The border between these two countries was created at the end of the American Revolutionary War in 1763, by the Treaty of Paris. This treaty was signed without the participation or approval of the Wabanaki Confederate Authorities on whose land the border was and is still situated.

One of the struggles facing Wabanaki peoples today is the refusal of the Canadian government to honour the Treaty of Amity, signed between Britain and the United States in 1794. Known commonly as the Jay Treaty, it guarantees, among other things, the rights of Indians living on either side of the border to pass and repass freely by inland navigation through the respective territories and countries of the two parties. The United States honours the right of free passage of Canadian Indians into the United States for living and working purposes without visas or permits, but the Canadian government does not honour the same rights for Indians born in the United States.[1]

The Terrorism of Church Residential Schools

During my time with gkisedtanamoogk and others, the discussion that had the most profound impact on me concerned the role of Christianity in the colonisation process. When my hosts discovered that I was a Catholic it all came out! Stories handed down through the generations; stories tinged with bitterness about the treatment of their peoples in the Catholic boarding school system, where priests and nuns dominated their lives. They told of severe beatings, the denigration of their culture, the breaking apart of families, and the destruction of their way of life. I saw great pain in the faces of my hosts, as if these cruel events had taken place the day before, and I recognised authenticity in their stories.

The Catholic Church was not alone in this terrorism. Indian children in other parts of North America were forcibly taken from their parents and placed in Methodist, Anglican and Presbyterian residential schools. Violence and abuse of various kinds was often used to maintain order in these institutions. Indian children encountered alien structures and routines, and were exposed to equally foreign child-rearing strategies and schooling techniques, including threats, taunts, deprivation, physical labour and corporal punishment. Sexual, physical and cultural abuse was not uncommon.

One of the main purposes of the residential school system was to separate children from their communities in a systematic attempt to rid them of their 'pagan lifestyle', including their language and spirituality. Indian children were regarded as 'dirty savages' and commonly told they were 'too dumb' to understand the instructions of their teachers. A prevailing missionary belief held that cultural, moral and economic inferiority also made Indian children vulnerable to dishonest and promiscuous behaviour. Some were told their parents were doomed to damnation because of their religious beliefs. In short, this school system aimed to *remake* Indian children by converting them to soul-saving Christianity, eliminating their own cultural identity, cutting their family ties, and fashioning them into 'pseudo-Caucasians'.[2] The system was, in the words of one Saskatchewan historian, 'an aboriginal nightmare'.[3]

The residential school system caused untold pain and lasting damage. In July 1991 at an Anglican residential school reunion held at Algoma College in Ontario, Chief Darrel Boissoneau of the Garden River Reserve in the Ojibwa Nation, himself a former missionary, argued that residential schools were an experiment in cultural genocide. He contended that Indians needed to undergo a healing process to overcome the damage done to them by these schools. 'Part of that process involved taking control of their own lives and well-being. And part of that self-empowerment, in turn, was the assumption of control of Native education by Native peoples.'[4]

The Catholic Church and Colonisation

Stories about the abuse of power in the Catholic Church are legion. I have personally observed and experienced this abuse of power in various forms. In 1967 I attended a congress in Rome involving lay people from over 100 countries. Pope Paul VI called the congress to obtain advice on church teaching, but on the issue of birth control the voice of the people was completely ignored. Any illusions I had then about the integrity of the institutional Catholic Church were shattered. Years later I remembered this experience while researching the role of Christianity, particularly that of the Catholic Church, in undermining indigenous cultures. The information I unearthed took me back 800 years and was even more appalling.

In the thirteenth century the Catholic Church, in addition to its evangelical mission, was also a secular world power, playing a pivotal role in colonising and dispossessing indigenous peoples. Pope Innocent IV, who reigned from 1243–54, held a relatively moderate position for his time.[5] He asserted that all human beings had basic human rights, including certain property rights and the right to choose their own rulers. These rights, however, were to be subordinated to the mission of the church. While he considered secular society legitimate, it was secondary to that of Christian society. He contended that as the vicar of Jesus Christ he had power not only over all Christians, but also over all non-believers. Therefore he could intervene in the affairs of other countries, but only indirectly.

The Pope's views were fiercely debated. His more orthodox opponents maintained that as the undisputed, ultimate authority of the church with final responsibility for evangelisation, the Pope had the right to intervene *directly* in the affairs of non-Christian societies. The canonist Hostiensis went further, arguing that the Pope could authorise military action in support of Christian missionaries. Such views later supported European expansion by providing the ideological justification for colonial conquests.

Although the Catholic Church believed it had a role in protecting the 'natives' in any particular country, the goals of evangelisation became subordinated to the colonisation process. The papal policy was pragmatic: papal support was given to European powers to invade new territories in return for the Catholic Church's right to convert 'the natives' to Christianity. During the fifteenth century Pope Eugenius IV (1431–47) gave the Portuguese authority to evangelise and civilise the Canary Islands; while his successor, Pope Nicholas V (1447–55), effectively gave the Portuguese a free hand to invade African countries and dispossess and enslave the indigenous populations. Later, in 1493, Pope Alexander VI promulgated a Papal Bull known as *Inter Cetera*, which authorised the invasion of America by Spain and gave

> full and free permission to invade, search out, capture and subjugate the Saracens and pagans and any other unbelievers and enemies of Christ

wherever they may be, as well as their kingdoms, duchies, counties, principalities and other property . . . and to reduce their persons to slavery.[6]

This decree clearly served to legitimise the actions of the colonising powers at the time, notably Spain and Portugal.

The papal policy of supporting colonisers to invade new territories in exchange for the right to convert indigenous populations did not go unchallenged. The most formidable and famous opponent was Father Bartolomé de Las Casas (1474–1566), who argued passionately for the rights of all people, including aboriginal peoples. He, too, was committed to conquering aboriginal peoples but hoped to do it less violently.[7] But his defence of the dignity of aboriginal peoples was ultimately rejected and he was marginalised.[8]

In what has been described as a high point of papal social teaching on the rights of aboriginal peoples, Pope Paul III (1534–49) wrote a key document called *Sublimis Deus* in 1537. In it he affirmed that all human beings have rights and the capacity to receive faith. Aboriginal peoples, he argued, were human beings—capable of understanding the Catholic faith, and wanting to receive it. He was silent on the issue of political sovereignty and never questioned the legitimacy of Spanish rule.[9] Aboriginal religions were subsequently disregarded as vague and useless, and no serious impediment to conversion to Christianity. The interests of the church and colonising powers remained paramount. In due course the Pope annulled the ecclesiastical sanctions that could have been used to protect American Indians from the rapacious Spanish conquistadors, a move reflecting the tension between evangelisation and the pressure to honour the system of royal patronage.

Over the next 400 years church missionaries and colonisers worked hand in hand conquering new lands and extending their empires. The majority of missionaries (Catholic and those of other Christian denominations) had a culture-bound theology in which evangelisation was synonymous with civilisation. Missionaries and colonial administrators were in the business of exporting European culture and religion to other parts of the globe. As J. M. Blaut has said: 'A missionary might have great love and respect for the people among whom he or she worked, but could not be expected to believe that the culture and mind of these non-Christians was on a par to that of Christian Europeans.'[10] Jesuit and historian Paul Prucha notes that, 'Not surprisingly, missionaries wherever they went fought hard for religious freedom for Christianity, but this freedom did not extend to the religions of indigenous peoples.'[11]

Cultural Genocide

George Tinker, a member of the Osage/Cherokee Nations and an associate professor of cross-cultural ministries, claims in his book *Missionary Conquest* that Christian missionaries of all denominations working among American Indian peoples were partners in cultural genocide. He defines cultural genocide as 'the effective destruction of a people by systematically . . . destroying, eroding or undermining the integrity of the culture and system of values that defines a people and gives them life'.[12] He argues that Christian missionaries, while no doubt well intentioned, were nevertheless 'guilty of complicity in the destruction of Indian cultures and tribal social structures [and] in the devastating impoverishment and death of the people to whom they preached'.[13] Tinker concludes that by and large Indian peoples were not liberated through the gospel of Jesus Christ.[14] Other indigenous peoples exposed to Christian missionaries may say the same.

Christian missionaries in such countries as the United States of America, Canada, New Zealand and Australia actively supported the passing of legislation to outlaw traditional indigenous religions. In 1890 in the United States they used their influence to promote legislation outlawing various indigenous ceremonies and making 'performance of the Plains Sun Dance and the Hopi Snake Dance, among others, a punishable crime'.[15]

Missionaries in Canada saw the potlatch ceremony as the main obstacle to Indians becoming Christians. The *give-away* custom integral to this ceremony was also seen as threatening to western economic practices and ideals of private property.[16] The potlatch was the hallmark of coastal Indian societies. At these gatherings political rank was determined, tribal decisions made, wealth distributed, and traditional rituals and dances performed. Celebrating and feasting capped the gatherings, at which conspicuous personal poverty was a chiefly requirement. In 1884 the Canadian Parliament amended the Indian Act making the potlatch illegal—law-breakers could expect six months' jail. The act was later amended again, enabling its enforcers to label any gathering of Indians, other than a Christian gathering, a potlatch. Those present again risked arrest and jail.[17] It was only in 1951 that the Canadian Parliament rescinded laws against the practice of traditional Indian religions.

In New Zealand the 1907 Suppression of Tohunga Act outlawed Maori traditional healers and religion.[18] Although designed and promoted by Maori politicians it was passed amid controversy. Some Maori supported it as by the early twentieth century they were deeply concerned at the inability of tohunga to heal the new western diseases using traditional methods. The Act was aimed at:

'Every person who gathers Maoris around him by practising on their superstition or credulity, or who misleads or attempts to mislead any Maori by professing or pretending to possess supernatural powers in the treatment or cure of any disease, or in the foretelling of future events.'[19]

However, the Act was also used for invidious purposes. The latter clause enabled the authorities to arrest (and silence) the Maori prophet Rua Kenana, whose prophecy about a Maori millennium involved driving out European settlers from New Zealand.[20] The Act also had the effect of outlawing Maori methodology and undermining the legitimacy of Maori knowledge in respect of healing, the environment, the arts and the links between the spiritual and the secular. The Act was repealed in 1962.

The Australian story is even more damning. For more than two centuries the Christian churches have been at the forefront of the systematic oppression and genocide of Australian Aboriginal peoples. In 1823 it became government policy to convert Aboriginal people to Christianity, 'teaching them the habits of clothes, prayer, work and industry'.[21] This policy was in direct conflict with a spirituality that had sustained Aborigines for more than 40,000 years. In enforcing this legislation many Christian missionaries essentially operated as agents of the Australian government, actively taking on extensive delegated powers and helping build a spirit of paternalistic contempt towards Aboriginal peoples. In some areas mission boards became the sole civil authority, exercising law-making powers and establishing and operating local institutions such as schools, infirmaries, hostels, jails and farms. The powers of the missionaries extended to prosecuting and jailing law-breakers, as well as counselling them, controlling their incomes, prohibiting their customs, and acting as sole legal guardians for adults and children.[22] Only recently have Christian churches in Australia begun to confront their role in dispossessing one of the earth's ancient civilisations.

A New Direction in Catholic Thought

Change in Catholic thinking on the rights of indigenous peoples came with the election of Pope John XXIII in 1958, who gave papal support to the political sovereignty and self-determination of indigenous peoples. Under his leadership the second Vatican Council, held in the early 1960s, recognised for the first time in Christian history the right to religious freedom for all peoples. It was only after this period that the right to maintain one's culture was explicitly recognised by the Catholic Church. In 1971, during the pontificate of Pope Paul VI, the synod document titled *Justice in the World* went further and made explicit the link between liberation and evangelisation. It stated that 'action on behalf of justice and participation in the transformation of the world fully appear to us as a constitutive dimension of the preaching of the Gospel'.[23] It was this kind of prophetic thinking that motivated many in my generation to become involved in justice struggles in our own countries.

While there were advances in thinking, some claims in the Vatican II document *Dignitatus Humanae* continued to promote a distorted view of reality. *Dignitatus Humanae* stated for example that 'it has always remained the teaching of the [Catholic] Church that no one is to be coerced into believing'.[24] This kind of claim compounded the historical denial of human rights by the Catholic

Church. Says Father Michael Stogre: 'As late as the 1950s, a Pope was still denying the right to religious freedom.'[25]

In the decades following Vatican II a theology of inculturation received increasing acceptance among liberation theologians and missionaries within the Catholic Church. Inculturation is the process of understanding the message of Christ within the framework of a particular culture. The purpose of inculturation is to defend human and cosmic life, and to affirm the presence of the spirit precisely where the colonisation process denied it: in the Indian, the African slave, the woman, the body and in nature. Interestingly, debate on this approach occurred as far back as during the first days of colonisation. Theologian and sociologist Richard Pablo argues that 'many missionaries, as well as some indigenous thinkers, offered inculturation as an opponent of colonisation, identifying it as the defense of life, especially the endangered life of the indigenous peoples and of nature'.[26]

It is extraordinary that the first Pope in history to recognise the uniqueness of aboriginal peoples was Pope John Paul II, who was elected in 1978. In a World Day of Peace message in 1988 he stated that to remove aboriginal peoples from their lands is to promote their destruction and eventually their extinction and is 'tantamount to ethnocide'.[27] But for many aboriginal peoples this statement was too little, too late. The gap between papal teaching and Vatican practice has significantly impacted on the credibility of the Catholic Church. Pope John Paul II went on to undermine the church's credibility when he disingenuously acknowledged the damage done by Christianity to aboriginal peoples but also claimed that the missionaries taught them 'to love and appreciate the spiritual and cultural treasures of your way of life'.[28] This assertion entirely failed to recognise the church's role in actively destroying and undermining indigenous cultures and religions, and was nothing less than insulting.

Throughout Latin America today many Catholic religious and lay people are fighting alongside indigenous peoples for human liberation, often at great personal cost. The assassination of San Salvador's Archbishop Oscar Romero in 1981 symbolised the fate of many church leaders who align themselves with the poor. In 1989 six Jesuit priests, their housekeeper and her daughter were murdered in El Salvador. The Jesuits were faculty members of the University of Central America, which played a leading role in efforts to resolve El Salvador's decades-long civil war. The Jesuits often spoke out against abuses of human rights perpetrated against the poor. A 1995 United Nations Truth Commission linked 19 graduates of the School of the Americas to the Jesuit slayings.[29] Notwithstanding the prophetic witness of individual Catholics such as these, the official Catholic Church continues to defend its institutional interests in South American countries and remains firmly aligned with the oppressors. As a final insult to those Catholics who struggle and die for justice the Vatican has just appointed six Latin American cardinals to top Vatican posts. Their main qualifications are their close personal supportive relationships with right-wing military governments and their opposition to liberation theology.[30]

The Way Ahead

A cursory look at history shows that the Catholic Church and Christianity in general were at the cutting edge of the colonisation process. They provided an ideology that affirmed European superiority and legitimised the invasion of the lands of many indigenous peoples. Catholic missionaries, with the support of the Roman Church, established institutions that helped to entrench and accelerate the colonisation process and at the same time undermine the fabric of indigenous ways of living. Many Catholic missionaries became the willing agents of colonial governments. The Catholic Church could have 'prophesied against the colonialism that was crippling the world' but it remained silent, choosing instead to become a willing partner in order to expand its own empire.[31]

The Catholic Church must re-evaluate its missionary history before it continues to canonise its missionaries. Should it canonise individuals who would be rejected by the people they sought to evangelise? Pope John Paul II is currently planning to canonise Franciscan Fray Junipero Serra for his missionary dedication to upholding the rights and dignity of North American Indians. Father

Serra worked among Native Americans in California in the eighteenth century when the use of corporal punishment, flogging, shackles and stocks by missionaries was commonplace.[32] Seen by many in the Catholic Church as a hero, Serra was on the payroll of the government and believed that punishment should aim to conquer and assimilate Native Americans. Today, the descendants of those whom Serra sought to convert to Catholicism take a different view of his place in history and are strongly opposed to his canonisation.

The Catholic Church is, of course, not alone. All Christian churches must realistically assess their role in undermining aboriginal cultures, and many have begun to do this. But although some important statements of regret have been made at an official level in New Zealand, Australia and Canada, many Christians in these countries have little awareness of their history and live comfortably with the myths of colonisation and the role of the missionaries. There is a tremendous amount more to do as we face the past, acknowledge what has happened and re-commit ourselves to the struggle for the liberation of all peoples.

The Catholic Church must own up to the crimes it has committed as a prerequisite to any credible apology and genuine healing. While some individual church leaders have offered apologies for past injustices, the institution still has a long way to go. Half-baked apologies, such as the recent Vatican document *Memory and Reconciliation—The Church and the Faults of the Past*, just won't do.[33] In this document the church blames anti-Semitism on the weaknesses of its members and attributes no responsibility to the institutional teaching authority. This overlooks the fact that Catholicism has a long history of anti-Semitism rooted in the perception that the Jews murdered Christ.[34] Historian Raul Hilberg has compiled a list of 20 canonical laws that were restrictive of Jews from the fourth to the fifteenth centuries and were paralleled by specific Nazi decrees.[35] This is the reason Rabbi Leon Klenicki insists that 'we acknowledge a continuity in the persecutions against Jews from the Constantinian period in the fourth century, all the way to the present day'.[36]

It took until 1959 for the term 'perfidious Jews' (Christ-killers) to be removed from the Holy Week liturgy by Pope John XXIII. In 1965 Vatican II officially rejected the idea of Jewish responsibility for the death of Christ. John Paul II has worked personally and assiduously to begin to heal the historic relationship. This history continues to be scrutinised with the continuing controversy of the role played by Pope Pius XII during the Nazi holocaust.[37]

The Achilles heel for the Catholic Church is its insistence that the 'teaching authority' of the institution cannot be wrong—only individuals. This premise is based on the institutional model wherein the church is 'a perfect society whose essence or core remains untouched by intellectual failure or moral fault . . . [This model] has failed to grasp that structural sin operates within the institution and must be confessed as such.'[38] Adding weight to this premise is the Catholic principle of the continuity of doctrine. This principle has long reinforced a view held by church leaders that any moral doctrine that has been taught by the church over many centuries must surely be right.[39] Any acceptance that the institution of the church may have been mistaken would strike at the heart of its claim to moral supremacy.

A parallel example can be found in the doctrine on slavery. From the sixth century the Catholic Church taught that 'the social, economic, and legal institution of slavery is morally legitimate provided that the master's title of ownership is valid and provided that the slave is properly looked after and cared for, both materially and spiritually'.[40] This teaching was supported by extensive Catholic pro-slavery documentation and such influences as the principle of the continuity of doctrine. It was only 'officially corrected' by the Second Vatican Council in 1965.

The Catholic Church must confront other contemporary challenges. The globalisation of poverty in the late twentieth century is unprecedented in world history. This poverty is not a consequence of a scarcity of human and material resources. It is the logical consequence of colonisation, which concentrated most of the world's resources in the control of about 750 global corporations.[41] Adherence to a global system based on the relentless accumulation of private wealth poses a huge challenge to any church professing the gospel of Jesus with a 'preferential option for the poor'. Richard Pablo argues that the Catholic Church must choose between inculturation and globalisation. 'If the Church chooses inculturation it will necessarily be opposed to globalisation.'[42] A church that follows the logic of globalisation will be unable to reach those who are marginalised or excluded. The standardised, paralysed, Europeanised, centralised, synchronised church will never reach those who are marginalised. Only a local church, the promise of Vatican II, grounded in the reality of the lives of local people, can achieve that goal.

Living with Paradox

I have spent my adult life working and searching for a more just and holistic world. Like millions of Catholics I have also lived with the paradox of a church that has inspired my journey, and that of many others, through its teaching on human rights and social justice. The problem has been that the teaching has so often been obscured by the abuse of power exercised by the institution.[43] It is a striking incongruity that in every country in which I have travelled I have met Catholics—inspired by the gospel of Jesus—taking huge personal risks in their work for human development and liberation.

In 1993 *Inter Cetera* was the focus of an unsuccessful petition by a group of indigenous peoples asking the Pope to rescind it. At the parliament of world religions in 1994 over 60 indigenous delegates drafted a 'Declaration of Vision', which read: 'We call upon the people of conscience in the Roman Catholic hierarchy to persuade Pope John Paul II to formally revoke the *Inter Cetera Bull* of 4 May 1493 which will restore our fundamental human rights'. In October 2000 a group of indigenous peoples staged a protest on the steps of the Vatican to reinforce their stand. A Vatican representative who received the petition was described as sympathetic but non-committal.[44]

Over 500 years after the promulgation of *Inter Cetera* by Pope Alexander VI, the indigenous peoples of the world are still awaiting a response to their 1993 petition to Pope John Paul II. They are seeking a formal end to the document that called for 'our Nations and Peoples to be subjugated so that the Christian Empire and its doctrines would be propagated'.[45] They have called on all bishops of the world to support their petition, believing that there is a direct causal relationship between this ancient papal document, the theft of native lands and the deaths of more than 96 million indigenous peoples: that 'this Papal Bull has been, and continues to be, devastating to our religions, our cultures and the survival of our populations'.[46]

In 2005 the petition is to be examined at the Pontifical Historical Commission. There has been no other response from the Vatican, other than to state that *Inter Cetera* is regarded as 'juridically not valid any more'. The Pope's formal revoking of *Inter Cetera* would be a symbolic call for an end to the subjugation that indigenous people have endured for 500 years, and an extremely important gesture of peace.[47]

However, the contemporary drive to centralise every aspect of the functioning of the Catholic Church and to exclude lay people from all but subservient roles does not augur well for inclusive, creative change envisaged by Vatican II, let alone future relationships with indigenous peoples.

In the midst of a hurting world, Joan Chittister, theologian, social psychologist and communication theorist, offers an inspiring reflection:

> Whatever the ennui, depression, the doubt, the fatigue we find ourselves adrift in God . . . nothing can stop the one who knows the whole truth has yet to be heard, that the Gospel is still being rejected by the very people who are responsible for telling it. It happened over and over again in the time of Jesus. Why not now?[48]

FOUR

Shattering the Myths

Robert Consedine

Waitangi, 6 February 1990

It was an oppressively hot day and an underlying tension permeated the environment. Police were everywhere, searching individuals, checking bags, confiscating placards and other protest materials and scrutinising the crowd. The area had been filling with people since early morning as various groups gathered to finalise their strategies for the day. The media were making last-minute preparations, expecting multiple news bites. Conflict was anticipated.

It was the 150th anniversary of the signing of the Treaty of Waitangi. Many people had made the journey to Waitangi to stand in solidarity with Maori demands that the Crown honour the Treaty. I, alongside many others, had spent the night before sleeping on the roadside in order to be part of the experience.

The waka, navy frigates and tall ships loomed in the distance as the restless crowd continued to await the arrival of the official party. Maori protesters, with some Pakeha support, were prepared for a major confrontation with the Crown. A group had been turned away from the Treaty grounds by the police but some individuals had managed to gain entry. Those who did not, blocked the bridge across to the Treaty grounds.

Queen Elizabeth II and the government representatives finally arrived by boat. As the official party made its way to the Treaty grounds someone threw a wet T-shirt at the Queen and the police moved in. Amid accusations and arrests the proceedings continued and the official party found their place. Then the speeches began.

Almost immediately Maori protesters began chanting: 'Honour the Treaty', 'Tino rangatiratanga' and 'Give back the land'. The speakers ploughed on. Two rows of protesters, each person presenting one large letter on a piece of cloth, stood on cue, raising their symbol in the air for all to read: HONOUR THE TREATY. It was a spectacular intervention—eye-catching and creative.

One of the official speakers, the Right Reverend Whakahuihui Vercoe, stood and publicly accused the Crown of marginalising Maori people. It was an extraordinary moment. After all the planning by the protesters for the Waitangi Day celebrations, a member of the official party had made a direct accusation against the Crown: the large crowd cheered but the officials sat stony-faced.

1990 was an important year in the history of New Zealand. In commemorating the 150th anniversary of the signing of the Treaty the government spent $30 million on various Treaty-related projects. For many Pakeha, Waitangi Day 1990 symbolised the beginnings of an awareness of the history of their country, in particular of the fact that promises made in the Treaty had not been kept by successive governments. The anger in the Maori community was very visible, symbolised powerfully in speeches and protest.

How did we get to this point in our history? Why so much protest? I decided that looking for villains would not be useful. Knowing what happened would be the vital clue. What I learned was that since the signing of the Treaty, every generation of Maori has engaged in protest against the colonisation of their country. The protest has taken many forms, including letters and delegations to queens and kings in London; petitions to Parliament; direct challenges to the authority and legitimacy of the government; armed resistance in the Land Wars; passive resistance at Parihaka; a variety of religious and political movements; court cases; appeals to the Privy Council; the formation of Maori political parties; the occupation of buildings and land; marches, pickets, blocking roads and bridges; the creative development of Maori systems (often started voluntarily) in language, education, justice, health and the news media. And the message has remained the same: Honour the Treaty.

Pre-European Contact

Hundreds of years earlier Maori had arrived in New Zealand, becoming the first human inhabitants of the country. They adapted rapidly to the physical environment, developing cultures deeply connected to the land and natural world around them. Over time, through interaction with one another, they evolved societies based on kin relationships. They established social systems to ensure their survival and development as tribal peoples. Each hapu operated independently and practised its own customs, which were maintained through a sophisticated oral system and rigorously enforced. The sovereignty of each hapu was grounded in a system of law based on custom. There was significant commonality among tribes in dealing with issues of justice, land, health and education, and some differences. Into this world, the first Europeans arrived.

Early European Contact

The Dutch explorer Abel Tasman sighted the Southern Alps of New Zealand on 13 December 1642. After naming it Staten Landt he sailed north, past Cape Foulwind to Farewell Spit, where Tasman and his crew became the first known Europeans to encounter New Zealand Maori. An early encounter resulted in a long boat off the *Heemskerck* being rammed by a canoe. Three crew were killed and another mortally wounded and exaggerated reports of the incident later circulated through Europe. Maori were described as murderers and New Zealand was seen as a dangerous place—impressions that influenced the perceptions and conduct of future exploration.

On 6 October 1769 a surgeon's boy, Nicholas Young, travelling with Captain James Cook on the *Endeavour* sighted Tuuranga-nui

(Poverty Bay). During its six-month visit the *Endeavour* circumnavigated the New Zealand coastline, anchoring in one harbour after another, visiting local settlements and welcoming Maori people on board. Accounts by Cook and Sir Joseph Banks noted that Maori were 'strong fit active and healthy . . . the men are of the size of the larger Europeans, stout, clean limbed and active'.[1] Anthropologist Anne Salmond suggests that Maori may have been more healthy than seventeenth-century Europeans, who 'lived about as long as pre-European Maori, but . . . overall they were more prone to disease and quite often less well fed'.[2] In the eighteenth century Maori life expectancy equalled that of the wealthier inhabitants of Europe and was 'well above that of countries such as Spain and Italy'.[3]

After the *Endeavour*'s visit, European ships began to visit New Zealand in ever-increasing numbers, guided by 'Cook's meticulous maps'.[4] Cook himself visited again in 1770 and 1773. Scientific exploration continued for a further 90 years with visitors from France, Spain, Russia, Austria and North America. From the late 1700s the most significant group of Europeans to roam around the shores of New Zealand were whalers and sealers, who interacted with Maori, coming and going at will. Long-term settlers began to arrive around 1800, along with timber workers and traders.[5]

At this point European relationships with Maori were mainly cordial and the contact mutually beneficial. Maori were still in control and could enforce their own custom. Early settlers were amazed at Maori fishing exploits—one fishing ground was located 77 kilometres from the shore.[6] Other evidence points to a significant scale of customary fishing practices, the use of sophisticated technology and a commercial motivation.[7] Joseph Banks, a botanist on board the Endeavour, described a net measuring 700–900 metres, while L. J. Nicholas, an early voyager, concluded in a record dating back to 1814 that 'their nets are much larger than any that are made use of in Europe . . . one of them very often gives employment to a whole village'.[8]

The Arrival of Protestant Missionaries

The next significant group to come to New Zealand was the

Anglican and Methodist missionaries who arrived from England in 1814 with their cultural beliefs and Christian idealism. The arrival of the Reverend Samuel Marsden in the Bay of Islands marked the start of formal contact with British missionaries. Conventional belief holds that in 1814 Marsden became the first missionary to lead a Christian service in New Zealand. In fact the first service had been held 45 years earlier on Christmas Day 1769.[9]

In the period leading up to the signing of the Treaty of Waitangi in 1840 Protestant missionaries engaged in the usual missionary activities. They built churches and schools, preaching and teaching in the Maori language. It was English Protestant missionary policy to be fluent in the Maori language to increase their effectiveness. Around 1820 onwards they began to record the Maori language, and by the 1830s a Maori-language version of the Bible was widely dispersed in Maori communities.

Missionaries introduced the first horses, cattle, sheep and poultry. Potatoes and other vegetables (introduced by Cook) were now available throughout the country and grown mainly by Maori. Sydney merchants were trading with Maori for flax, timber and produce. Such industry would have been applauded by Samuel Marsden (and his contemporaries), who 'ardently believed that Commerce promotes Industry—Industry Civilisation and Civilisation offers the way for the Gospel'.[10]

The Protestant missionary promotion of the Treaty of Waitangi also needs to be seen in the light of their rapacious land acquisition before 1840. Prior to the Land Claims Commission hearing in 1841, Anglican missionaries initially claimed they had fairly purchased 240,000 hectares from Maori. They subsequently reduced their claim to 87,800 hectares and the commission approved 27,000 hectares.[11] Tens of thousands of hectares were also claimed by other settlers and land speculators. However, the commission was ineffective and no land was returned to the Maori owners, as wasteland was now deemed to be Crown land. Land ownership by Anglican missionaries was the subject of fierce controversy in the 1840s between Anglican Bishop Selwyn, the Rev. Henry Williams and Governor George Grey. Williams's refusal to return Maori land resulted in his being dismissed from his post at the Church Missionary Society.[12] It is worth noting that many families became financially well established in New Zealand because of the dubious acquisition of land by their forebears.

Commenting on the role of these missionaries, one New Zealand historian concludes that these Protestant missionaries were at the cutting edge of British imperialist policy:

> The effectiveness of missionaries as unwitting components of Britain's imperial machine was due largely to the anglo-centric conception of Christianity which was held by many missionaries. This was a chaotic and confused concoction of religion, with concepts of monarchy, Empire, duty and civilisation, all tied in.[13]

The Civil Wars

In 1820 Nga Puhi chief Hongi Hika went to England as a guest of missionary Thomas Kendall, where he obtained a small arsenal of muskets. The civil wars between hapu, which had started earlier, intensified following Hongi Hika's return. Lawyer R. D. Crosby estimates that between 50,000 and 60,000 Maori were killed, enslaved or forced to migrate from 1810–1840.[14] However, demographer Ian Pool, on whom Crosby partly draws, points out that '100,000 persons could have been expected to have died over this thirty year period in the "normal course of events" with or without wars'.[15] Historian James Belich postulates a mortality rate of about 20,000.[16]

Nonetheless, casualties of constant raiding eventually became unendurable, causing many hapu to look for safer territories. This new type of warfare made it difficult for tribes to unite. Weaker tribes suffered terribly and later may have been more inclined to look to external mechanisms such as the Treaty of Waitangi for protection.

In 1835 Ngati Mutunga and Ngati Tama, two major hapu of Te Ati Awa from Taranaki, made a violent and tragic claim on the Chatham Islands, which had been occupied by the Moriori for over 400 years. The story that the Moriori were a separate race arriving in New Zealand before Maori and were subsequently driven out by Maori is one of New Zealand's most persistent myths.[17] This myth has been used to justify colonisation since the colonial government began dispossessing and marginalising Maori after the signing of the

Treaty of Waitangi. In fact, Moriori are Polynesians just like New Zealand Maori. They just happen to live on Rekohu—the Chatham Islands. The ancestors of the Moriori are the same peoples as the ancestors of the New Zealand Maori. The name Moriori was used after contact with Europeans and Maori, and is the same word as Maori in a different although closely related language.

At that time 500 men, women and children of Ngati Mutunga and Ngati Tama emigrated to the Chatham Islands. They chartered a European ship and many were sick on the journey. Moriori could have killed them with ease on their arrival but, in keeping with their pacifist tradition, offered them hospitality.[18] The invaders responded by beginning to kill the Moriori with muskets, clubs and tomahawks, and claiming the land. After a three-day meeting Moriori maintained the decision of their elders: there would be no killing by their side.

The outcome of that decision was tragic. It has been estimated that 300 died at the time of invasion and a further 1300 died subsequently of despair. There were only 101 Moriori alive in 1862.[19] Even before the invasion the European presence had already brought measles, influenza and venereal disease, which had by 1835 lowered the population by at least 400 to about 1600 in 1835.

The final injustice occurred in 1870 when the Native Land Court awarded 15,520 hectares of the Chatham Islands to Maori claimants and 240 hectares to Moriori in a decision that represented a rout for the Moriori. It is an astonishing paradox that subsequently back in Taranaki 'the Moriori were confronted by the spectacle of the people who had conquered and killed them forty years before now adopting a pacifist ideology; and choosing as their emblem the albatross feathers originally worn by the Moriori followers of Nunuku'.[20]

European Numbers Build

By the 1830s a mix of Europeans began to arrive in New Zealand. Some were traders who wanted to do business with Maori, some were settlers, some escaped convicts from Australia, and others were seamen jumping ship. Its potent mix of lawlessness, alcohol and prostitution established Kororareka (Russell) as the hell-hole of the Pacific in the eyes of the missionaries, although it was probably no worse than any English port town. It is estimated that a thousand ships visited the area during the 1830s. By the end of the decade Europeans living in New Zealand totalled around 2000.

Estimates of the Maori population at the time of the signing of the Treaty of Waitangi vary widely. Some are as high as 200,000, although this figure is thought by some more likely to represent the Maori population in the early 1800s, before hapu wars and introduced diseases had reduced the Maori population significantly. The most reliable estimate comes from Professor Ian Pool, who worked back from the Census of 1874 and that of 1857–58 to establish an estimated figure of 70,000–90,000. This would mean that in 1840 Maori probably outnumbered Europeans by about 50 to one.[21]

New Zealand had two potential colonisers, the French and the English. The French landed in two or three different parts of New Zealand in the early 1830s and began to negotiate with Maori for land and sovereignty. By the late 1830s they had a definite plan for the colonisation of New Zealand and had drafted a deed of purchase for the South Island.[22] As the decade wore on there was mounting pressure on Britain to respond to the situation in New Zealand, in particular to concerns about law and order, interest from other nations (France and the United States), continuing discussions within Maori society about establishing a national form of governance to unite the tribes, and the successful participation by Maori in international and local trading and other areas of European life.[23]

Britain Stakes a Claim

The British response in 1833 was to extend the laws of New South Wales to cover New Zealand and to appoint James Busby as British Resident. In 1834 Busby presented northern Maori chiefs with a flag to enable them to trade internationally. A year later, without any support from the Colonial Office, he was instrumental in forming what became known as the Confederation of United Tribes of New Zealand, an assembly of 34 leaders of northern hapu, whom he persuaded to sign a document he had prepared entitled 'A

Declaration of the Independence of New Zealand' (see Appendix I).

The declaration proclaimed New Zealand to be an independent state under the designation of the United Tribes, established as 'a congress, a legislative authority, which would meet annually at Waitangi to enact laws, dispense justice and regulate trade'.[24]

A principal aim of the declaration was to sideline assertions of sovereignty by a Frenchman called Baron Charles de Thierry, who had declared an intention to establish a sovereign and independent state on behalf of France on the banks of the Hokianga River.[25] But Busby also had humanitarian concerns about the plight of Maori, and indeed the colony, in the face of growing lawlessness among settlers.

Mason Durie notes that 'the intention in 1835 was to create a Māori nation state, a departure from the exclusively tribal orientation which prevailed, and the introduction of a confederated approach to governance'.[26] In the face of booming trade opportunities, some Maori saw benefit in building more cohesion among the tribes. Others were less convinced, seeing no need for foreign recognition of a sovereignty that, as far as they were concerned, already existed.

The British government duly acknowledged the declaration and offered Maori qualified protection. According to Durie, 'Though the Māori legislature never eventuated, the declaration was recognised in Britain as evidence of a Māori nation and served to support a unified front by Māori as settlers from other countries arrived.'[27]

Busby was also becoming increasingly concerned about the high rate of disease among Maori in the wake of the settlers' arrival and soon recommended to the governor of New South Wales that New Zealand become a protectorate. In a report to the British House of Commons in 1837, the Committee on Aboriginal Peoples soon backed up his concerns when it noted that native races tended to die out with the impact of European settlement. The anti-slavery movement also wanted Britain to intervene to protect Maori.

The Declaration of the Independence of New Zealand, witnessed by the Crown resident, is an international declaration, which acknowledges the sovereignty of the independent tribes of New Zealand. As a forerunner to the Treaty of Waitangi, it followed the adoption of a flag in 1834, which symbolised tribal rights to trade as independent nations.[28] Ranginui Walker concludes that 'it was the ceremonial raising of this flag beside the Union Jack at Waitangi, witnessed by the British resident James Busby and 25 chiefs, which signified the recognition of Maori sovereignty over New Zealand.'[29]

Meanwhile Captain William Hobson, another representative of the governor of New South Wales, had come up with a plan for New Zealand, similar to the 'factory plan' implemented in colonial India.[30] At this point, writes historian Claudia Orange, some sort of treaty became inevitable as Britain sought a method by which to legitimise its activities in the new colony.[31] Mason Durie goes so far as to say:

> There might never have been a Treaty at all were it not for the Declaration of Independence signed five years earlier in 1835. Having recognised Māori sovereignty and independence then, Britain needed a mechanism to justify imposing its own will on Maori . . .[32]

Meanwhile the New Zealand Company was promoting its own plan for colonising New Zealand, supported by an abundance of British capital and talk of cheap land, plentiful raw materials and unlimited trading opportunities in a distant paradise. Britain was in a state of domestic crisis, and a population excess, coupled with pressing poverty, were other factors influencing prospective settlers.

It was close to 1840 before the Colonial Office finally decided to appoint Hobson, as a consul representing the Crown, to return to New Zealand to negotiate a treaty with the Maori people. Maori had requested intervention to deal with the lawlessness of British settlers. Hobson's initial appointment as consul (rather than governor) may suggest, as historian Paul Moon argues, an intention of the British government 'to curtail the extent of British rule in New Zealand'.[33] The Colonial Office gave Hobson specific instructions: he was to negotiate a treaty which both sides understood fully and with the 'free and intelligent consent of chiefs'; he was to obtain sovereignty, but only if Maori were willing to cede it; and he was to obtain land, but on the condition that Maori retained enough for their own purposes and would not be disadvantaged. His instructions were clear: Maori 'title to the soil and to the sovereignty of New Zealand is indisputable and has been solemnly recognised by the British Government'.[34]

Sovereignty or Governance? The Treaty of Waitangi

During the first week of February 1840 northern Maori chiefs were invited to Waitangi in the far north to meet with Captain Hobson, British Resident James Busby and other representatives of the Crown, along with Reverend Henry Williams and other missionaries. The purpose of the gathering was to facilitate the signing of a treaty between the British Crown and Maori chiefs.

On 3 February Hobson drafted a treaty in English, assisted by Freeman, his secretary, and Busby. The English text acknowledged that the chiefs had collective *sovereignty* over New Zealand, which they agreed to cede to the British Crown and in return were promised undisturbed *possession* of their lands and estates, forests and fisheries, yielding an exclusive right of pre-emption to the Crown over such lands as the chiefs wished to alienate at prices agreed upon by both parties. Maori were also granted all the rights and privileges of British subjects.[35]

Overnight the Anglican missionary Reverend Henry Williams and his son Edward then translated this English version into a dialect of the Maori language. But there were important differences between the two versions, rendering the Maori text more saleable.[36] In the Maori text of the Treaty, the Maori signatories gave the Crown kawanatanga (governance) over their land and the Crown promised to protect the tino rangatiratanga (the unqualified exercise of authority) of the chiefs over their lands and villages 'and all their treasures'. The Crown also promised to protect Maori peoples and extended to them the same rights and duties of citizenship as the people of England.

Clearly the Maori were ceding a lot more than they thought they were. The final draft of the Maori text was presented to the chiefs for signature on 6 February. Some Maori were very suspicious of British motives, believing they would be deceived over authority and land, and initially rejected the idea of a treaty outright. It took considerable reassurance from British representatives, Protestant missionaries and some of the pro-Treaty chiefs to persuade them to sign. The advantages of British settlement were stressed, while the effects on Maori independence were downplayed.

In particular, Hobson repeated assurances that the Queen had a loving and protective concern for Maori; that she did not want the land, but rather the authority to govern her (British) subjects effectively and to punish those guilty of crime. Hobson emphasised that land would never be forcibly taken, and that truth and justice would always characterise the proceedings of the Queen's government.[37] The English Protestant missionaries presented the Treaty as the personal wish of the Queen and as her act of love; a persuasive argument given that by 1840 many Maori were deeply engaged with Christianity.[38] Inspired by missionary arguments, some Maori interpreted the Treaty as a new covenant between the two peoples.

In the middle of the negotiations Catholic Bishop Pompallier intervened and requested a promise that people be free to follow the religion of their choice. After some divisive debate a statement was drawn up whereby the governor guaranteed that the faiths of England, the Wesleyans and of Rome and Maori custom would be protected by him.[39]

While these persuasive arguments supported the Crown's intervention, they did not capture the entire picture. The Colonial Office had made it clear to Hobson that Maori were to be told only half the story:

> Hobson was told to explain to the chiefs that Britain was intervening especially on their behalf because there was no other way to protect them. The Colonial Office meant that Britain was intervening partly to protect the Maori from lawless Europeans, other colonisers, especially France, and bring peace within the country. It was also to protect the British settlers in New Zealand and the interests they had created. Hobson was not directed to emphasise this, nor to explain the Government's new willingness to promote the systematic colonisation of New Zealand.[40]

The meaning of 'sovereignty' was obviously pivotal. Under English law the sovereignty of the British Crown over its territories was exclusive and indivisible, making shared authority impossible. The

British Crown shared sovereignty with no one.[41] On the other side of the coin, Maori chiefs were not in a position to cede sovereignty to the British Crown. The very notion of *sovereignty* was located in a European legal and political framework, which was based on entirely different premises from a Maori world view. While the chiefs at Waitangi may have represented their respective communities, they did not have the authority to *give away* what the Europeans understood as *sovereignty*. Says Paul Moon: 'No chief, however high his [or her] rank, could dispose of a single acre without the concurrence of his [hapu].'[42]

In this environment of deception why did Maori sign? Dr Claudia Orange explains that the deception was

> couched in terms designed to convince chiefs to sign, explanations skirted the problems of sovereignty cognisable at international law and presented an ideal picture of the workings of sovereignty within New Zealand. Maori authority might have to be shared, but Hobson would merely be more effective than Busby, and British jurisdiction would apply mainly to controlling troublesome Pakeha. Maori authority might even be enhanced.[43]

It is likely that those Maori who signed the Treaty expected a new relationship with Britain based on shared authority. Maori understood that the Crown would govern the settlers and that Maori would continue to control their own affairs, exercising full authority over their own communities, lands and other treasures. They anticipated that troublesome Europeans and land issues would be controlled, intertribal fighting would cease and the benefits of trade would increase. For Maori the Treaty was not only a written document but also a spoken agreement. All that was discussed at Waitangi was integral to the spirit and intent of the new relationship.

About 43 Maori signed the Maori text of the Treaty at Waitangi.[44] Some Maori left without signing, including two paramount chiefs— Te Wherowhero of the Tainui tribes and Te Heuheu of the Tuwharetoa Confederation. Ranginui Walker says: 'Although the meaning of the Treaty was disguised by the word governance, Te Heuheu intuitively understood its true intent.'[45] Other chiefs, such as Taraia of Thames and Tupaea of Tauranga, refused to sign because they wanted to retain full control over their affairs, which they feared would be restricted by the governor. One chief present at Waitangi later returned his gift of blankets to Hobson 'with a letter signed by fifty of his tribe. He wanted his name removed from the Treaty. Hobson was highly annoyed and would not listen.'[46] Other chiefs were never given the opportunity to sign the Treaty.

The Maori text was eventually signed by 512 Maori throughout New Zealand over a seven-month period, including five Maori women. Most did not see or sign the English Treaty at Waitangi. At Waikato Heads the names of 33 Maori were *appended to* an English text and at Manukau another six names were added.[47] In May 1840 Hobson proclaimed British sovereignty over the North Island by right of cession, and in June over the South Island by right of discovery, even though some South Island chiefs had signed the Treaty. Inevitably both sides had different understandings; they were operating from different texts and different world views.

British imposition of sovereignty over New Zealand was 'gazetted' in London in October 1840. In May the following year the Letters Patent established New Zealand as an independent colony of Britain (and separate from New South Wales). Hobson then took the oath of office for his new position as governor. 'It was at this point that the Crown formally subsumed the powers of governance and sovereignty from Maori—without a single Maori signature in sight, and still with no Maori mandate for this sovereignty to be extended to cover Maori.'[48]

Honoured in the Breach

The colonisation process now moved rapidly. Governors were appointed successively and large numbers of settlers began to arrive. The huge influx of settlers coupled with the continued decline of the Maori population through disease meant that the settler population equalled that of Maori by 1858.

A serious attempt was made by the second colonial governor, Robert FitzRoy (1843–45), to respect the promises made to Maori in the English text of the Treaty. FitzRoy, although convinced of his own cultural superiority, was a proponent of the humanitarian idealism that had earlier championed Maori rights. Soon after assuming his post, however, he found himself in an impossible situation, charged with developing a colony without adequate financial resources. On the one hand he believed in the honour of the Crown and upholding Treaty promises made to Maori, and on the other he faced the increasing expectations of settlers and a growing financial crisis exacerbated by the enormous pressure exerted by the New Zealand Company.

FitzRoy introduced policies such as waiving pre-emption, printing money and introducing direct taxes to deal with the financial crisis, without authority from the Colonial Office.[49] His intention was to both protect Maori interests and help the settlers purchase cheaper land, but these policies were often at odds. His recall to London after two years, engineered by the New Zealand Company, was a bitter blow for the missionaries and humanitarians. The company was determined to pursue its goals for systematic colonisation with little regard for the Crown's Treaty obligations or Maori as a sovereign people.[50] George Grey, who was anti-missionary and more sympathetic to the New Zealand Company, replaced FitzRoy.

From 1846 the legislative process became increasingly anti-Maori and anti-Treaty. The new governor soon restored the right of Crown pre-emption with the Native Land Purchase Act of 1846, which directly overrode the provisions of the Treaty. This Act also made Maori land ownership uneconomic by outlawing leases and restricting trade in timber and flax, which put pressure on Maori owners to sell.

When Maori had signed the Treaty they understood that the right of pre-emption was a protection clause that gave the Crown the first right of refusal; that it was primarily a mechanism to protect Maori from unscrupulous Europeans. In fact the Crown used its right of pre-emption to acquire Maori land at low prices, onselling much of it to settlers at significant profits in order to raise funds to develop infrastructure in the rapidly growing colony. Many Maori, who were initially welcoming of settlers, became willing sellers in the belief that they were entering into the equivalent of a leasing arrangement, only to find later that private title meant that the land had gone for ever.[51]

Maori soon found that the Crown, manipulating the law to its own advantage, began removing land from Maori ownership by any means, including deception. The Kemp purchase was the largest block of land ever bought by the Crown. In 1848 the Crown purchased 8 million hectares (almost a third of the country's land area) in the South Island from Ngai Tahu for £2000 on the condition that the tribe would retain their villages and homes, their gardens and natural food resources, as well as substantial additional lands. Not only were these conditions never honoured but the Crown also manipulated the sale to obtain further land without the knowledge or consent of Ngai Tahu. The deal had the effect of reducing Ngai Tahu's remaining lands to 'a pitiful remnant of their previous vast territory'.[52]

In 1852 the New Zealand Constitution Act created the first New Zealand Parliament. Voting was based on individual title to land, which had the effect of excluding Maori from political power because Maori land was communally owned. Despite the fact that Section 71 of this Act allowed for Maori authority over certain areas of the country (by establishing Native Districts where Maori rules would apply), successive settler governments refused to implement it.

By the late 1850s settlers were pouring into the country with an expectation of land but were met with increasing Maori resistance to sell. While settlers had been in the minority, the colonial government was limited in its ability to enforce British rule, but as settlers became the majority population and the demand for land outstripped supply, the Crown exerted its own determination to control the manner of land acquisition, often defying Maori wishes.[53]

In 1858 the King Movement emerged within the Tainui Confederation of Tribes, proposing a parallel parliament based on shared sovereignty and seeking to stop all further land sales.[54] The settler parliament refused to recognise or resource this or subsequent efforts by Maori to establish their own parliament and proceeded to develop coercive mechanisms to ensure that the alienation of Maori land continued. War was inevitable. A series of events starting at Waitara in 1860, where the Crown attempted to take land that Maori leadership refused to sell, quickly led to a period known as the Land Wars, also referred to by New Zealand historian Claudia Orange as Wars of Sovereignty.[55]

Simultaneously, legislation was passed from 1862 in the form of Native Land Acts, effectively requiring many Maori owners to attend lengthy court hearings, prove ownership and then sell land to meet costs. Title could be granted if there were no Maori challenge, even if the real owners did not know of the claim. The Native Land Court established in 1865 (known to Maori as the 'land-taking court') became a vehicle to transfer and privatise ownership of Maori land, regardless of Maori consent and in opposition to Maori customary tradition. The effect of the legislation, aimed at individualising Maori land ownership, was to make sales easier for settlers and to destroy the power of the tribal system.

Apart from the Native Land Acts, two other laws of the 1860s deserve special note. The 1863 New Zealand Settlements Act enabled the Crown to confiscate land and property from any Maori who were believed to be in rebellion, whether the land belonged to the 'rebels' or not. Some 1.3 million hectares were confiscated under this Act, with the assistance of 28,000 imperial troops brought to New Zealand from 1856 by Governor Grey to subdue Maori. The Settlements Act was underpinned by the 1863 Suppression of Rebellion Act (direct from Ireland), which suspended basic rights for those found to be in rebellion against the Crown, carrying a penalty of confiscation and death. The main beneficiaries of these acts were the Crown and land speculators.

Another issue arose for the colonial government as a consequence of transferring Maori land to individual title. Because voting eligibility was subject to a property qualification (having title to land), meaning Maori could not vote while their land was held communally, the move to individualise titles had the effect of increasing the voting eligibility of Maori. The colonial government's response was to establish four Maori parliamentary seats in 1867. These seats did provide a very limited avenue for Maori representation in a political system dominated by wealthy, landowning European men. Their main purpose, however, was to prevent Maori from gaining significant political power. For a few eligible Maori the property qualification was additional.

In 1877, in *Wi Parata v. the Anglican Bishop of Wellington*, Maori sought to reclaim title to land earlier gifted for the purpose of building a church that had never eventuated. In its decision the court declared the Treaty of Waitangi a legal nullity because it had not been incorporated into statute. The ruling failed to uphold aboriginal common-law rights firmly embedded in English law, which guaranteed that the first occupants of a country had a natural right to the lands occupied by them. This landmark decision was directly contrary to the Treaty of Waitangi, the New Zealand Constitution Act 1852 and some colonial statues of the 1860s.[56] Yet it was to inform legal thinking for the next hundred years.

The extent and rate of Maori land deprivation overall was incredible. By the late 1860s almost all the 14 million hectares of the South Island and about 3 million hectares in the North Island had been purchased by the Crown. By 1899 a further 4.5 million hectares was acquired under the Native Land Acts.[57] Such was the confusion in law and practice relating to land that in 1891 the government set up a commission of inquiry chaired by William Rees. The purpose was to inquire into the working of Maori land law. In the final report the authors concluded 'that lawyers of high standing and extensive practice have testified on oath that if the legislature had desired to create a state of confusion and anarchy in native land titles it could not have hoped to be more successful than it had been'.[58] Dom Felice Vaggioli, an Italian monk whose observations of life in New Zealand in the late nineteenth century were so critical of British settlers that his book was eventually banned, offered a more colourful description. He wrote: 'The legal fraternity had no qualms about joining with settlers in their rapaciousness and greed in sucking Maori dry in the Native Land Courts.'[59]

Maori resistance to the land-grabbing continued, taking another form in the 1890s. In 1894 Kotahitanga mo Te Tiriti o Waitangi (1891–97)—the Maori Parliament—attempted to introduce a Maori rights bill into Parliament. Consistent with the Maori text of the Treaty, the bill sought Maori control over their own lands, fisheries, oyster beds, shellfish beds, tidal estuaries and other Maori food resources. When the bill was tabled, Pakeha members refused to form a quorum, and walked out of the House. Two years later the Pakeha Parliament formally rejected the bill.[60]

Maori were allocated four seats in Parliament in 1867 as a measure to allow token representation and limit Maori political power. The figures tell the story. Each Maori MP was required to represent 12,500 constituents while each Pakeha MP represented only 3500 constituents with a total of 72 seats. There was no way Maori would have been allowed the 15 seats in the house due to them on a population basis. When the four Maori seats were reaffirmed in 1896, a definitional change meant half-castes were given the choice of being enrolled for a Maori or European constituency; however, Maori seats were excluded from any provision for revision under the Electoral Representation Commission. So while European electoral boundaries were redefined every five years according to population increases, the Maori electorates were left unchanged. Not until 1967 were Maori candidates legally entitled to stand for general seats.[61]

The new century saw more land acquisition. Between 1900 and 1930 nearly 2 million more hectares were purchased, mostly under the Native Land Act 1909. Historian Alan Ward notes that this happened 'at a time when many Maori communities had little land left, when the Maori population was known to be stable or growing and when the Maori leadership made very clear their wish to retain and farm most of the remaining land and to receive State support to that end'.[62] By 1975, at the time of the great Land March from Te Hapua in the north to Wellington in the south, there was less than 1.2 million hectares of land left in Maori ownership. Long forgotten by most were the Colonial Office instructions to Hobson that only land Maori did not need to sustain their way of life and that they wished to sell should be acquired by the Crown under the right of pre-emption.

Maori: Dispossessed and Marginalised

From the time of the signing of the Treaty until the mid-1970s Maori went from being an industrious, vibrant, economically viable and entrepreneurial society successfully adapting to a rapidly changing world to a dispossessed, marginalised, threatened and involuntarily minority population in their own country. Maori were becoming strangers in their own land, seen as useful only for entertainment, tourism, sport, the armed services, and for marketing New Zealand as a South Pacific paradise with the best race relations in the world.

The Education Ordinance introduced by Governor George Grey in 1847 began a process of continuous government policy designed to accelerate the process of settlement, to establish and strengthen Pakeha institutions, and to encourage assimilation. That ordinance offered subsidies to Methodist, Anglican and Catholic missions to run boarding schools for Maori children, removing them from their villages, placing them in a culturally foreign environment and exposing them to 'religious education, industrial training and instruction in the English language'.[63]

Later, near the close of the 1860s, 'Native Schools' aimed to 'civilise' Maori children and prepare them for manual or labouring work, emphasising order, discipline, respect for the British Empire and the development of practical skills, with little regard for Maori cultural values. 'Their goal was not to extend the pupils intellectually but rather to provide them with sufficient schooling to become law-abiding citizens.'[64] English was the medium of instruction and many Maori children were physically punished for speaking their own language in the classroom and playground, a practice that was to continue well into the next century. These practices served to discourage many Maori from maintaining their language—the lifeblood of any culture. However, part of the impact of colonisation also meant that many Maori parents petitioned Parliament to teach English and forbid Maori language in schools. Further, many Maori refused to speak Maori to children so the acquisition of English was hastened. English was seen as the medium for success in an English-speaking world.

Successive governments passed legislation and implemented policies in an unrelenting attack on the foundations of Maori society. The Native Reserves Act 1864, for example, allowed the Crown to lease all remaining Native Reserves to Pakeha farmers at token rentals. In the 1890s Maori were forced to pay a 'dog tax', with penalties of jail and hard labour, in a move to reduce the numbers of stray dogs in Maori communities as they were considered a menace to stock.[65] In the early 1890s, responding to the Rees Commission, the government passed a series of laws such as the Native Land Purchases Act (1892), the Native Land Purchase and Acquisition Act (1893), the Native Land (Validation of Titles) Act (1893) and the Native Land Court Act (1894).[66] Historian Tim Brooking sums up the result:

> Most of the Maori land was actually acquired in the 1890s (2.7 million acres) by the state and about 400,000 by private individuals), despite the determined and vociferous opposition of Kotahitanga, Kingitanga and all the Maori MPs other than James Carroll. The penultimate grab of farmable Maori land ensured that most first class land had passed from Maori hands by 1900.[67]

The story of Parihaka serves as the ultimate illustration of the determination of the Crown to undermine Maori society and override the human rights of Maori. In the 1870s Taranaki Maori, led by the inspirational Te Whiti o Rongomai and Tohu Kakahi, set up a model, self-sufficient village with some European-style housing and market gardens. Te Whiti, himself inspired by the teachings of the Bible, preached temperance and peace to his followers and developed a series of creative, non-violent tactics 50 years ahead of Mahatma Gandhi.

The Crown, acting in the belief that the land had been legally confiscated in the 1860s, sent Pakeha surveyors to peg the area ready for sale. Under Te Whiti's leadership Maori women went out at night to rearrange the pegs. Te Whiti also instructed teams of ploughmen to plough and plant the land, and to build fences to block the roads.

In response, during the late 1870s and 1880s the Crown passed some of the most shameful legislation in New Zealand history to expedite the confiscation of land at Parihaka—ultimately 800,000 hectares. This legislation eventually suspended *habeas corpus*, a right guaranteed in the Treaty, enabling Maori to be jailed indefinitely with hard labour and without trial. The Crown sent in 1589 troops to destroy the village and to ultimately arrest 636 of Te Whiti's followers, who filled the jails in Taranaki and in Mount Cook, Wellington. Historian Sean Brosnahan records that 215 prisoners were shipped to Dunedin in four separate groups: 74 men from Pakakohi (the Patea district) 1869–72; five from the East Coast 1871–75; and 136 supporters of Te Whiti and Tohu 1879–81. Te Whiti and Tohu themselves spent 18 days in Dunedin in 1882.[68] Prisoners provided hard labour all over Dunedin. The *Deed of Settlement of Ngaati Ruanui* records that 18 prisoners died before release, 'prison conditions were hard' and 'oral sources refer to prisoners being housed in caves'.[69]

By the 1890s Maori were seen by the settlers as a disappearing race. The Maori population, possibly as high as 200,000 at the beginning of the century, was by its end a mere 45,000, while the European population had climbed to 770,000.[70] Most Maori lived in appalling conditions. Living in makeshift camps without sanitation, they suffered a high infant mortality rate and succumbed easily to infectious diseases. There was little medical assistance and traditional remedies had minimal impact. Dr Alfred Newman, an influential physician and businessman, maintained at the time that the 'disappearance of the race is scarcely a subject for much regret. They are dying out in a quick, easy way, and are being supplanted by a superior race.'[71] His opportunistic arrogance reflected widely held beliefs at the time, with Victorian racism pervading Pakeha colonial culture, including science.[72]

Maori were often also denied government assistance available to the rest of the population. Under the Advances to Settlers Act (1894) low-interest loans were made available to Pakeha settlers only. At the turn of the century many older Maori found themselves excluded from receiving the newly introduced old-age pension because they could not prove their age and it was assumed they had land resources to rely on. After World War I, Pakeha returned servicemen went into a ballot for a farm, while their Maori counterparts were excluded on the basis that Maori communities already had land of their own.[73] During the Depression unemployed Maori men were entitled to only half the unemployment benefit received by Pakeha men. The assumption was that Maori had land resources to sustain them. Yet this contravened Article Three of the Treaty which guaranteed Maori the same citizenship rights as Pakeha.

By the end of World War II, 75 per cent of Maori still lived in tribal areas, often around their marae, but the war, rural poverty and the search for work initiated a period of rapid urbanisation.[74] The government was also offering inducements for Maori to labour in manufacturing and assembly plants. By the mid-1960s more than 60 per cent of Maori were living in urban areas.[75] However, Maori well-being remained tenuous and the 1961 Hunn Report presented an improving but still largely dismal picture of Maori health and social conditions. It advocated a new government policy of integration, which 'espoused the retention of Maoritanga within an overall Pakeha framework'.[76] But the rhetoric did not match the reality. Policies of integration worked to disguise a continued push towards assimilation, or absorbing Maori into Pakeha society.

Until 1960, for example, responsibility for Maori children was usually shared between the extended Maori family and the community. A policy of integration required that from 1962 adoptions be conducted under the Adoption Act 1955, supplanting the role of the extended Maori family. 'The Act was based on the concept that the adoptive parents should completely replace the birth parents . . . and all records of the baby's origin were sealed for ever.'[77] The mechanism for the change was the revoking of the adoption powers of the Maori Land Court in 1962.[78] For many Maori, 'adoption' moved their children from being an open community responsibility to a closed Pakeha system shrouded in secrecy, with no recognition of the possible long-term impact. Despite this whanaungatanga continues.

The negative impact and outcomes of colonial structures and policies are the focus here, with particular reference to the significant exclusion of Maori from the structures of the nation state, loss of the right to exercise their tino rangatiratanga, loss of their economic base and consequent poverty. It is generally established that settler prosperity rested on Maori dispossession.

However, despite their subordination to the dominant European society, Maori have responded to and engaged with the nation state in a variety of ways over the last 165 years.[79] Giselle Byrnes, in a critique of the work of the Waitangi Tribunal, notes that

> in historical scholarship outside the Treaty claims process, 'fatal impact' interpretations have largely been abandoned . . . [although] historians do not deny the negative and destructive consequences of colonialism they have persuasively argued that Maori political and social systems were dynamic, highly adaptive and increasingly pragmatic in response to changing circumstances and the long-term effects of that change.[80]

The tribunal, however, is a commission of enquiry; its role is to answer a question by receiving and investigating claims, weighing the evidence, making a judgement on the balance of probabilities and then formulating recommendations. It is the forum where the Maori story can be officially told, heard and recorded, often for the first time, although many of the assertions Maori are making are not new. A variety of political activities highlighted their anger and discontent throughout the nineteenth and twentieth centuries. They were made at the time grievances happened. Ngai Tahu made their first complaint in 1849. This is not judging 1849 by today's standards. The issues were named and known at the time. The Waitangi Tribunal deals with evidence about which judgements can be made. Some examples: Tainui lost vast areas of land because of confiscation; the government attack on Waitara was unprovoked; and Ngati Whatua were rendered landless. Maori common-law rights were guaranteed and not upheld. The challenge is how to make reparation for that, decades after the event.

In this generation we are concerned with *consequences*. Maori did not have the power to maintain their position as the European state was imposed. They never stopped asserting their right of tino rangatiratanga—unqualified exercise of authority—of their tipuna, which was reaffirmed in the Treaty of Waitangi. Simultaneously, the Crown has never stopped ruthlessly subverting and undermining the exercise of that same Maori authority. A classic example is the number of committees set up by Maori in the nineteenth century— by kainga, hapu, iwi, district, or according to a particular goal. One of the primary aims of these committees was the abolition of the

Native Land Court and regaining the right to determine ownership of their own lands. But Maori were 'consistently denied this right and instead subjected to an institution which distorted their customs, denied them the tribal ownership guaranteed by the Treaty and quietly and efficiently denuded them of their lands as a result'.[81]

There can be little doubt that policies of successive governments largely overrode Maori advice and protest and served to erode the fabric of Maori societies by systematically dismantling Maori institutional life. Today, 165 years after the signing of the Treaty, less than 1.2 million hectares of land remains in Maori tribal control, compared with about 27 million hectares originally. Maori are over-represented in the negative social statistics. They have the highest unemployment rates, poorest health statistics, highest youth suicide rates, highest conviction and incarceration rates as well as lower home ownership. With their survival as a people so long threatened, their legal rights (until recently) overridden in the courts, their power in the political system restricted, the 20,000 Maori protesters at the 2004 foreshore and seabed hikoi were walking in the footsteps of their tipuna in the tradition of a long history of creative resistance.[82]

FIVE

Confronting the Myths

Robert Consedine

Christchurch, 1970s

On the fringe of inner-city Christchurch sits an old, run-down church, painted Canterbury red and black on the outside and Superman red and blue on the inside. Concrete stucco peels from the exterior walls and rusty spouting leaks. Since World War II this building has housed Corso, New Zealand's leading non-governmental international aid and development agency. Many other organisations, such as Trade Aid, Catholic Overseas Aid and Medical Aid Abroad, have since decamped.

This was my office base when I was the Corso organiser for Canterbury, the West Coast, Nelson and Marlborough in the 1970s. Despite the surroundings, it was here that I, with hundreds of committed and inspiring volunteers, remained totally preoccupied with fundraising for Corso's overseas world aid and development projects. Our focus was overseas development assistance and emergency relief, and we were also committed to developing consciousness-raising projects aimed at educating New Zealanders about poverty in developing countries.

Celebrities were roped in to help raise the profile of these projects among the New Zealand public. Educators such as Paulo Freire and Ivan Illich, theologians such as Tissa Balasuriya and Hans Kung, liberation leaders such as Walter Lini of Vanuatu and Jose Horta of East Timor all found their way to Christchurch. We also hosted visits from United Nations agencies, Hollywood actor Danny Kaye, country and western singers Tex Ritter and Tom T. Hall, and others who assisted in fundraising for Unesco. Mother Teresa came to town and inspired us all. All Blacks including Colin 'Pine Tree' Meads generously allowed themselves to be 'kidnapped' and 'held to ransom' in support of various fundraising projects. Prime Minister Norman Kirk dropped in occasionally, inspiring us with his vision of justice for every human being.

In the midst of this manic activity Maori activist Dun Mihaka appeared on the scene, more than once. His challenge to Corso supporters was direct: how can you focus on injustice in the Third World and ignore the plight of Maori people in New Zealand? It was the first time since the activities of Nga Tamatoa at Auckland University and the Auckland Committee on Racism and Discrimination that I was forced to think about New Zealand history. With little concrete knowledge of my own I had accepted many of the myths of my childhood and couldn't see the problem. It wasn't until after the 1981 Springbok tour that I internalised the extent of the situation and felt a need to respond.

The Beginnings of Public Awareness

In the late 1960s the challenge facing Maori must have seemed overwhelming: how to raise awareness in a majority population that had almost no knowledge of New Zealand's colonial history and was largely in denial about domestic racism. Maori also had to contend with an unsympathetic media, which reflected the conventional majority view that New Zealand had the best race relations in the world and that Maori had had a good deal. The 1960s initiated an era of protest movements in many western countries, and New Zealand was no exception as Maori protesters began the daunting task of alerting the New Zealand public to long-held and deep-seated Treaty grievances existing in Maori communities since 1840.

The sort of challenges facing Maori in advancing social change were not new. The (anti-slavery) abolitionists, suffragettes, the women's movement, trade union leaders, peace movements and every liberation struggle in history has faced similar challenges. In the passion of wanting change, people must decide how far to go to confront the injustice. Protest movements in Ireland and South Africa had adopted both non-violent strategies and armed struggles. Contemporary Maori struggles by contrast have always been non-violent.

The political activities of Nga Tamatoa, the great land march of 1975, the occupation of Bastion Point and the work of the Waitangi Action Committee dramatically increased the visibility of Maori protest. Highlighted and often misrepresented in the media, these activities contributed to significant social change in New Zealand. They helped promote a growing Pakeha awareness of New Zealand's colonial history, of the effects of government policy and court rulings, of the background to the development of the Waitangi Tribunal and the expansion of parallel Maori institutions. Many Pakeha began to better understand the highly contested debate on the constitutional status of Te Tiriti o Waitangi and the tangata whenua status of Maori peoples in New Zealand society.

At the heart of Maori protest was the loss of land, taken by destructive legislation passed as recently as 1967.[1] Maori activist Eva Rickard explained the significance of land to Maori in this way:

> Whenua is land. It is also the placenta within the mother that feeds the child before birth. When the child is born the whenua is treated with respect, dignity and taken to a place in the earth and dedicated to Papatuanuku—the earth mother of the Maori people. There it will nurture the child because our food and our living comes from the earth. It says to the child that this is your little piece of land—no matter where you wander in the world I will be here. And at the end of your days you can come back and this is your Papakainga and it will receive you in death. This, I believe, is the spiritual significance of the land to the Maori people.[2]

However, this does not apply to all Maori. Some choose to sell.

From the early 1970s Maori protest focused on Waitangi Day (6 February—a national holiday commemorating the signing of the Treaty in 1840). Nga Tamatoa (the Young Warriors) stated that 'unless the Treaty was ratified the Maori would declare Waitangi Day a day of mourning.'[3]

Maori protests on Waitangi Day were to take many creative forms over the next 30 years. In the year 2000 Prime Minister Helen Clark refused to attend the ceremonies at Waitangi where they had been held since 1953. Instead, she commemorated the day at Onuku Marae, near Akaroa. Crown–Maori relationships in the new millennium have been even more conflicted. At Waitangi in 2004 Prime Minister Helen Clark was reportedly 'caught in a crush', and Opposition leader Don Brash was 'hit in the face with a clump of mud'.[4] Both had previously made speeches hostile to the aspirations of many Maori. In the *Government Proposals for Consultation* document, released the previous year, the government had declared that the foreshore and seabed 'were in general, vested in, or owned by, the Crown' and would become public domain, despite a 2003 Court of Appeal decision to the contrary (see Chapter 10).[5] Dr Brash had also made a speech that many Maori believed was hostile to their aspirations, as well as racist.[6] With the advent of a new Maori Party, led by former Labour Minister outside Cabinet Tariana Turia, and a polarised electorate, Treaty issues and relationships may well be central to the 2005 parliamentary elections.[7]

1975 Land March—Te Roopu o te Matakite (The People with Foresight)

It was an event resplendent with symbolism. The land march Te Roopu o te Matakite, formed by Syd Jackson, Whina Cooper and others began on 13 September 1975 at Spirits Bay in the far north of New Zealand. In legend the spirits of the Maori dead pause here before beginning the long journey to Hawaiiki, resting place of the ancestors.

The march started at the water's edge, with others joining along the way. At Te Hapua, New Zealand's northernmost marae, the main body assembled. Two trucks and a bus accompanied the marchers to carry supplies, the injured and the old.

Media coverage ensured the month-long march was noticed by tens of thousands of New Zealanders, who lived in transcendent ignorance about the colonial history of New Zealand. Although Pakeha struggled to grasp its meaning, the land march, which stopped overnight at 29 marae for late-night discussions, had a highly politicising effect on Maori. It was a continuing protest at the alienation of Maori land—te whenua o te iwi. The slogan was explicit: 'Not one more acre of Maori land to be surrendered to the Pakeha.'[8] Ranginui Walker sums up the impact thus: 'As a consequence of the land march, Maori people throughout the land were politicised in a unity of purpose to a level unprecedented in modern times, in the endless struggle against colonisation.'[9]

The marchers converged on Wellington and Parliament on 13 October with their demand: control of Maori land in perpetuity. It was a momentous intervention—the beginning of a process to put the Treaty back on the contemporary political agenda.

1976–78 Bastion Point: Stepping Outside the Law

The struggle to reclaim the land intensified after the great land march. Two years later a government plan to subdivide 24 hectares of Crown land at Bastion Point triggered an extended and high-profile occupation of the site. The genesis of this protest lay in a land grievance dating back nearly 140 years.

Auckland, the largest city in New Zealand, was once a fishing village on the shores of the Waitemata Harbour owned by the Ngati Whatua o Orakei. In 1840 the Crown, using its power as sole land agent and setting a pattern for future land dealings, bought the Auckland isthmus—1215 hectares—for £241 and within nine months Hobson had onsold 17 of those hectares for £24,275.[10] Ngati Whatua were naturally aggrieved and determined to retain the remaining 285 hectares they still held for their own livelihood. Until 1976, their continued protest had always been lawful.

For over 100 years after the first intervention of the Native Land Court in 1868, the Ngati Whatua had protested, but until 1976 they have always protested within the law. They launched eight actions in the Maori Land Court, four in the Supreme Court, two in the Court of Appeal, two in the Compensation Court, six appearances before Commissions or Committees of Inquiry and 15 parliamentary petitions. The 'occupation' of Bastion Point by the protesters, from 1976 to 1978, was the first time any part of the tribe had stepped outside of the law.[11]

The protest was led by Joe Hawke, who as a boy had witnessed the burning of the papakainga (ancestral village) at Okahu Bay in 1951. This savage act of inhumanity was the culmination of a series of blunders carried out by the government, which was determined to get the land to cover up previous mistakes. On 25 May 1978, after 506 days of occupation, 600 police officers, supported by the New Zealand army, arrested 222 protesters for wilful trespass on Crown land. The use of army and police, ordered by Prime Minister Robert Muldoon, received dramatic media attention, which reverberated through the country. That event symbolised a national day of shame for New Zealand. Professor Ranginui Walker described it as 'a sordid tale of colonial oppression of the once proud owners of Tamaki Makaurau'.[12] Walker concluded that 'few people drew the conclusion that the Crown had been down that road against Rua Kenana, Te Whiti and Te Kooti. Fewer still realised that the Maori is not intimidated by power . . .'[13]

Waitangi Action Committee

During the late 1970s and the 1980s public consciousness continued to be outraged and/or challenged by the activities of the Waitangi Action Committee.[14] In 1979 the committee initiated a 'raiding party' against a group of engineering students at the University of Auckland who were parodying a haka, as they had done for years. They had tried to negotiate a solution with the group but had failed to convince the students that their actions were culturally offensive. During the 'raid', haka skirts were ripped off the students.

An anti-Maori media misrepresented the raid as a gang rampage. The protesters were charged with rioting and, despite strong community support, were convicted and sentenced to community service. Yet even conservative Maori leadership came out in support of the protesters and against the insulting behaviour of the engineering students. Ranginui Walker observes that 'the He Taua [the avengers] attack on the engineers' haka party effectively exposed the raw nerve of racism in New Zealand society, which for so long had been concealed by the ideology of Maori and Pakeha as one people living in harmony'.[15] The Waitangi Action Committee, with Maori and Pakeha support, continued to engage in protests, focusing attention on Waitangi Day, using highly charged slogans such as 'The Treaty is a fraud' and 'Cheaty of Waitangi'.

During this period increasing numbers of Maori around the country were becoming involved in protest actions against local governments. They protested against the confiscation of Maori land because of unpaid rates, zoning restrictions that prevented Maori communities from building on their own land, and attempts to claim coastal land and reserves for open space. A highly visible example was the struggle of Tainui Awhiro, led by Eva Rickard, to reclaim ownership of land at Te Kopua Whaingaroa (Raglan). In World War II the Crown had taken the land for an emergency airstrip but it had never been used for this purpose and was subsequently placed under the control of the Raglan County Council, which leased it to the Raglan Golf Club. Traditional burial plots were used as greens. After lengthy protest some of the land was eventually returned.

The 1981 South African Springbok Tour
The protest movement to stop the 1981 Springbok rugby tour of New Zealand galvanised the nation and became another point of awakening for many Pakeha. Twenty years earlier the 1960 'No Maoris, No Tour' campaign had captured media interest and aroused public attention in its attempt to halt New Zealand's collaboration with the racist South African sporting administration, which required the exclusion of Maori from the All Blacks. By the late 1960s the focus was on the apartheid sport system in South Africa, in support of calls for a complete boycott from a variety of black South African groups. A growing minority of Maori and Pakeha New Zealanders stepped up the campaign to stop all apartheid sporting

tours and in 1973 Prime Minister Norman Kirk called off a tour of New Zealand by a racially selected South African rugby team, citing the threat to law and order. His Labour Party suffered at the ballot box as a result.

In 1981 the country was polarised when the rugby administration and the National government determined that the proposed tour should proceed. Many New Zealanders took to the streets in a series of planned protests and hundreds were arrested and charged with various offences. The tour divided families and communities.

The anti-apartheid, anti-tour campaign gave rise to a period of civil action and law-breaking unprecedented in New Zealand since protests by the Anti-militarist League prior to World War 1.[16] The campaign demonstrated a capacity in New Zealanders, pushed far enough, for significant social disorder. Many Maori and Pakeha agreed on this issue and came together to support the protests in a watershed for New Zealand, which again exposed the raw nerve of racism underpinning our society and challenged New Zealanders to think more deeply about their own country.

In this climate of political protest, two major official reports signalled a growing concern about race relations. *Racial Harmony in New Zealand* prepared by the Human Rights Commission in 1979, and *Race Against Time* produced by the Race Relations Conciliator two years later, indicated that New Zealand race relations were at a turning point. 'The myth of New Zealand as a multi-cultural utopia is foundering on reality . . . We are now seeing the conflict of culture in very real form.'[17]

A New Direction: The Waitangi Tribunal

Ratification of the Treaty of Waitangi became a new focus for Maori demands. Maori argued that if the Treaty had legal or constitutional standing then they would be more able to pursue their claims in the courts. Matiu Rata, Minister of Maori Affairs, sponsored the Treaty of Waitangi Act, which was passed into law by the Labour government in 1975 and represented a new era in New Zealand's journey with the Treaty of Waitangi. It established the Waitangi Tribunal as a commission of inquiry to hear claims by any Maori or group of Maori people relating to *future* actions or omissions of the Crown deemed inconsistent with the principles of the Treaty of Waitangi. The Act did not define these principles; rather it gave the tribunal the exclusive authority to determine the meaning and effect of the Treaty, referring to both English and Maori texts and deciding on the differences between them. The tribunal was required to report on its findings and make recommendations to the government.

Historian Marcia Stenson notes that from a number of tribunal decisions—spread over 20 years—a series of common core principles can be found:

- The essential bargain was the exchange of the right to make laws for the obligation to protect Maori interests.

- The Treaty implies a partnership, with mutual obligations to act towards each other in good faith.

- The Treaty is able to be adapted to meet new situations.

- Compromise is needed on both sides, so the needs of both Maori and Pakeha can be met.

- The principle of redress for Treaty breaches flows from the Crown's duty to act reasonably and in good faith as a Treaty partner.[18]

During its first 10 years the Waitangi Tribunal's accomplishments were minimal and many Maori subsequently viewed it as another Pakeha trick. One tribunal member, Paul Temm, says that on his appointment to the Waitangi Tribunal in 1982 he thought it would sit for 'only one or two days a year'.[19] However, during that first 10 years the tribunal made some significant recommendations that had practical outcomes ultimately benefiting all New Zealanders.

The 1983 Motunui claim focused on the contamination of traditional fishing grounds and reefs by industrial waste and sewage. The 1984 Kaituna claim responded to a proposal by the Rotorua City Corporation to divert treated sewage into the Kaituna River, affecting the quality of fisheries. The tribunal upheld both claims, accepting that the claimants' spiritual and cultural values would be prejudiced as a result of any effluent in their waterways. But the tribunal's recommendations were mild and conciliatory, aimed at effecting a practical solution that both parties would accept. In the Motunui claim 'the immediate result was the suspension of the proposed effluent outfall off Motunui'[20] and in the Kaituna claim the tribunal recommended that 'the Rotorua City Corporation investigate alternative land-based sites for disposing of the effluent that would avoid Lake Rotorua and the Kaituna River'.[21]

The Waitangi Tribunal's Te Reo Maori (Maori language) report in 1986 was another peg in the ground. It detailed active attempts by previous governments to stamp out Te Reo Maori,[22] the threatened state of the language,[23] and persistent efforts by Maori communities to retain and cultivate their language. In the report Te Reo Maori was interpreted as a taonga (treasure) essential to Maori culture and protected under the Treaty of Waitangi. The tribunal's report led to the passing of legislation in 1987 declaring Te Reo Maori an official language and conferring the right to speak Maori in any legal proceedings. But the Act, like the tribunal's recommendations, did not meet radical demands, and made no provision for Maori to be spoken in dealings with public authorities or for public documents, notices and newspapers to be published in both English and Maori. The Act did, however, establish Te Taura Whiri i te Reo Maori—the Maori Language Commission—to promote Maori as a living language and advise and assist the Crown in implementing Maori as an official language.

Tribunal's Powers Expanded

A fourth Labour government passed the Treaty of Waitangi Amendment Act in 1985, following a decade of Maori agitation on Treaty issues and motivated by a desire to retain the Maori vote. This Act gave the Waitangi Tribunal an expanded membership and the authority to investigate claims against the Crown retrospectively. The Orakei claim, regarding 280 hectares of land, was taken to the Waitangi Tribunal by Ngati Whatua in 1985. The first historical land claim presented to the tribunal, this claim arose from the Bastion

Point protest and two subsequent land occupations. In 1987 the tribunal made a series of recommendations for redress to Ngati Whatua o Orakei, which were later partially implemented by the government in 1991.[24] The recommendations were restrained but achievable. They included the return of some land, much of which was to remain in public reserves, the cancellation of a debt of $200,000, and a $3 million payment. The payment was not calculated on the value of lost land, the bulk of which had already passed into private ownership and would have been worth many millions of dollars. Rather it was calculated on a minimum amount 'needed to provide an economic base—or least adequate housing— for those members of the tribe who wished to return to Orakei'.[25] The payment represented only a fraction of the value of what the Crown had taken and the tribe was generous in accepting it.

To date the tribunal has produced over 100 publications, including more than 65 claim reports and more than 40 overview, thematic, district, occasional and review reports. They cover breaches of the Treaty of Waitangi relating to land, fish, waterways, radio spectrum rights, flora and fauna, petroleum, foreshore and seabed, and the right to sovereignty, among other issues. As at 30 June 2004, 1178 claims had been registered: 427 had been disposed of; 333 were in research and hearing; 207 were in report writing; 20 were consolidated claims; 109 were still to be investigated and one claim number was not allocated.[26]

Crown guidelines for the resolution of historical claims are:

- The Crown will explicitly acknowledge historical injustices— that is, grievances arising from Crown actions or omissions before 21 September 1992. 'However, a comprehensive settlement will still allow a claimant group or a member of a claimant group to pursue claims against the Crown for acts or omissions after 21 September 1992, including claims based on the continued existence of aboriginal title or customary rights. The Crown also retains the right to dispute such claims or the existence of such title or rights'.[27]

- Treaty settlements should not create further injustices.

- The Crown has a duty to act in the best interests of all New Zealanders.

- As settlements are to be durable, they must be fair and equitable with all claimant groups.

- Settlements do not affect Maori entitlements as New Zealand citizens, nor do they affect their ongoing rights arising out of the Treaty or under the law, and

- Settlements will take into account fiscal and economic constraints and the ability of the Crown to pay compensation.

To complement the Crown guidelines, in 2000 the government developed a set of six negotiating principles intended to ensure that settlements are fair, durable, final and occur in a timely manner. They are good faith, the restoration of relationship, fairness between claims, just redress, transparency and that they be government negotiated. There are four stages in the process between claimant groups and the Crown: preparing the claim for negotiation, pre-negotiations, negotiations, and ratification and implementation. After agreement in principle is finally reached and signed by both parties, a draft deed of settlement is installed, ratified and signed, a governance entity is established and legislation is introduced. The deed of settlement would include historical account, Crown acknowledgements of breach and Crown apology, and financial, commercial and cultural redress.

Most historical Treaty claims involve one or more of the following types of land loss:

- Pre-1865 land transactions, including pre-Treaty purchases later investigated and validated ('Old Land Claims'), Crown purchases, and post-Treaty private purchases made during the Crown's waiver of its pre-emptive right to purchase Maori land.

- Confiscation of Maori land by the Crown under the New Zealand Settlements Act 1863, and/or

- Transactions after 1865 under the various native/Maori land laws.

Recently a new fast-track procedure has been developed in the Central North Island inquiry. Tribes from Rotorua, Taupo and Kaingaroa wanted a 'quick, fair and transparent public process, without the full researching and hearing of all 150 claims'. This new process will enable potential settlement by 2005. Future claimants will then be able to choose between a full enquiry and this speedier process.[28]

The tribunal process serves many positive purposes. For one thing, many tribes and hapu have researched their own histories with a view to establishing claims before the tribunal. For another, it gives Maori an opportunity to tell their histories and express their grievances in a forum that ensures they are respectfully heard—some feel for the first time since the Treaty was signed. The protocols observed respect Maori culture and tribunal hearings are now routinely held on local marae. The process contributes to the process of healing required to resolve long-standing grievances.

Another benefit is the production of tribunal reports which document large sections of New Zealand's colonial history, often for the first time. The tribunal's reports are remarkably comprehensive, well indexed and quite outstanding in terms of layout, narrative and detail. They will provide valuable material for generations to come and have already served to encourage public debate on the Treaty and provide the government with considered views on a wide range of Treaty issues, taking into account Maori customary and ancestral law.

Drawbacks in the Tribunal Process

There are, however, significant weaknesses in the tribunal process. Historian Paul Moon identifies the main drawback as being that the Waitangi Tribunal is not independent—that the government has 'unconcealed political involvement in the Tribunal's operation'.[29] Certainly the tribunal operates in a conservative political framework and must acknowledge and work within the given political climate. And while its findings have been potentially radical, its recommendations have often been mild and accommodating, providing solutions that 'could be achieved without much pain or expense to the predominant Pakeha community'.[30]

The tribunal's recommendations are generally not binding on the Crown, except in regard to exotic forests, surplus railway land and state-owned enterprises land.[31] The Crown can otherwise ignore the recommendations of the tribunal when considering whether and how it recognises Treaty claims. The tribunal is required to function on the assumption that the Crown's sovereignty is indisputable.

By law the tribunal is also bound to take both texts of the Treaty into account, despite their differences. It has upheld a view advanced by Lord McNair in *The Law of Treaties* 'to the effect that in the absence of a provision to the contrary neither text is superior to the other, but that it [is] permissible to interpret one text by reference to the other'.[32] This view puts the tribunal at odds with the *contra-proferentem* principle in international law, which requires that an indigenous language text of a treaty takes precedence when there is dissonance between the texts. The US Supreme Court more than 100 years ago laid this guiding principle for interpreting treaties with Native Americans. In an 1899 ruling it stated that treaties should be construed 'in the sense which they would naturally be understood by Indians'.[33] It is astonishing that a government commission such as the Waitangi Tribunal should be required to even consider the English text of a treaty neither signed, nor sighted by most Maori. Furthermore, it is widely believed that the government in the mid-1980s set up the Waitangi Tribunal primarily to turn protest into a paper trail and to reassert the shaky legitimacy of the Crown. Jane Kelsey captures this view in her assertion that 'colonial leopards do not change their spots, they just stalk their prey in different ways'.[34] The slow progress made by the tribunal and recent governments would support that view. The tribunal has also created the illusion of partnership while marginalising the more radical elements of Maori society.[35]

In defining and interpreting Treaty principles the Waitangi Tribunal draws not only from the two Treaty texts but also from historical documents that shed light on the intentions and understandings of the original signatories and the historical context in which the Treaty was signed, as well as contemporary legal interpretations. This consideration of the circumstances surrounding the Treaty signing allows for a fuller appreciation of its meaning then and its implications now. However, many Maori and others do not support the view that the English text has equal status to the Maori text.

Inadequate funding has been an ongoing issue for the tribunal, delaying the process and creating a backlog of claims. Moreover, the Crown has not moved to spread the settlement payments over a longer period, as has the government in British Columbia, making larger amounts of redress more affordable.

Despite these significant limitations, the tribunal's achievements have been considerable and promise some positive long-term outcomes. Treaty settlements where they have occurred are enabling Maori to strengthen their economic base through local, national and international business initiatives.

The New Zealand Institute of Economic Research undertook for the first time in 2003 an in-depth analysis of the Maori economy.[36] The conclusions transform the frequently promoted myth that Maori are a drag on the New Zealand economy, painting a very different picture:

- The Maori economy is more profitable than the general economy, has a higher savings rate and is a net lender to the general economy.

- Maori households contribute more in tax than they receive in benefits and other fiscal transfers. Maori households receive $2.3 billion in fiscal transfers and make a tax contribution of $2.4 billion from the Maori economy.

- The Maori economy grew faster between 1997 and 2002 than the general economy.

- The Maori economy is more exposed to international trade than the general economy.

- The apparent trade-off between Maoriness and economic success is mostly a failure of the existing institutions to reconcile the two better.

- There are difficulties getting finance but Maori institutions themselves could fill the gap.

- The return on equity and assets is lower than in the general economy, which reflects a need for big governance changes.[37]

The Effect of a Market Economy

The Labour Party's rise to power in 1984 led to the opening up of a traditionally protected economy to a world economy. As a result it voluntarily embraced and implemented an economic policy based on a philosophical belief in the total rationality of the market. This policy shift resulted in the lowering of trade barriers, destroying many New Zealand businesses, the promotion of foreign investment and the turning of traditional government departments into profit-earning enterprises with the ultimate goal of privatising state assets. Political commentator Bruce Jesson argues that

> speculative finance has gutted New Zealand's productive economy since the barriers to the global market place were dropped in 1984–85, and society as a whole has been gutted with it. It is no exaggeration to say that while the means of the financial dealers may be sane—and in fact highly rational—their purpose is mad if viewed from any perspective other than their own self interest.[38]

Some Maori leaders and many Pakeha viewed Labour's economic policies as being in direct conflict with the Treaty of Waitangi Amendment Act (1985). On the one hand Maori were being encouraged to work with the Crown to settle Treaty grievances. On the other hand, state-owned enterprises had the authority to sell all surplus state assets to the highest bidder, including foreign owners, which meant there would be little left for Maori to claim. Moreover, it was argued that while the Crown had obligations under the Treaty, the private sector, both local and international, was free from such obligations. Academic Jane Kelsey sums up the contradiction:

> The structural goals of government's policy were to shift resources and control from the Crown to the private sector . . . When the state transferred its resources through privatisation, or its power through

devolution, it would also divest its ability to perform, and to be held to account for, its Treaty responsibilities. There would be very little in the hands of the Crown for Maori to exercise rangatiratanga over. The interests of capital would be left more secure while Maori would remain economically and politically destitute.[39]

This policy of privatisation was concretised in the State Owned Enterprises Act in 1986. The Act enabled Crown land to be sold into private ownership by the new state-owned enterprises, which took over the land from previous government departments and were required to run at a profit. Once in private title, the land could not be subject to a claim under the Waitangi Tribunal. Of a total of 27 million hectares (the land surface of New Zealand), 3 million were intended to be transferred to Landcorp and 880,000 hectares to Forestcorp.[40]

There were strong Maori objections to this legislation until, acting on advice from the Waitangi Tribunal, the government inserted a Treaty clause in an amended Act. Section 9 states: 'Nothing in this Act shall permit the Crown to act in a manner that is inconsistent with the Principles of the Treaty of Waitangi.' This section, however, was contradicted by Section 27, which ultimately allowed a state-owned enterprise to dispose of Crown land.

In 1987 the New Zealand Maori Council went to the Court of Appeal in the so-called state-owned enterprises case. The court ruled against the passage into private hands of Crown land that might be subject to Waitangi Tribunal claims. The Court of Appeal further stated that Section 9 was overriding in its protection of Maori claimants and that the transfer of state assets was contrary to the principles of the Treaty, and would be unlawful. The government then passed the Treaty of Waitangi State Enterprises Act (1988), protecting Crown land transferred to state-owned enterprises which might be subject to claims before the tribunal. The tribunal has (in these cases only) the power to make a binding recommendation on the Crown to return such land to Maori owners. All land titles were to carry a memorial (caveat) protecting potential claims, but state-owned enterprises could apply to the tribunal to have the memorials lifted.

The Principles of the Treaty of Waitangi

One of the features of the contemporary debate is the emergence of the principles of the Treaty of Waitangi. The fact that they have provided a broad framework for creative and visionary change is one of the strengths. Parliament, in the meantime, has wisely refrained from trying to define them precisely. Different versions have emerged from the Court of Appeal, the government, the Waitangi Tribunal and the New Zealand Maori Council.

The Court of Appeal in 1987 stated:

- The Treaty provides for the acquisition of Sovereignty in exchange for the protection of rangatiratanga.

- The Treaty requires a partnership and the duty to act reasonably and in good faith.

- The Treaty provides for the freedom of the Crown to Govern.

- The Treaty bestows on the Crown a duty of active protection of Maori people in the use of their lands and waters to the fullest extent practicable.

- The Crown has a duty to remedy past breaches of the Treaty.

- The Treaty provides for Maori to retain Chieftainship (rangatiratanga) over their resources and taonga and to have all the rights and privileges of citizenship.

- The Treaty bestows on Maori a duty of reasonable co-operation.[41]

The Labour government defined the principles in 1989, and these were then modified in 1990 by the National government as:

- Principle of government (kawanatanga).

- Principle of self-management (rangatiratanga).

- Principle of equality.

- Principle of reasonable co-operation between iwi and government.

- Principle of redress.

It should be noted that these are the government-redefined principles of the Treaty. They are not the terms of the original Treaty of Waitangi. Maori were not consulted. At best they are an important step. Here is the New Zealand Maori Council's version of the principles:

- The duty to make good past breaches of the Treaty.

- The duty to return land for land.

- That the Maori way of life would be protected.

- The duty to consult Maori.

- That the parties would be of equal status.

- That priority would be given to Maori values with regard to taonga.[42]

The principles are constantly evolving. An excellent guide to the principles of the Treaty of Waitangi, as expressed by both the courts and the Waitangi Tribunal, was published by Te Puni Kokiri in 2001.[43]

The Role of the Courts

The decision of the Court of Appeal in the state-owned enterprises case represented a new direction in the courts' interpretation of the Treaty and was informed by previous findings of the Waitangi Tribunal. This decision and subsequent others evolved the following Treaty principles, which, although contested, still represent a giant leap forward on previous decisions. They include:

- That sovereignty was ceded to the Crown in exchange for the protection of Maori interests.

- That the Crown's freedom to govern (which requires reasonable co-operation from Maori) is balanced by its obligation to actively protect tino rangatiratanga.

- That the Treaty established a fiduciary relationship akin to a partnership and imposes on the Crown a duty to act reasonably, honourably and in good faith, which incurs a further duty to make informed decision (which will often require some form of consultation), and a duty to redress past breaches of the Treaty.

These principles cannot be taken as a definitive list as the court is likely to continue to reinterpret the meaning of the Treaty in applying it to new cases. They are, however, fairly settled in the understanding of the courts and the Waitangi Tribunal.

The basis of the developing understanding of the courts is that the Treaty is 'essential to the foundation of New Zealand' and 'part of the fabric of New Zealand society'.[44] Court rulings make it clear that the Treaty must be viewed as 'a living instrument capable of adapting to new and changing circumstances', and that 'what matters is the spirit and the positive and enduring role of the Treaty'. The way ahead, says constitutional law expert Philip Joseph, 'calls above all for generosity of spirit'.[45] In signing the Treaty, Maori expected to retain their tino rangatiratanga over all their resources and treasures.

The courts are presented as a place where citizens can obtain justice and will be treated with respect, dignity and fairness. As we know, this was not the case in the past for many Maori communities and individuals. Justice Prendergast's decision in the 1877 Wi Parata case—that the Treaty was a legal nullity—was in the view of legal academic Paul McHugh 'a judicial annihilation of Maori status and rights under the Treaty of Waitangi'.[46] McHugh believes further that 'its most important judicial consequence remains: the establishment of the absolute sovereignty of the Crown and the incapacity of the Treaty of Waitangi to act as any form of qualification upon that sovereignty'.[47]

One hundred years after Prendergast's decision the courts in New Zealand finally recognised the solemn commitments made to Maori in the Treaty. Even without the Treaty the courts always had the power to uphold common-law guarantees yet rarely chose to intervene. Far from being independent, the courts actively served certain interests over others and became a vehicle for the dispossession of

Maori, legitimising the corrupt acquisition of land perpetrated by the Crown in collusion with wealthy landowning Pakeha. The argument that Parliament makes the laws and the courts have the freedom to interpret and enforce them remains unconvincing in the face of the historical role of the courts in permitting obvious wrongdoing by the Crown and illegality. Maori communities continue to live with the negative outcomes of past biased court rulings: the court system owes Maori an explanation. A demonstration of justice and independence would go a long way.

In the mid-1980s that long-sought-after demonstration of judicial justice and independence emerged as the political changes in the country impacted on the courts. Canadian Professor Doug Sanders captures the consequences of the change:

> The record in the courts had been dismal, as in Canada and Australia. But again, the changes in thinking in the country meant the courts had to abandon their racist past. The first sign of judicial respect came in the *State Owned Enterprises* case in 1987, later confirmed in the judicial decisions on fishing rights. The change in judicial attitude was profound, going well beyond the limited statutory provisions that had mandated respect for the principles of the Treaty. A sea change had occurred in the recognition of Maori rights.[48]

Arguably it was the historical decision by the Court of Appeal in 2003 over New Zealand's foreshore and seabed (discussed in Chapter 10) that finally demonstrated the level of judicial independence which Maori had sought.

Crown Policy and the Fiscal Envelope

In 1989 the Crown developed a set of principles to guide Crown action on the Treaty of Waitangi. These principles reinforced the Crown's right to govern, redefined rangatiratanga as self-management (as opposed to self-determination), upheld redress of past Treaty breaches, advanced a duty of reasonable co-operation and promoted equality under the law. Many Maori saw this policy as another attempt by the Crown to repackage the Treaty in a way that reinforced Crown power, i.e. the status quo.

A few years later the wider claims process was brought to a head with the introduction of what is known as the fiscal envelope. This proposal offered a total of $1 billion to be shared among all claimant tribes as full and final settlement of all historical claims. Payments were to be spread over 10 years. Developed over three years and launched by Prime Minister Jim Bolger on 8 December 1994, this proposal was roundly rejected by Maori throughout the country.[49]

Although the Crown claimed it had intended to seek Maori opinion over the following months, elements of the proposal were clearly beyond discussion, including the concept of a fiscal cap, and proposals regarding the conservation estate and the ownership of national resources. In addition, a climate of secrecy and unilateral declaration surrounded the proposal, suggesting a lack of good faith by the Crown and an undisclosed motivation.[50] Many Maori saw it as just another insult—an attempt to try to settle 150 years of theft, fraud and dishonour with a token amount.

It is now widely believed that the fiscal envelope was primarily designed to appease Pakeha voters rather than to deal justly with Maori claims.

Following universal rejection of the fiscal envelope, two of the largest tribes, Tainui (1995) and Ngai Tahu (1998), settled their claims.[51] The 1992 pan-Maori Commercial Fisheries Settlement of $170 million had already been concluded.[52] As at 30 June 2004 a further 13 settlements had been achieved, bringing the total to 16. In 2004 there were over 25 claimant groups from around the country involved in negotiations or pre-negotiation discussions with the Crown.

To date $679,074,000 has been committed to final and comprehensive settlements, plus $35,262,000 for the value of gifting for claims that have been settled or part settled, part settlements and claimant funding. There are a further four Heads of Agreement or Agreements in Principle still to progress to signed Deeds of Settlement.[53]

Considerable confusion remains among the public about the purpose of Treaty settlements. Many New Zealanders see the Crown's Treaty settlement policy as the Crown giving taxpayers' money to Maori as a form of special assistance, failing to realise that the settlements represent token redress for past grievances. What recipients of settlements do with the money is for them to decide. It is their money. If the Crown were to decide this for them it would be committing another breach of the Treaty, as Maori were promised full authority over their property and other resources. This confusion is likely to continue while many New Zealanders remain unaware that much of the nation's wealth was built on land and other resources taken from Maori communities by successive settler governments.

Maori Development Initiatives

The hikoi of 1975 marked a pivotal point for Maori in the process of nation-building. From this point on, the Maori renaissance was clearly visible to all. Little wonder, then, that from the early 1980s alternative Maori systems and institutions began to emerge. Iwi and urban Maori authorities began to develop structures to deliver a wide range of services to Maori and build the economic base of their peoples. These initiatives symbolised Maori taking control of their own destiny and reclaiming their right to exercise fully the authority or tino rangatiratanga long denied by the state.

The policy informing these new initiatives was Maori development. The aim was to deliver education, employment, health and social services 'by Maori for Maori in a Maori way'. A number of these initiatives began on a voluntary basis, eventually receiving some government support through contracting for services. Many remain under-resourced and face ongoing financial difficulties. Some have now become a normal part of the political and economic landscape and present a new horizon of possibilities for the future.

Te Kohanga Reo

Te Kohanga Reo, or Maori language nest, is one among a number of highly successful Maori initiatives.[54] There are four cornerstones to the kaupapa of Te Kohanga Reo:

- Total immersion in Te Reo Maori and Tikanga Maori.

- Management and decision-making by whanau.

- Accountability to the creator, the mokopuna (children), the Kohanga Reo movement, whanau, hapu, iwi and the government.

- Commitment to the health and well-being of the mokopuna and the whanau.[55]

Te Kohanga Reo is committed to the revitalisation of Maori language and has been operating for more than 20 years, although its genesis lies in traditional Maori customs. It offers total immersion in the Maori language from birth and is described as a programme of Maori development that operates according to Maori principles, values and practices. In Te Kohanga Reo, Maori control the context, content and style of learning. In 2004 there are over 500 kohanga reo providing immersion education for over 10,500 mokopuna and their whanau.[56]

The creation of Te Kohanga Reo marked the second period of substantial Maori involvement in the early-childhood sector. Following the Hunn Report in 1961, the proposal to establish a Maori Education Foundation was quickly enacted. Hunn had argued that 'if a Maori Education Foundation could be established it would transform the scene within ten years'. The foundation was charged with the task of 'lifting Maori education standards to a level equal to that of the Pakeha'. One of the first areas the foundation worked in was early-childhood education. However, despite impressive results it was unable to sustain its initial success. M. Pewhairangi identifies two reasons: lack of Maori language and withdrawal of field officers.[57]

Titoki Black et al. note the following factors as illuminating why the kohanga reo movement has been so successful. Te Kohanga Reo:

- Were a dream of kaumatua.

- Were developed with Matauranga whanau/hapu/iwi Maori as their core; had immersion in the Maori language, culture and whanau development as their central aims.

- Were designed with a long-term aim of preparing Maori children for a life of learning, including participation in formal schooling programmes as well as those based in the Maori education system.[58]

The early success of Te Kohanga Reo was born of the visionary commitment and remarkable voluntary dedication of Maori communities, particularly Maori women. 'The ultimate objective . . . [was] nothing less than the rebirth of the Maori nation as an equal but separate element contributing to the common good of New Zealand society'.[59]

In 1990 the responsibility for kohanga reo was transferred from the Department of Maori Affairs to the Ministry of Education. There was a greater emphasis on more regulatory controls, with huge implications at the grassroots level and a heavy cost to the kaupapa. The government provides operational grants to the extent that in 1999 government financial compliance requirements were described as suffocating the movement to the detriment of its main goals.[60]

The kohanga reo model for the revitalisation of ancestral language and culture is flexible and portable across cultures. It has global significance well beyond the South Pacific. A number of nations of the South Pacific have adopted the model for their own use, including Samoa, Tokelau, the Cook Islands, Tonga and Fiji.[61]

Te Kohanga Reo has pioneered:

- A model of education that is global in its relevance and impact.

- Improved participation rates in early-childhood education for Maori.

- Learning Te Reo Maori through immersion.

- Whanau development.

- The creation of a unique, intergenerational learning environment.[62]

In the late 1970s only a small percentage of the Maori population over 50 years of age were fluent in the Maori language. However, the 2001 census cites that one in four Maori could speak te reo, compared with 30,000 non-Maori. Nearly half of the Maori language speakers were under 25 years of age.[63] The figures tell the story.

Kura Kaupapa Maori

The graduates of kohanga reo were catered for in another highly successful Maori initiative, begun in 1985. Kura Kaupapa Maori schools, where the principle language is Te Reo Maori, now number 62, catering for nearly 5000 students accounting for 3 per cent of all Maori enrolments in schools (1 July 2001). A further 12 per cent of Maori students are involved in Maori medium education for at least 31 per cent of their schooling. The curriculum is based on Maori values, philosophies, principles and practice.[64] Geographically the kura, which are within the New Zealand state system, are spread from the Far North down to Southland—only five are in the South Island.

Te Wananga

The growth in participation rates for Maori in tertiary education in the 1990s has been spectacular. At the centre of this remarkable increase are the three wananga now operating throughout New Zealand: Te Wananga o Raukawa, Te Wananga o Aotearoa and Te Whare Wananga o Awanuiarangi. They are undoubtedly building on the visionary kohanga reo and kura kaupapa Maori.

This is a transformation of the historical approach where, as Walker notes, 'Maori were required to participate in an education sector controlled by past policies of assimilation, integration, multiculturalism and bilingualism, which for Maori has been a process of humiliation and shame.'[65] The key to the success of the wananga is the provision of education programmes that are Maori centred and Maori focused.

As at July 2002 there were 11,010 Maori student enrolments at universities, 22,775 at wananga, 14,970 at polytechnics and 1397 at colleges of education.[66] However, the overall picture is even more significant. According to the Ministry of Education, the total increase from 1999 to 31 July 2003 has been from 32,825 to 62,574, the majority of these students enrolled in wananga. Te Wananga o Aotearoa alone had 23,468 enrolled at 31 July 2003. Half were studying part-time and had no school qualifications, and about one-third were studying extramurally.[67] Central to this expansion have been the formal relationships between tribal groups and the government. Nine iwi education partnerships have been established so far.[68]

Sarah-Jane Tiakiwai and Lani Teddy name four key obstacles that emerge as issues for Maori in relation to their participation within the tertiary education sector. (Note that these are less relevant for wananga.)

- Financial barriers, academic restrictions, differences in philosophy that are culturally based.

- The ability to participate in decision-making at all levels of the institution, and to engage in meaningful consultation, particularly as guaranteed under the Treaty of Waitangi.

- The scope to maintain te reo, tikanga Maori and a strong Maori identity.

- The lack of awareness of what constitute Maori issues at the tertiary level.[69]

The aspirations of Maori for their educational advancement were defined by Professor Mason Durie at the Hui Taumata Matauranga hosted by Tuwharetoa at Turangi in 2001.[70] He advocated 'the ability of Maori to move freely and comfortably between two worlds without compromising their Maori identity or the need to participate within the global context. These concerns relate to power sharing, greater autonomy, and the ability of Maori to participate fully in and throughout the education system, as guaranteed by the Treaty of Waitangi'.[71]

Towards the New Millennium

The 1990s saw increasing intensity in public debates on the Treaty, illustrating a diversity of views in both Maori and Pakeha communities and usually a limited understanding of New Zealand's colonial history. Race relations remain a hot topic in the media and Maori claims over resources not specified in the Treaty (such as minerals, new technology and radio spectrum) continue to fuel outrage among many Pakeha over what they perceive as a 'Treaty grievance industry'. Some Maori fear that increasing immigration will result in a watering down of Treaty obligations by the Crown.

While the Crown principles of the Treaty are now incorporated into over 40 pieces of legislation, this legislation does not protect the Treaty itself. The texts of the Treaty have never been incorporated into or protected by legislation. Some Acts require that decision-making processes have due regard for Crown Treaty principles or Maori interests, but they fall short of specifying the Treaty of Waitangi as an obligation on the Crown. Where the Treaty is mentioned, it is normally by way of a clause limiting aspects of an Act, or a clause limiting the administration of an Act.[72] Most Acts of Parliament contain no reference to the Treaty, but even here the courts may imply an obligation on the Crown to give effect to Treaty principles or take Treaty principles (or relevant administrative law principles) into account in decision-making.

Despite advances in court rulings and Waitangi Tribunal findings, the unique status of Maori as tangata whenua (with pre-existing common-law rights) and as Treaty partner remains highly contested, as does the constitutional role of the Treaty. The Crown still operates on the basis that sovereignty was ceded in the Treaty, while many Maori dispute this claim, continuing to demand that barriers to tino rangatiratanga be removed. In current debates the multicultural nature of New Zealand society is used by some to promote the equal status of other (non-Maori) New Zealanders and diverts the guilt and shame many Pakeha feel when confronted with historical injustices against Maori. The latter drives a sustained desire among many non-Maori New Zealanders to forget the past and proceed forward as one people. Maori for the most part do not seek to engender guilt or to blame Pakeha today for wrongdoing in the past, but they rightly expect the Crown to redress breaches of the Treaty by previous governments and ensure that Treaty obligations are fully honoured today.

At the turn of the new century the Crown accepts the Treaty as the founding document of the country and as the basis for constitutional government.[73] At the start of 2005 the coalition government remains committed to resolving historical grievances, but there is increasing pressure on claimants to bypass the Waitangi Tribunal process and proceed to direct negotiation with the Crown. While this approach may serve to accelerate Treaty settlements and soothe public impatience, it would fail to address a need of some claimants to tell their history in a respectful forum as part of a larger healing process. It may also put the Treaty claims process at risk. If injustices are not resolved properly, then grievances may continue to fester.

Limited public understanding on the Treaty continues to serve as a barrier in the government's ability to observe its Treaty obligations. The public backlash against the insertion of the principles of the Treaty into the New Zealand Public Health and Disability Act (2000) is indicative of the challenge ahead. A clause aimed at reducing health disparities, which mentioned Maori, survived, and a mechanism to enable greater Maori participation in decision-making was also inserted. However, despite the commitment to getting the principles of the Treaty into social legislation, the government's approach to Treaty obligations remains equivocal.[74]

In 2004 Dr Don Brash, leader of the Opposition National Party, and Labour Cabinet Minister Trevor Mallard made a number of speeches attacking Maori rights and alleged privileges.[75] The public response revealed a simmering hostility and a significant level of racism against Maori that permeates New Zealand society. It also revealed how little Maori Treaty rights are understood.

The last word goes to Mason Durie: 'What is missing is a secure understanding, based on both Maori and Crown views, that commits the country to a position on the Treaty so that litigation, protest, alienation, and dispossession fade into history.'[76]

SIX

Why Don't We Know?

New Orleans, 1992

The sounds from the street outside at 3 a.m. sent a chill up my spine. Was it an engine backfiring, a car door slamming or a gunshot? The rattle of the shutters didn't help. The sound of muffled voices and a dog barking lingered. The heat was intense and for the tenth time I rose from my bed on the floor to look through the barred windows at an empty street. Nothing moved. I returned to bed and tried once more to sleep.

It would be morning soon and again I would meet with a group of anti-racism trainers from the People's Institute for Survival and Beyond, a national multiracial network of veterans of broad-based movements for justice, including civil rights, anti-war, welfare rights, farm worker and indigenous rights.

The institute's trainers were experienced in community work and movement-building. They had taken me in—a total stranger—to share their stories, struggles and some anti-racism strategies. They had allowed me to sleep on the office floor in their headquarters in an old converted house in the middle of a black ghetto in New Orleans. I was locked in their headquarters at night for my own safety: this was not a neighbourhood where white people could walk alone on the streets. In the midst of the surrounding poverty and struggle, their hospitality and friendship were extraordinary.

I had landed in this city of astonishing contrasts earlier that week. With time to fill, I followed the tourists to the French Quarter to hear some of the best jazz in the world. As I wandered down Bourbon Street towards the mighty Mississippi the sounds of jazz wafting from the restaurants and nightclubs was magical.

In this environment it would have been easy to forget the brutality of the past, except for the fact that the history of slavery had become a marketable commodity here. There were plenty of tourist visits on offer to see the old plantation houses—but no such routes to view the present-day legacy of slavery in the black ghettos.

In American cities many African Americans live in inner-city enclaves while most white North Americans inhabit the suburbs. Race and class are inevitably intertwined in New Orleans as elsewhere. The railway tracks and a motorway overpass mark the division, and staying in a black ghetto heightened my awareness of the line.

As I lay awake that morning my thoughts drifted to what we had discussed at the institute the day before. A primary focus of the institute was to lead anti-racism workshops throughout the country. The director explained that the North American school systems had historically programmed people not to think, not to question authority, not to challenge the status quo—simply to memorise. Such systems obviously reinforce the world view of the dominant European culture and as a result students learn how to maintain racism, not how to undo it.[1] A new way of 'seeing' was required and the institute's anti-racism workshops used a variety of exercises to engage people in an educational process that enabled them to experience a new way of understanding.[2]

This explanation challenged me to think about parallels with the education system in New Zealand. Was this the reason so many New Zealanders were ignorant of the colonial history of their country? Had we been taught to think in a certain way about our colonial history—or simply not taught this history much at all? Was this lack of knowledge a product of institutional racism? These questions preoccupied me as I continued my travels.

Uncovering Institutional Racism

Ten days later I found myself at a meeting of anti-racism workers in Cleveland, where I met Joe Barndt, a Lutheran minister based in the Bronx, New York. Joe had spent the past 14 years travelling all over the United States training anti-racism workshop leaders. Some years earlier, while living in Germany and confronting Germans about the Nazi holocaust, Joe had been challenged by references to Native American genocide in his own country. He returned home with new insight and direction.

At the meeting Barndt and others discussed the notion of institutional racism, which is when a society perpetuates the world view and values of the dominant group through institutional policies, practices and procedures that advance their interests and serve to disadvantage other racial/ethnic groups. Members of the dominant culture often deny the existence of institutional racism because they do not experience it.

I was familiar with Barndt's work on racism. In a book published a year earlier he explained:

> Institutional racism is practiced in two ways, which we will call 'direct' and 'indirect'. Direct institutional racism, as the name suggests, is always conscious and intentional; it is openly and publicly practiced without apology or shame. It has also been, until recently, quite legal. Indirect institutional racism may be intentional or unintentional. When it is intentional, indirect racism is deliberately disguised or hidden so that the public will be unaware of it. When unintentional, indirect racism is far more complex. It can exist as though it has a life of its own and is extremely difficult to eradicate.[3]

Now in Cleveland, Barndt made another powerful statement. He argued that institutional racism starts out as being intentionally racist and overt (visible), moves to being intentionally racist and covert (hidden), and later becomes unintentionally racist and covert. The task of an institution in dismantling institutional racism is to retrace its journey and identify ways in which the values and interests of the dominant culture have been entrenched in the foundations of the institution and perpetuated through its organisational life and functioning.

Was Barndt's definition applicable to the education system in New Zealand?[4] In colonial times a range of mechanisms were used in schools to reinforce Pakeha privilege and values, including rigid time periods, European symbols around the room, and the exclusion of Maori language. Were the curricula another tool used to reinforce and maintain the interests of Pakeha? Was it compulsory anywhere in the primary or secondary curricula to learn about New Zealand's colonial history and the Treaty of Waitangi? If so, whose knowledge, world view and values were being taught? Was it the colonisers' perspective? Exactly what was taught about the Treaty of Waitangi?

Examining New Zealand School Texts

School curricula state the guidelines for what is to be taught, but many other factors, such as teaching methods, class numbers, the restrictions that examinations impose, the political climate and the texts used, all contribute to the way in which it is delivered in practice. Nevertheless the impact of texts cannot be underestimated.

> Most social science research shows that children's racial attitudes are formed not so much by actual contact with people of other races, but by contact with the prevailing attitudes in their communities about those other races. In those societies in which books for children are an integral means of communication, they serve as an important tool for socialising children into the inherent values, assumptions and beliefs of those societies.[5]

With the impact of Barndt's argument about institutional racism in my mind, I wondered if the texts used in teaching history and social studies in New Zealand schools had begun as 'intentionally racist and overt'. Did the texts move to being 'intentionally racist and covert'? Were they now 'unintentionally racist and covert'? Is the reason why many New Zealanders don't understand the connections between New Zealand's colonial history and the issues confronting this country because the texts from which they have learned have reinforced the viewpoint and needs of the colonising English culture?

In examining some of the texts I knew I was applying twentieth-century knowledge. Nevertheless, my findings were illuminating.

Up until as late as 1960 a policy of assimilation dominated in New

Zealand. This system was underpinned by 'conscious and intentional' institutional racism at every level. The notion of assimilation as a social policy developed out of the nineteenth-century European belief that the races of the world were arranged hierarchically from 'savage' races through to civilised races. Naturally the British saw themselves as representing 'the pinnacle of civilisation'.[6]

The policy of assimilation was directed at absorbing Maori into the Pakeha way of life, and many people involved in administering these policies probably believed they were bestowing benefits upon Maori by 'civilising' them.[7] The curricula and texts used in schools from 1877–1960 demonstrate how the policy of assimilation affected what was taught to both Maori and Pakeha about themselves, the Treaty of Waitangi and New Zealand's colonial history.

English History Dominates

The Education Act of 1877 made primary education in New Zealand compulsory and listed the subjects to be taught. One of Reverend W. J. Habens' first tasks as Inspector-General of the Department of Education was to write the regulations for the curriculum. History was not compulsory,[8] and where it was taught it was English history exclusively.[9] In the 1878 regulations only the geography curriculum included references to New Zealand.[10]

The Act made no provision for a national system of secondary education, but secondary schooling was available to those who could afford it. There were no national curricula for secondary schools. The school principal, with permission from the school's board of governors, would determine the curriculum for the school and decide on the texts used.[11] The primary syllabus was reviewed in 1885 but emerged practically unchanged.[12]

A new syllabus was written in 1904, primarily by George Hogben, Inspector-General of the Department of Education from 1899. This syllabus contained a new history component for standards three to six. 'Cook and his discoveries', 'Colonisation and the early government of New Zealand' and 'New Zealand and other forms of colonial government' were some of the options.[13] New Zealand was explicitly mentioned twice in the list of 67 topics: European (mostly British) history still dominated. No detailed prescriptions were given, with each school having discretion over what was taught and how, with reference to 'the surroundings of the children'.[14] In practice there was no uniformity in what teachers taught.

In 1913 the primary syllabus was again revised and reorganised but the content remained the same.[15] Teachers were, however, given more freedom to interpret the syllabus instructions and were encouraged to integrate subjects. In 1919 the syllabus was further revised, removing the compulsory aspect of history.[16]

Under the Secondary Schools Act 1903 free places for secondary education were given to pupils who had their proficiency certificate, which was one of the entry criteria, and the numbers attending secondary school escalated. Curriculum changes followed and in about 1915 history became a compulsory subject for free place-holders,[17] yet little change occurred immediately in terms of history curriculum content. Marcia Stenson notes: 'Emphasis on the history of England and the Empire persisted, until the 1930s saw the emergence of a greater New Zealand content and of world history.'[18]

Colonial Texts: 'Intentionally Racist and Overt'

So what was the tenor of the texts used to teach history? Race was high on the list of topics, says University of Canterbury historian Colin McGeorge: 'From the 1890s until the syllabus was extensively revised in the 1940s, New Zealand primary school texts employed the concept of race to explain the growth and glories of the British Empire and New Zealand's unique place in that Empire.'[19] Primary school textbooks in the 1870s and 1880s were imported from England and mirrored the social thinking of the time, notably Social Darwinism, which emphasised survival of the fittest and a hierarchy of races based on biological differences.

In one text of 1879 it was noted that: 'Whites form by far the most important race, for they have the best laws, the greatest amount of learning, and the most excellent knowledge of farming and trade. There are five great races of men and of these the white race is highest.'[20] Another text, printed in 1888, said: 'Here is a white man.

This race is at present the most powerful. White men are the best scholars and the best workers. In their lands the people have more peace, more comfort and more freedom than the inhabitants of other lands enjoy.'[21]

These texts demonstrate how the education system explicitly taught racial superiority to primary school children, shaped their thinking about their own place in the world and began to entrench their beliefs of how to view people of other cultures. Teaching racial superiority shapes behaviour and underpins a set of assumptions about normality in terms of the way life should be lived, the way institutions should work and whose knowledge should be validated. This historically entrenched mindset supplanted Maori values: the Maori way of life was not 'normal'.

While the Treaty of Waitangi was not officially listed as a syllabus topic, information on it was available from around the turn of the century. *The New Zealand Graphic Reader Sixth Book* (circa 1900) included 'Lesson 20. The Treaty of Waitangi'. This lesson, based on the English translation of the Treaty of Waitangi, concluded that:

> Although the Maoris have many times since the signing of the Treaty of Waitangi waged fierce wars against the colonial government, it must nevertheless be remembered that Britain's authority in New Zealand was peacefully acquired, and was in the main established in response to the voluntary request of the natives. Generally speaking too, the rights of the natives under the Treaty have been respected, and they themselves do not complain that any of its provisions have been unduly strained or arbitrarily set aside.[22]

This lesson conveniently ignored the endless demands, delegations, petitions, political actions, meetings and conferences, calling for the Maori text of the Treaty be honoured. Although the Colonial Office in London took the existence of the Treaty seriously, it took no responsibility for what actually happened at the frontier of New Zealand settlement. On paper the office expressed concern for the well-being of the 'natives', with promises of protection, citizenship rights, tribal authority, participation, relationship and honouring Treaty commitments, yet it did little, once settlement gained impetus, to honour those commitments and promises.

Race remained a dominant theme in the new primary syllabus in 1904, with one teaching text noting that:

> the strongest reason for the maintenance of the Empire is the influence for good that it may exercise over the whole world. Britain is at the head of the most progressive and most just of modern nations. It is, therefore, fitting that she should guide and control the destiny of new and infant countries; to her and to no other should be committed the fate of the lower races of mankind, who are, many of them, engaged in an unequal struggle for very life with powers whose rule is not so merciful.[23]

By 1905 New Zealand published texts were available but the notion of the hierarchy of races was still strong.[24] British settlers in New Zealand were by this hierarchical standard 'naturally superior to Asians and Africans because they were white, [and] superior to other Europeans because they were racially British'.[25] And 'While there was no general agreement on the Maori's place on the racial ladder, there was universal agreement that he was a very superior savage.'[26]

The first *School Journal* appeared in 1907 and was made compulsory in state schools from 1914.[27] Until the early 1930s about one-third of the journal's space is estimated to have been devoted to 'imperial, military and patriotic matters'[28] and the 'moral superiority of Britain was asserted as a fact'.[29]

New Zealand History More Evident

The 1928 primary history syllabus made a leap forward, stating that: 'New Zealand history and stories connected with the life of the Maoris have been introduced into the syllabus for the first time.'[30] This was untrue as it overlooked the New Zealand content in the 1904 *History and Civic Instruction* curriculum. However, the 1928 syllabus devoted more space to New Zealand topics. Even though they were optional, this new syllabus listed topics such as 'The coming of the Maoris', 'How the Maoris lived', 'First settlements by white men—whalers, sealers, missionaries', 'Abel Tasman and Captain Cook', 'Famous missionaries', 'The Treaty of Waitangi', 'Famous Governors', 'Early arrangements for governing New Zealand', 'The New Zealand Association' and 'Progress of settlement in North and South Islands compared'.[31]

However, the colonisers' perspective still clearly pervaded in the way these topics were to be taught. One explicit aim for form one students was to learn 'how England became a great colonising nation'.[32] Form two students were to be taught about 'the building up of the British Empire'.[33] Teaching 'love of country' and 'patriotism', so that the child may learn 'joy and pride to play his part, however humble it may be, in the advancement of New Zealand and the Empire' was still paramount.[34]

Selective entry to secondary school and proficiency exams were abolished in 1936 and during the 1940s the Minister of Education H. G. R. Mason appointed William Thomas (formerly rector of Timaru Boys' High School) as chairman of a committee to overhaul the secondary school curriculum. Schools were required to develop a wider range of subject choices, catering for those for whom the traditional academic secondary school courses were reckoned inappropriate. The Thomas Report of 1944 introduced social studies as a new compulsory subject, based on a combination of history, geography and some other subjects.[35] The Treaty of Waitangi was not specified as a subject area; rather the report stipulated that 'within wide limits schools should be free to work out courses in harmony with their special aims and adapted to their local circumstances'.[36]

In 1947 a social studies syllabus was issued for primary schools.[37] This did include the Treaty of Waitangi alongside other New Zealand history topics such as: 'Tasman', 'Cook', 'D'Urville', 'an early trader (e.g. Maning)', 'a whaler (e.g. Guard, Barrett)', 'the missionaries (e.g. Marsden, Williams, Selwyn)'.[38] So what exactly was taught about the Treaty?

The Colonial View Dominates

Our Nation's Story was a series of four history texts developed for children from standards three to six to accompany the 1928 syllabus revision. Although it was, at some level, up to teachers what they taught, *Our Nation's Story* meant considerable uniformity and the series was used widely until the late 1940s. Just under one-third of the whole series referred to New Zealand.[39]

Our Nation's Story is a good example of how the education system promoted the attitudes and beliefs of the dominant culture and particular models of citizenship.[40] It presented the Treaty of Waitangi as 'the fairest Treaty ever made between Europeans and a native race; indeed in many ways, it was much fairer to brown man than to white'.[41] The missionaries explained that

> Captain Hobson . . . had not come to take New Zealand away from the Maoris. All he asked was that the Maoris should acknowledge the Queen of England as their ruler. If they would do this, the Queen would leave them in possession of their lands, and would also protect them against their foes.[42]

As we have seen, despite the Colonial Office's insistence that the Treaty be upheld, it was effectively discarded by the mid-1840s, and *Our Nation's Story* demonstrates that in the late 1920s this was the dominant understanding:

> The Treaty of Waitangi is acknowledged as a very important document; its signing was an historic moment . . . but there is no sense of the Treaty as a living document and no suggestion that it might be basis of future claims for restoration.[43]

McGeorge concludes that the *Our Nation's Story* series 'repeatedly assumes a Pakeha readership; and there is no suggestion that its Maori readers might have heard another account of the wars or felt any lasting sense of loss or dispossession as a result'.[44] School children were assured that 'the bond between the white New Zealanders and the brown is a very strong one'.[45] *Our Nation's Story* thus promoted the philosophy of assimilation, where Pakeha and Maori were seen as one, and where national identity overrode any differences in cultural identity. It was another means by which the government legitimatised its behaviour and actions under the policy of assimilation.

The racism, too, was explicit:

> *Our Nation's Story* . . . implies a hierarchy of races with particular inherent qualities and capacities . . . Maori are described again and again as brown and European New Zealanders as white, and the series as a whole gives the clear impression that lighter inevitably overcomes darker. Fair-haired

Angles conquered Britain, Maori drove out the darker Moriori, and naturally enough, the 'white man' prevailed over the 'brown man' in New Zealand.[46]

1960s: Slow Progress

Our Country: A Brief Survey of New Zealand History and Civics, published in 1927, was a text widely used in junior forms of secondary schools. By 1960, still in use and on its thirteenth printing, the text had been substantially revised and contained the following: 'The Treaty was carefully translated into Maori by the missionary Henry Williams and his son.'[47]

At least the Maori Treaty was mentioned, but only within the terms of the incorrect assumption that both the English and Maori texts of the Treaty were identical. Williams did not 'carefully' translate the English text into Maori; rather he fashioned a palatable Maori version.

The government officially abandoned the policy of assimilation in 1960.[48] J. K. Hunn, then secretary of Maori Affairs, acknowledged that the policy had not achieved its expected goals and accepted that Maori culture was an ongoing part of New Zealand life.[49] The new official policy was integration, but there was little change in practice. A policy of 'cultural deficit' began to dominate thinking during the 1960s and 1970s, in which it was asserted that Maori had failed to assimilate fully because of deficiencies in Maori culture.

The Treaty of Waitangi was not a prescribed topic in either the 1961 primary school social studies syllabus or the secondary syllabus in 1978. 'As with other syllabuses', the 1978 guidelines read, 'the prescriptive element is kept to a minimum. The intention is that teachers will devise school programmes that are, as far as possible, adapted to local circumstances and to the needs of their students.'[50]

In the 1960s New Zealand's economy was booming. 'We have the best race relations in the world', 'Maori are just like us' and 'we are all New Zealanders' the world was told. In this climate, Carol Mutch notes:

The content of the social studies curriculum was designed to preserve and celebrate the status quo . . . people of English descent still called England 'home'. Studies and supporting textbooks included a preponderance of historical examples from the Anglo-European heritage and geographical examples from countries that were politically, economically or historically linked to New Zealand.[51]

Yet there were texts available in the 1960s and 1970s to accompany the teaching of the Treaty of Waitangi and New Zealand's colonial history if schools chose to do so. In 1967 *Suggestions for Teaching Social Studies in the Primary School Index: Parts 1, 2, 3, 4* listed the Treaty of Waitangi as one of many optional New Zealand topics.[52] A *Teachers' Index of Core Materials for Social Studies*, published in 1971, listed resources that could be used in conjunction with the social studies curricula and contained 'full reviews, or brief synopses, of almost every Bulletin and thematic Journal published by the School Publications Branch since 1948'.[53] An updated edition was published in 1978.

The wide use of the social studies teachers' guides would suggest the articles listed were likely to be used, if the topic was taught, but did many teachers choose it as an option to teach? And exactly what did they teach?

The 1971 *Index*, for example, contained some additional information for teachers about Wakefield's scheme, stating: 'We must not be too quick to say that the Maoris were robbed of their land. One-tenth of all the land bought was set aside for the use of the Maori people and that tenth after the white man had settled became more valuable than the whole lot beforehand.'[54] The lie was still being taught. The information in the *Index* contained the promise of the Crown, but the practice was quite different. For example, in the case of Kemp's purchase Ngai Tahu retained 6359 acres; 0.32 per cent of the 20 million acres for which the Crown paid less than one farthing per acre.[55] This was part of the Treaty claim that Ngai Tahu settled with the Crown in 1998.

Te Tiriti o Waitangi, written by Ruth Ross in 1958, was the only resource listed in the 1971 and 1978 *Index* that had reference to the Treaty in the title, suggesting the topic was not regarded as a very significant or important part of a school pupil's education. Ross's article was progressive for its time. The story focused on the Treaty-signing process at Mangungu, a Wesleyan mission station on the

Hokianga, a few days after the Treaty was signed at Waitangi. The story has characters that canvass both Maori and Pakeha perspectives, and reference is made to the translation of the Treaty into Maori language. The differences between the English and Maori texts of the Treaty are evident in the story, and the hurried nature of the signing process and the regret of some of the Maori chiefs about signing was referred to also. Near the end of the story Mr Hobbs the missionary says: 'How *can* one explain in Maori the meaning of sovereignty?...Why, I'm not sure I know myself all that sovereignty implies.'[56] This statement is symbolic of how confused the Treaty debate has always been. Amid this confusion, the Crown has been able to maintain the status quo.

In contrast to Ruth Ross's article, *The Maori and the Missionary* (1953) was also included as a resource in the 1971 and 1978 *Index*, representing the colonisers' perspective. Missionaries went 'to the aid of the backward races'.[57] Maori were fortunate to see how missionary families lived—'such a change from the rough and wild and frightening ways of the Maori pa'.[58]

Interestingly, teachers did receive a 'special note' in regard to this bulletin stating:

> This bulletin, in the opinion of an independent reviewer, contains some material which places incorrect interpretations on the impact of the missionaries. It has also been claimed that the contents could be harmful to Maori-Pakeha relationships, as in many places the Maori is shown in an inferior light to the Pakeha, and the common theme appears to be acceptance by Maori children of the superior value system of the white Christian way of life. *It is strongly recommended that teachers read this publication critically, and assess its possible impact on children's attitudes before making use of it.*'[59]

Yet, how serious was the commitment to challenge the colonisers' perspective when this misleading and potentially harmful material was allowed to remain in circulation?

During the 1970s the concept of multiculturalism emerged with its emphasis on valuing cultural diversity. This was partly in response to the fact that New Zealand was becoming an increasingly multicultural society. A decade of Maori activism followed, aimed at the revival of Maori culture, language, values and self-determination. Some activists pushed biculturalism, arguing that until the unique status of the indigenous people of New Zealand was recognised, a multicultural society was not feasible.

1980s and 1990s: Time for Change

As the political climate began to change, so did the school curriculum. In the 1980s Labour Minister of Education Russell Marshall instigated a formal curriculum review. More than 21,000 submissions were received by the review committee and the draft report noted:

> A high number of responses stated that a truthful version of New Zealand history be taught in school. In their opinion, insufficient history about New Zealand was being taught, and when it was taught much of it was from a viewpoint that gave neither an accurate nor full record of what had occurred. Teaching a romantic view of the history of any of our country's peoples did not serve the interest of New Zealanders in the long term.[60]

This suggests that many New Zealanders recognised that the education system was failing to adequately teach school pupils the history of this country and that something needed to be done.

By 1991 a handbook for social studies teachers was produced to accompany the 1977 social studies syllabus. This was after four draft books had been produced in 1989 and distributed to high school teachers on a trial basis. The 1991 handbook redefined the aim of the 1977 syllabus to incorporate an emphasis on cultural differences into social studies.[61] The themes of 'Social Control' and 'Social Change' remained, providing the framework within which to establish courses of study which included: pre-colonial Maori society; the effects of early contact with Pakeha on Maori; why European settlers emigrated to New Zealand and the different European customs and heritages they brought with them; life in colonial New Zealand today; and the Treaty of Waitangi and the contemporary issues surrounding it.[62]

A questionnaire distributed to selected schools in 1993 found that 96 per cent of teachers had used the handbook.[63] This would suggest that aspects of the Treaty of Waitangi and New Zealand's colonial history were more likely being taught in some schools.

The Syllabus Today

The most recent social studies curriculum implemented over 1999 and 2000 represents a dramatic contrast to previous syllabuses. It is very thorough. Under one of the five summary of requirements, *Essential Learning about New Zealand Society*, it states:

> Students will have opportunities to develop their knowledge and understandings about New Zealand society through studying: the effects of colonisation for Maori and Pakeha; the Treaty of Waitangi, its significance as the founding document of New Zealand, how it has been interpreted over time and how it is applied to current systems, policies, events; and the development over time of New Zealand's identity and ways in which this identity is expressed.[64]

Yet while schools are more likely to teach the Treaty today, and to see it as essential for their school, it is still not *compulsory* that they do so.[65]

Both social studies and history are elective subjects in the senior school. However, only one in seven of the Year 11 school population studies history as a subject. The proportion decreases at Year 12 and slightly increases at Year 13 (1 in 10; 1 in 5). While there are eight New Zealand history topics available to teach at Year 11, the most popular four topics that are taught are the origins of World War 2, the black civil rights movement, Palestine–Israel and Ireland. In Year 12, very few history students across the country study New Zealand history topics at all, while in Year 13, 60 per cent study England (1558–1667) rather than the alternative paper on New Zealand in the nineteenth century. Most New Zealand history learned by senior students is through local research studies undertaken for six to eight weeks a year at each level *and internally assessed*.[66] While learning the history of other countries is important, studying New Zealand history remains vital as well, if students are going to understand the contemporary treaty debate.

Under the summary of ministry requirements in the social studies curriculum there are five perspectives to be used, and schools must be able to show that students' learning 'reflects a balance of the perspectives within any two-year period'.[67] One perspective is 'multicultural' in recognition of the fact that

> students from a diverse range of cultural groups are present in many New Zealand classrooms. When exploring cultural experiences and cultural diversity, social studies programmes in schools will . . . examine issues related to racism and explore ways to promote non-racist attitudes and behaviour in the school and wider community.[68]

Yet how are the teachers who have themselves been educated under an earlier curriculum able to teach this topic adequately? Of those who are motivated to do so, how are they supported in developing teaching strategies that account for diversity of opinion, downright resistance, racism, prejudice, disinterest and 'Treaty fatigue'?

The current curriculum is by far the most progressive, yet sociology lecturers Avril Bell and Vicki Carpenter note that this is often only a starting point for pupils.

> Official curriculum knowledge is not the only knowledge taught at school. Much of what gets taught . . . is part of what is often called the 'hidden' or 'covert' curriculum. These terms refer to the knowledge that is taught *unintentionally* through the organisation of schools and classrooms, the relationship between teachers and students, the 'curriculum in use' (i.e. what is actually taught rather than what is in the official prescriptions) and the pedagogical styles used.[69]

Where do teachers explore their own racism and how their own values, attitudes and world view may be affecting what and how they teach?

Some commentators are even more pessimistic. Bishop and Glynn argue that

> no significant advancement is being made in addressing diversity in society in general or . . . education institutions, including classrooms, because current educational policies and practices in most western countries were developed and continue to be developed within a framework of colonialism.[70]

Can the new curriculum be successful when it is entrenched in a system that is so historically one-sided? Is it enough to make changes in the curriculum, or does the entire way the system functions need to be addressed?

However, some of the texts available today offer us hope. *In Tune*, a student activities book, is used to teach social studies to year 9 and 10 students. Published in 1997 by the Office of the Race Relations Conciliator, in conjunction with the Ministry of Education, it canvasses the Treaty debate in a way that enables students to work through learning activities, finding answers to their own questions and forming their own conclusions.[71]

Our Treaty: The Treaty of Waitangi 1840 to the Present by Ruth Naumann is another excellent resource that is useful for social studies in intermediate and secondary schools. Information is provided in a variety of easily accessible and attractive formats, and a range of interactive 'challenges' are provided to encourage students to engage with the material. It has a broad scope covering the Treaty from 1840 to the present day.[72]

While *The Cultures Collide* by P. Woodcock and *The Story of the Treaty* by Claudia Orange are in circulation for more able social studies students, one of the most widely used texts in conjunction with the current curriculum is *Te Mana o Te Tiriti: The Living Treaty*.[73] The text is also a more accurate account of New Zealand's colonial history and includes activities that enable students to increase their understanding of the present Treaty debate.

There is now an official Treaty of Waitangi website funded by the government, which could be potentially useful to schools and the community. The site is embryonic and it remains to be seen whether it lives up to its stated goal of providing the public with a *comprehensive* source of information on the Treaty of Waitangi. This is a government-funded and -controlled project under the authority of the State Services Commission.

A Legacy of Treaty Illiteracy

Many New Zealanders have not been taught the colonial history of this country or the truth about the Treaty of Waitangi because it has never been compulsory in schools. This means there is a significant information gap for many adults today. In her address to the Pacific

Vision Conference in July 1999, Prime Minister Helen Clark acknowledged that: 'In our shared history . . . I regret in New Zealand today so few young people come to learn about the history of our country and our region.'

This information gap was confirmed for the Waitangi Associates team when, facilitating Treaty education workshops in April and May 2000, we surveyed 397 teacher trainee students at the Christchurch College of Education. Some 88 per cent had never heard of the New Zealand Declaration of Independence (1835); 61 per cent were not familiar with the differences between the Maori and English texts of the Treaty of Waitangi; and 80 per cent had no familiarity with any of New Zealand's native land legislation. Of the 397 students, 83.5 per cent had left high school in the 1980s or 1990s.

This is an extraordinary result in the year 2000. Given this level of ignorance, how are these students placed to participate in informed discussion about the Treaty, let alone teach our children the fundamental ingredients of New Zealand society?

David Jenness states that 'perhaps history is not written until, in the particular society, there is some ideological ground to be occupied, and until it becomes consequential which *version* of the national story shall prevail'.[74] The eras of assimilation, integration, multiculturalism and biculturalism have all influenced which version of the national story has been, and is being, told. Yet, the failure historically of the history and social studies curricula to teach *both sides* of our national story has left a legacy of Treaty illiteracy, where people remain ill-informed, clinging to the myths and stereotypes they have absorbed.

The importance of what we are taught, even at primary school, cannot be underestimated. Family, friends, the media and schooling contribute to shaping our attitudes, beliefs, viewpoints, behaviour, morals, values and understanding of what it means to be responsible citizens. Children can begin to learn at any age, providing the way they are taught is appropriate to their level. If we continue to abrogate our responsibility in this regard it is our children and society who will suffer. For, as outlined in the 1961 social studies syllabus, unless [children] have begun to develop open-minded, sympathetic and generous attitudes to peoples and opinions, a determined loyalty to truth, and strong feelings of humanity, they are much less likely to achieve a mature development of these attitudes later.[75]

Until New Zealanders are informed about New Zealand's colonial history, the potential remains for increased social polarisation and disintegration of social relationships.

PART TWO
The Healing

We can know a great deal about the history of indigenous–settler relations. But knowing brings burdens that can be shirked by those living in ignorance. With knowledge, the question is no longer what we know but what we are now to do, and that is a much harder matter to deal with.

Henry Reynolds
Why Weren't We Told?

SEVEN

Getting Involved

Chicago, 1968
Avoiding the FBI had become an art. The late-night meetings in the African American suburbs of Chicago were surrounded with secrecy. Venues changed nightly. Cars came from different directions, arriving at varying times. Occasionally a car would not stop. The meetings were brief and involved small numbers. Afterwards, the participants dispersed at speed. Phones, illegally tapped by the government, could not always be used.

When I arrived in Chicago I met a number of African American groups living in the ghettos and was able to observe some of these meetings. Such groups had created a pipeline for draft dodgers to enter Canada under cover to avoid the insanity and obscenity of fighting in the Vietnam War. It was dangerous for both draft dodgers and supporters, all of whom could be charged with federal offences, yet despite the danger, the commitment of the supporters remained firm. Their philosophy was succinct: why should we go to Vietnam to fight for democracy when we are still fighting for democratic freedom in America?

The 1960s was a time of political turmoil in the United States, with anti-Vietnam protests and civil-rights marches. Images of protests alongside pictures of body bags containing dead young Americans screened nightly on television networks, followed by

President Lyndon Johnson reassuring the nation that the war was going well. Whole blocks were burned down in Detroit. In Chicago civil unrest nearly closed down the Democratic national convention in 1968.

The Civil Rights Act in 1964 outlawed discrimination against people on the basis of race, colour, religion, sex or national origin in all areas of social, economic and political life. The Voting Rights Act the following year aimed to ensure that African Americans could vote by outlawing the use of literacy tests.[1] Yet these laws failed to address what many saw as the most invidious forms of discrimination.

> These were the de facto systems of segregation not codified in law, but practiced in unwritten custom and longstanding habit. In large areas of America, de facto segregation locked blacks out of suburbs, kept them out of decent schools, barred them from exclusive clubs and denied them all but the most menial jobs.[2]

The groups I met in Chicago lived with the reality of segregation: racism was a part of their daily existence. Democracy kept them poor, hungry, unemployed, homeless and often in jail. I learned a valuable lesson while in Chicago. Legal discrimination creates a climate in which evil can be perpetrated. Laws that aim to halt discrimination against people based on gender, colour and class can start the process of change. But laws in themselves do not change behaviour.

Professor Martha Minow of the Harvard Law School captures the essence of this anomaly:

> When you're dealing with the subtleties and complexities of human relationships, law is an extremely blunt instrument . . . Law can tell people to stop doing something . . . it can't make people behave differently in a day-to-day way . . . I worry there is a false hope that law can solve the problem, when, at best in many circumstances, law can create a clearing, a space where other kinds of difficult work at building human relationships can go forward.[3]

The law does not create goodwill. Challenging colonial mindsets, racist actions and assumptions about 'the other', and creating the time, space, energy and commitment to build holistic relationships and promote personal and social change, even with goodwill, is a lifelong process.

The following year, 1969, I attended the World Assembly of Youth conference in Liege, Belgium, with my wife Trish. When we got there we discovered most of the liberation movements in the world were represented, including the African National Congress, the Palestine Liberation Organisation, the political wing of the Irish Republican Army and the Zimbabwe liberation movement. We later found out that the meeting had been funded by the CIA as part of the Cold War programme to win the allegiance of national youth movements engaged in political struggle.[4] Nevertheless the conference had a highly politicising effect on me, giving me a political understanding of the world that was largely new to me. Combined with what I had seen in Chicago the year before, it caused me to think differently about what was happening to people all over the world in the struggle for land and human rights.

Finding My Way

Growing up in the 1960s I thought of race relations as a problem in other countries. Like many other New Zealanders I had been lulled into the popular belief at the time that New Zealand had the best race relations in the world. I had very little contact with Maori and had no awareness that there was any problem. I had never read the Treaty of Waitangi and was ignorant of the myriad land and other laws passed in order to exclude Maori people from the system and take their resource base.

Looking back, I now see that my travel overseas was preparing me for the next (unknown) step in my life. While my work for Corso in the 1970s had kept my focus overseas, that experience, combined with the emotional impact of being in jail in 1981, brought into question all that I had assumed about poverty and racism. Why did I know so little about colonisation in New Zealand and what had happened to Maori?

After I left jail I could not forget what I had seen and heard. I began listening to Maori activists more closely and reading everything I could lay my hands on about this topic. I spent hours at night poring over books trying to cram in years of colonial history about New Zealand that I had not been taught.

My journey of self-discovery was tremendously liberating as I came to see, feel and experience issues with a new clarity. I realised how hugely disadvantaged I had been, growing up in a country where the media and the education system had been feeding me either misinformation or, as at school, no information at all. Like so many Pakeha, I had to learn to distinguish between truth and political propaganda. I had to accept responsibility for my own learning about New Zealand's colonial history.

Reading and listening to other people enabled me to realise that there was a wide variety of views, opinions and interpretations on New Zealand's colonial past and its impact on the present. This new appreciation transformed my picture of the colonisation of New Zealand. It enabled me to comprehend the complexity of the debate and begin to gain a more *informed* point of view, knowing both sides of the story.

Much of what I read and learned shocked me. It occurred to me that much of what had happened to Maori as a result of colonisation paralleled what had happened to my ancestors in Ireland. Making this connection enabled me to understand that healing history involved connecting my own ancestral story with the journey of my country. It also enabled me to stand alongside Maori and honour their struggle, while considering what this history meant to me as a Pakeha New Zealander.

Making a Response

Initially I had no idea where this new knowledge would lead or what my contribution would be. Others were already working actively in addressing race relations in New Zealand. In the early 1970s the Auckland Committee on Racism and Discrimination (ACORD) produced research papers on racism and discrimination, in particular to do with the police, courts and local bodies. The research papers found their way around government departments and follow-up education became difficult because of ACORD's high-profile political tactics. The need for alternative strategies meant some people from ACORD, along with Nga Tamatoa and the Polynesian Panther Party, set up New Perspectives on Race (NPR). This team consisted of Maori and Pakeha members who led anti-racism workshops for Pakeha belonging to church groups, community groups and government departments.

There were several outcomes. The Churches Programme on Racism emerged and has continued to offer excellent workshops. A group of staff in the Department of Social Welfare undertook critical research and produced a report called *Institutional Racism in the Department of Social Welfare Tamaki-Makau-Rau*. This led to another report, *Puao-Te-Ata-Tu*; both of them were ground-breaking. In 1978 a group called Urban Training to Combat Racism (UTCR) was formed in Wellington, and other anti-racism groups followed, including Double Take in Wellington and Fight Against Institutional Racism (FAIR) in Palmerston North.

In 1985 Project Waitangi succeeded in gaining government funding for a five-year education programme that would enable Pakeha to learn about the Treaty of Waitangi. A small office was set up in Wellington and groups were formed around the country. In time, training methods were developed, drawing on the experience of members of all the different groups.

As a co-founder of Project Waitangi in Christchurch I became part of a team leading Treaty workshops and networking with Maori and Pakeha interested in the Treaty. We experimented with a variety of education programmes, with the focus on the majority Pakeha population. As with all social change initiatives, we encountered knockbacks along the way. Public opinion was vehemently opposed to any issues related to Treaty rights for Maori, and at the outset many Pakeha approached the idea of doing Treaty education with reluctance. They did not see the point: knowing about the Treaty 150 years after its signing seemed irrelevant.

Any suggestion of racism invariably resulted in an instant denial. Many were puzzled that a group of Pakeha were teaching the Treaty of Waitangi—did we have Maori ancestry? The idea that Pakeha would take responsibility for learning and teaching Treaty commitments mystified them.

Project Waitangi members who chose to facilitate workshops faced a steep learning curve. We knew our workshop process had to be good, because we were dealing with a subject that was highly controversial and contained information that many Pakeha people did not want to know. We were often confronted with considerable hostility and resistance at the start of workshops, but it usually dissipated as the workshop continued. Through trial and error we eventually developed an educational process that worked. Participants were positive in their evaluations and support for the process began to grow. We were inspired to further refine the workshop, our persistence strengthened by a strong belief in what we were doing. We remained confident that what we were teaching would help us achieve our vision of Treaty education for all New Zealanders.

We also had the support of a network of local iwi, including Ngai Tahu, the Otautahi (Christchurch) Runaka, and a growing network of Maori from Cape Reinga to Bluff. These contacts had a profound impact on our approach to Treaty education. The philosophy of Pakeha taking responsibility for learning about the Treaty of Waitangi and colonialism received their unconditional support. If Maori were to regain self-determination, they needed the solidarity of well-informed and committed Pakeha who understood the power-sharing nature of the Treaty relationship. Pakeha taking responsibility for their learning freed Maori to focus on their own issues.

Reverend Maurice Gray, upoko (head) of Te Runaka ki Otautahi o Kai Tahu, shared his wisdom and guidance, calling our work 'creating the space'. I understood this to mean that Maori did not want to be 'helped' by Pakeha, but wanted the space to achieve self-determination. I have never forgotten these words and continue to think of them as a guiding principle in my Treaty work with Pakeha today. The opportunity to attend the Runaka and other hui remains a real privilege. I am able to witness Maori addressing the daunting challenges facing their people, and benefit from the wisdom being expressed. This level of relationship enables me to be in contact with local Maori when I need to be. It also encourages me to get on and address issues of Pakeha responsibility, while Maori energy is directed in pursuit of meeting their own personal, social, economic and political needs.

Getting involved in Treaty education meant that alongside learning about racism, history, culture, networking, leadership, development and accountability, I had to confront my own fears and acknowledge and work through my own prejudice and racism. I came to recognise that 'change only occurs when you allow yourself to be what you are, instead of trying to be what you would like to be'.[5] I integrated changes in my thinking and functioning in a way that still retained my own authenticity and identity.

Refining the Process

As time went on, members of Project Waitangi became divided over how Treaty education workshops should be run. The classic dilemmas of the left—the conflicting ideologies of feminists, Christians, Marxists and trade unionists—came to the fore. People who brought a feminist or socialist perspective argued that without that agenda anti-racism work would be futile, and so on. The challenge was to find a common purpose. What aspects of these ideologies should be incorporated into the anti-racism process? Was the movement primarily educational or should it also have a high political profile? Increasingly, agreement became impossible. Each leader had an unfailing commitment to the goals, but a vehemently different view on how to carry them out. Workshop leaders who didn't fit the prevailing political agenda at any particular time were frequently marginalised and political differences often degenerated into personal differences.

I've always believed Marxist, socialist, feminist and globalisation perspectives are all relevant, valid strands of the whole. All need to be acknowledged as each contributes to our understanding of the complexities of healing our history—so much so that they warrant workshops in their own right.

The challenge in Treaty education workshops is to keep the focus on racism, colonial history and the failure by governments to honour agreements with indigenous peoples. Says American anti-racism activist Paul Kivel:

> We must notice when we try to slip into another identity and escape being white. We each have many other factors that influence our lives, such as our ethnicity, gender, sexual orientation, class, personality, mental and

physical abilities. Even when we are talking about these elements of our lives we must keep whiteness on stage with us because it influences each of the other factors.[6]

One of the most insightful exercises we conduct in advanced Treaty workshops focuses on 'white privilege'. It is aimed at understanding the invisible knapsack that 'white' people take for granted in a society in which they are the majority. Peggy McIntosh, associate director of the Wellesley College Center for Research on Women, has produced from her own experience a list of 26 ways 'white' people are unconsciously privileged in a society in which they are members of the dominant group.[7] Although the research was conducted in an American setting, many New Zealand workshop participants accept the validity of the list. (See Chapter 10 for New Zealand analysis.)

During this time of refining the process (1983–90) I attended a variety of workshops around New Zealand and experienced different ways of delivering Treaty education. In one workshop, which stands out in my memory, 28 Pakeha, including myself, were confronted with their own racism and accused of all the behaviours associated with colonialism. Amid an atmosphere of hostility to everything Pakeha, I and the others were blamed for being part of a system that maintained white racial superiority and a Eurocentric world view. The leadership of the three-day workshop were Maori and Pakeha and as a white male I was particularly confronted. By the end of the workshop many participants were shattered and left feeling appalled at the level of abuse. For my part I was convinced that this approach was counter-productive to the purpose of Treaty education.

Confrontation is not appropriate as an educational method for Treaty education, because it is designed to engender guilt and to make people feel negative about their own cultural identity. This kind of workshop process does not treat people as individuals, but as representatives of an historical and contemporary system. It has the potential to force people to become more entrenched in their beliefs and to take more extreme positions and engage in behaviours designed to alleviate the guilt. Inflicting guilt on workshop participants is a poor substitute for solid analysis and information aimed at enhancing understanding.

Confrontation does have a role in social change. The courage of political activists and those the media labels as 'Maori radicals' ensures that the Treaty of Waitangi and its implications remain at the top of New Zealand's political agenda. This in turn keeps the Treaty in the consciousness of all New Zealanders as high-profile, non-violent protest continues to highlight the gross injustices perpetrated against indigenous peoples. But in an educational workshop setting confrontation is destructive and dangerous.

Developing a New Approach

After 1990 the National government withdrew all funding from Project Waitangi. This group devolved into Network Waitangi, encouraging the groups already formed to continue the educational work on a regional basis as best they could. As the now-redundant full-time Project Waitangi worker for Christchurch, I set about creating my own Treaty education business. I continued to do extramural study specialising in New Zealand history and aimed to read for a minimum of two hours every day. As the level of debate becomes more complex there is always more to learn.

I worked independently for the first four years, mainly with community groups, and continued to fine-tune the workshop process. As word spread I began to be invited to facilitate Treaty workshops in a variety of workplaces and was soon required to recruit others of like mind and spirit to work with me in order to meet the demand. Once again my vision of being part of a team of workshop leaders became a reality. Our team now works in over a hundred New Zealand organisations, from community groups to the highest levels of government.

Early on I knew that if Treaty education were to be successful then I would have to offer a process that was twice as good as any other educational experience. The women's movement influenced my thinking here. I recalled women saying that in order to succeed at the same job as men, they had to be twice as good as men. I realised that because of the level of resistance to the topic of the Treaty, the workshops had to be dynamic, credible, informative, interesting and fun.

The major hurdle was how to encourage attendance among those people who simply weren't interested in Treaty matters. Workshops based on confrontation were clearly not the answer: in fact the opposite was required. Instead of inviting hostility and defiance, I needed to create an hospitable environment. Somehow we needed to engage and include all types of participants, wherever they were in their thinking on the topic. It all came down to leadership.

I continued to develop my own leadership style, grounded in my experience at a seminar led by Brazilian educator Paulo Freire in Christchurch in 1972.[8] I remember that seminar well. Freire sat in the middle of a crowd of eager participants who were waiting to hear his wise and profound insights on education . . . but nothing happened. Thirty minutes passed. What did he have planned? Finally, someone asked him a question. He replied with a question, a statement, then more questions. He did not supply answers, rather he encouraged each person to develop and share his or her own answers. The experience had a profound impact on me and shaped my thinking on Treaty education. Paulo Freire's idea was to ground all education in the experiences of individual participants and develop a continual shared investigation.

In trying to empower people to be confident and full participants in a society confronting its colonial history and changing the traditional relationship between the colonisers and the colonised, I realised it was not up to me to give participants the answers. My role was to give them the tools to find their own answers. The life experience of each person needed to be central to the task and process of the workshop, and the information needed to be introduced and discussed in a way that enabled each person in the group to feel connected to the issues and part of the process of addressing them.

Questions, Questions, Questions

I worked at creating an educational process that would allow a safe level of openness to exist, enabling people to raise their questions, explore their opinions and participate in the debate. This meant an ideal group size of no more than 20. I knew some would resist as we live in a climate of fear around these issues. Empowering people to work through the resistance required a process that was challenging, but not anti-European. The workshop needed to honour each person's own cultural journey and validate any, and every, question participants had. I would start this process with a creative warm-up that invited acknowledgement of current issues being canvassed in the media, as well as the impact of the Treaty debate of New Zealand society. Here is a list of typical questions that arise in this session of a Treaty workshop:

- What are the major issues that Maori people have with Pakeha people?

- What is in the Treaty of Waitangi? How many versions are there? Which one do we believe?

- Was the mistranslation of the Treaty deliberate or unintentional?

- Surely all treaties are broken. Can't we just forget about it?

- Is the Treaty struggle taking place overseas or just here in New Zealand?

- How will implementing the Treaty help Maori today?

- Who are the 'real' Maori leaders? Which ones do we listen to?

- Surely Maori benefited from the Pakeha settlement?

- When are Maori going to stop moaning and work like the rest of us?

- Everyone has equal opportunity. Why can't Maori take advantage?

- What defines a Maori?

- What is an indigenous person?

- Why can't Maori own their Pakeha side?

- Maori seem to have a lot of unused land. Why are they claiming more?

- What has 'being Maori' got to do with health?

- Our schools are open to everyone. Why can't Maori just fit in?

- I don't believe Pakeha people have a culture. Aren't we all New Zealanders?

- Is it true that Maori get all these privileges such as scholarships?

- Why should we go back 150 years to solve problems?

- Maori traditionally took over land by force. Surely Pakeha people just did the same?

- What about the Maori taking over the Moriori? Who was here first?

- Why should Maori have preferential treatment at law school and medical school?

- What do Maori expect from health professionals?

- Maori are claiming the airwaves. There were no airwaves in 1840. What's next?

- Should I learn the Maori language?

- How can Maori claim mineral resources they did not know about in 1840?

- Who will benefit from Maori land claims?

- I've heard the Maori are now claiming private land. Is this true?

- This is all about Maori. What about other cultures in New Zealand?

- I've heard that the word Pakeha is an insult. What does it mean?

- What do Maori see as the role of Pakeha in New Zealand today?

- How are these issues being dealt with in Australia and Canada?

- Are there any Australian and Canadian examples of successful solutions?

Throughout the two-day workshop process participants often find answers to their questions by absorbing the information presented and engaging in discussion. When their questions are taken seriously, they inevitably feel 'freed up' to participate further. In that process the complexities of the issues unfold and the questions asked enable each person to continue or, in some cases, begin the journey of 'integrating' knowledge about this country's colonial history.

Sociodrama: Learning by Doing

Integration involves building on what is already there in order to take the next step. In the firm belief that experiential learning is the key, I employ the tool of sociodrama. This approach invites participants to integrate their thinking and analysis while participating in a fun learning experience that fully engages their emotions and senses.[9]

It has been said that we learn 10 per cent of what we read, 15 per cent of what we hear, but 80 per cent of what we experience.[10]

In order to get people to look at the Treaty and racism in a different way I knew I needed to get the group thinking in different ways. I needed to use methods that engaged their heads and hearts, so that it got them enjoying themselves. To this end I invited people to enact historical roles, such as being an early settler, Queen Victoria, a colonial clerk, a Treaty negotiator, a Crown representative, a drunken convict, a prostitute, a governor, an indigenous chief or a member of a tribe. I wanted them to be their ancestor of 200 years ago. This could mean a Scottish clan chief, a starving Irish peasant, an English aristocrat, a mother of 17 children, a landless peasant, a craftsperson, a smuggler, a missionary, an escaped convict.

Given this opportunity to use their imaginations to enact central figures in history, the participants would be able to experience the pressures and understand the constraints under which an historical figure or group operated. They could explore how this person would have thought, and experience emotions such as powerlessness, anger, fear, paralysis, rejection and invisibility. They would, through this process, gain insights into a wide range of issues, including how the dominant culture has the power to exclude.

Through these constructed experiences, participants can come to new ways of viewing the Treaty of Waitangi and New Zealand's colonial history. As the information becomes more integrated into their own experience, they become able to explore the alternative positions, compromises and solutions canvassed in the current debate.

The potential for humour through the workshop process is enormous. In one workshop a participant described the first frozen shipment of meat from New Zealand to England in the 1880s by being a sheep's carcass on board a ship. He described to the group what he was doing and how it felt—suffice to say his future looked bleak! My task was to fill the gaps in historical information where necessary. Obviously, certain types of humour would be inappropriate, but so many of the views, fears and prejudices we collect on our life's journey are, when examined, verging on the absurd. By holding a mirror to them, and creating an outlet, I learned that I could allow people to let go of them through humour and move on.

Information v. Propaganda

In Treaty education, as in any other type, it is important not to replace one set of myths with another. The purpose of the workshops is not manipulation or propaganda. The integrity of the teaching process is always on the line and I can relate to Australian historian Henry Reynolds who said of himself: 'I never doubted the contemporary relevance of what I was doing or lacked a sense of the great responsibility which rests on the shoulders of those who interpret the nation's past.'[11] I aim to use educational techniques to enable participants to view issues from multiple perspectives and gain the tools to find their own answers. To this end I will present a range of views and identify key sources. I encourage participants to read, search out their own sources, judge each view against the others and draw their own conclusions.

The declared focus of the workshop is to explore what happened to indigenous peoples as a result of colonisation. Many New Zealanders have been denied this view of history and instead have been conditioned by a view that reflects the dominant Pakeha colonial ideology. While it is appropriate, for example, for New Zealanders and Australians to commemorate Gallipoli, El Alamein and Cassino, why is it that in New Zealand we do not commemorate the domestic wars of sovereignty fought in our own country in the 1860s? Invasions against indigenous peoples within colonial countries have traditionally been excluded in the teaching of colonial history. As a result of this ignorance there is often an overwhelming desire to protect, minimise and excuse the behaviour of European settlers when new information about colonial history is presented.

It is necessary to elevate the outcomes of colonial history and place them alongside other views of that history in order to address historical and contemporary issues. Only then can we see how the picture of colonial history changes with new information:

> Learning from history is never simply a one-way process. To learn about the present in the light of the past means also to learn about the past in the light of the present. The function of history is to promote a profounder understanding of both past and present through the interrelation between them.[12]

New Zealand historian the late Michael King adds: 'the past can only be understood in, and on, its own terms. People are limited always by the viewpoints of their own age, and by the amount of information and the degree of insight that has reached them'.[13]

We explore the relationship and tension between past and present in Treaty education workshops, taking care not to 'explain away' or excuse collective acts of violence in terms of the culture and context of the time in which they happened. We see that 'forgetting history' or saying 'it happened all in the past' does not work for either party. The end result of this thinking is to continue the advantage in favour of the colonisers. Theologian John O'Donohue captures the paradox:

> There is a tendency now in revisionist history to explain the past in terms of movements and trends of the contemporary time. This is inevitably reductionist. The suffering of the people is forgotten; they become faceless, mere ciphers of a trend or dynamic of history. To sanitise history is to blaspheme against memory. Equally, to become obsessed with the past is to paralyse the future.[14]

There are dangers in educating a population at large. Information on its own does not necessarily produce change. Early on in developing the New Zealand Treaty education process we were aware of the danger of turning ill-informed racists into well-informed racists. People do not make decisions on facts; rather on how they feel about the facts. This remains a real danger as information becomes more widely available without opportunities to process and integrate it.

Other Teaching Tools

Mini lectures, video clips, audiotapes, and small and large group discussions are some of the tools I use alongside sociodrama to familiarise participants with a wide range of perspectives on any given issue. Participants soon become well equipped to debate the issues. Here is an example of the activities that might take place in a typical workshop:

• Participants are offered six different historical positions on the Treaty of Waitangi. Six different groups of participants are invited to take one position each and make an argument in favour of their position. This serves to familiarise the participants with the language of the Treaty and show them the complexity of the Treaty debate.

• Participants are invited to debate the land claims of different groups. They might take the part of the original Maori owners from whom the land was taken, or the contemporary owners (Pakeha) who obtained legal title from the Crown and have developed the land over four or five generations. The participants are invited to work together to create just solutions.

• The land confiscation issue is further developed when participants are divided into groups to represent different stakeholders. For example, one group represents the Crown/government. A second group represents taxpayers. Other groups represent particular tribes. Participants are required to develop their particular role fully and engage in negotiating a politically workable outcome.

- A further activity relates to Treaty settlements currently being offered to Maori tribes by the Crown. Participants assume the role of individual members of a particular tribe and are required to debate whether or not to accept the settlement offer.

- Participants explore the future of sovereign authority in New Zealand by examining each position in the sovereignty debate. A variety of positions are canvassed, including a separate, parallel parliament for Maori peoples, a senate/upper house based on shared authority and tribal representation in the existing Parliament, and full autonomy for Maori within existing political and economic structures.

Through engaging in these debates participants become thoroughly familiar with the subject and realise how people are able to hold a variety of arguable positions passionately. They learn that some positions are mutually exclusive. In this process we as workshop leaders never present any position as 'the answer'; rather, we engage people in the complexity of trying to find resolution. Many of these issues are still being debated in society and new issues will continue to emerge.

The process is not intended to answer all the questions, but to create a framework within which people will find their own answers. We don't expect people to agree with one another, or to start and finish in the same place. Knowing *what* your opinion is becomes less important than understanding *why* you hold it. The role of the workshop leader is to assist the group to make connections and to motivate each person to engage in further learning. I encourage people to live with the questions, as a 'solution focus' is often a barrier to change in this arena. The path is not clear and is still unfolding. As a society we need to live our way into the solution. Life is a journey and it is through the journey that the answers will emerge.

'I despise the media for making us afraid'[15]

Healing history clearly requires challenging the internalised stereotypes and assumptions we hold about Maori. With rare exceptions, the media has fuelled Pakeha fear and ignorance around the Treaty debate. Maori are portrayed in extreme positions. They are losers at the bottom of the heap, or they are unreasonable, loud, confrontational activists making excessive demands, or occasionally they are articulate speakers discussing colonialism and the Treaty of Waitangi in an informed manner.

A journalist is a conduit between the interviewee and the public. Journalists therefore need to know about New Zealand's colonial history and its impact in order to ask informed questions. If a journalist does not have adequate knowledge to conduct an informed interview, then the public is short-changed, further fuelling prejudice in the Pakeha community as the journalist fails to elucidate the issues properly.

After he appeared on a prime-time television current affairs show, Member of Parliament Willie Jackson described the interview as 'unbalanced' and 'ill-informed'.[16] In a *Mana* news radio interview Jackson argued that many well-known Pakeha broadcasters are out of their depth on Maori issues:

> What we have unfortunately at the moment is a virtual Pakeha monopoly of broadcasting in this country in the TV news, radio and print area. I'm not talking about presenting the news . . . it's about who shapes the news, who directs the news, who asks all the major questions and, really, there's so few Maori faces there.[17]

In workshops, participants are given an opportunity to reflect on how the media has presented the Treaty debate to the public. They critically evaluate what is presented in light of the new information gained in the workshop and make up their own minds.

Transporting the Workshop Model to Canada

In 1996 I extended my work by becoming an international trainer of trainers in anti-racism/Treaty education. I was invited to Victoria, British Columbia, by a group of European Canadian anti-racism workers to share the New Zealand Treaty education workshop model. On this visit I also met groups in Edmonton, Calgary, Lethbridge and Winnipeg. I introduced the model to trade unions, secondary-school teachers, local police in Vancouver, RCMP Federal Police in Ottawa, First Nations groups, non-government organisations and university students.

The challenge that faced all people and groups in the field was how to develop an holistic, engaging and popular anti-racism/Treaty learning process. I discovered that personal experiences were often not incorporated into the teaching of history, but the feedback I received about our New Zealand workshop process was that integrating the personal and political worked well. The positive reception from a number of groups in Canada convinced me this experiential learning process was transportable to other countries dealing with the outcomes of colonial history, provided it was adapted to be well grounded in the local history, culture and political struggles confronting that particular region or country.

Following my visit, Te Huirangi Waikerepuru from Taiporohenui Marae, Te Hawera, Taranaki, travelled to Canada to share his culture and wisdom with First Nations communities and non-indigenous peoples. Reports from Canada indicate Huirangi provided inspiration to Coast Salish, Nuu Chah Nulth, Cree and Metis families in the realms of language revitalisation, traditional art forms and schools, traditional medicine, indigenous self-governance and economic development to name a few, and by addressing climate change and traditional dispute resolution.

The Indigenous Governance Program at the University of Victoria approached Huirangi to teach indigenous students internationally via online education. He has acted as external advisor to a master's degree defence and provided encouragement for indigenous doctoral students. He shared his knowledge about the protection of water from a Maori perspective, contributing towards a sustainable future for generations to come. His work in Canada strengthens the process of building solidarity among all peoples working for indigenous rights.

Ongoing Challenges

Treaty workshops began as a creative attempt to educate Pakeha people about New Zealand colonial history, and offer a unique combination of anti-racism/Treaty education strategies, enabling participants to engage in holistic learning. The process works. Workshops are now regularly delivered at all levels of New Zealand society, including community groups, government departments and private-sector organisations. My experience demonstrates that participants are often hungry for knowledge about the issues confronting New Zealand today and simultaneously can feel anxious about what they might learn. Yet, many participants report that their attitudes are transformed through attending a Treaty workshop and that they feel more confident in dealing with the issues.

Being creative in itself is insufficient. Treaty workshops must remain interesting, current, innovative and marketable in today's society. This challenges those of us engaged in Treaty education to continue to reflect on and learn from our experience, develop fresh learning strategies, keep abreast of new information, maintain our accountability to indigenous peoples, provide a consistently high-quality service, be open to opportunities, and identify, train and supervise new workshop leaders.

Originally it was thought that any motivated person could lead a workshop, but experience has shown that using untrained, unaccountable people can be completely counter-productive. Participants attending workshops led by inexperienced trainers have emerged rejecting the entire process and vowing to avoid any further involvement. Leading Treaty workshops requires exceptional skills.

Evaluations of Treaty workshops over the past 10 years affirm that the experience has transformed the way many participants view New Zealand society. This, in turn, has motivated many to create a climate where it is possible to address a new way of collaborating with Maori in a relationship working towards shared authority. Everyone benefits. Treaty workshops are an essential contribution towards healing history because it is only in understanding where we have been that we can begin to address past injustices and move positively together towards the future.

EIGHT

Honouring Our Stories

The Celtic Twilight—Aran Islands, 1992

It was dark. The sea had disappeared as driving sleet made its way across the bleak landscape of Inishmore. It was well after midnight and I was lost, completely disoriented and soaked to the skin. The rain and the wind were so fierce that I could not see the ground I was standing on. I knew I had about five kilometres to walk down the winding road, but in this weather staying on the road—even walking—seemed an almost impossible task.

Suddenly I stepped into space and I landed on my back in two metres of water in a ditch. At first I couldn't move. My shoulder was numb and I felt scared. Then gradually, for no apparent reason, my fear and anxiety left me. Complete calm entered my whole being and I felt the support of my Celtic ancestors around me. I was utterly lost, soaked to the skin and numb, yet I felt peaceful and sustained. It was an extraordinary feeling.

I cautiously dragged myself out of the ditch and, despite having no idea where I was, began to walk with a new confidence. I was guided back to the correct track by the life that surely existed within the land on which I was walking. The feeling of being connected to the land, of being cared for and not being alone in this ancient country, was one that will remain with me for the rest of my life.

Although I had been on the island for less than 24 hours, this was not the first time I had been lost. Earlier in the evening I had walked to the west coast on the edge of the Atlantic Ocean, climbing over many stone walls to inspect old ruins of fourth- and fifth-century monasteries belonging to Celtic monks. There were other Celtic ruins pre-dating Christianity, giving testimony to the lifestyle of the Celts. The Irish language is still the first language on the Aran Islands and many elements of the Celtic lifestyle remain alive.

So who were the Celts? They have been described as one of the great barbarian peoples of the world, given to ferocious, excitable and warlike behaviour. Despite their small numbers, they made a major and lasting contribution to western civilisation. From the plains of Hungary they migrated through Austria, Switzerland, southern Germany and France, then across the water into Scotland, Wales and Ireland. The Celts left behind no written records, unlike the Greek and Roman civilisations. The main access to Celtic history is through what they made rather than what they wrote. The oral tradition is also strong.

At the height of their development the Celts constituted an archetypal European people: tribal, familial, hierarchical and agricultural. They were not a political people and did not achieve or desire a cohesive political nationhood, but their motivation and the unity of the tribe make a compelling political model. They were not an imperial people, although wherever they went they left behind a dominant cultural imprint.

A French definition says that prehistory stops with the first written document. By this principle the Celts qualify as a prehistoric people. Like any civilisation, they emerged rather than arrived, developing over several centuries. By 800 BC the Celts were clearly identifiable in Europe, and 700 years later, by 100 BC, a Celtic society of some depth and richness had gained ground in Ireland.[1]

It is not my intention to tell the story or even attempt to summarise the history of the Celts. Rather, it is to make connections between this civilisation and the ancestry of many Pakeha New Zealanders, who are now discovering their own heritage and making meaning of it in light of their New Zealand roots. It is my belief that in exploring the cultural heritage of our ancestors, we can begin to develop an awareness of where we feel most grounded.

Being Grounded

I define 'being grounded' as making connections that enable a feeling of belonging. We posssess the connections intrinsically, but many of us are unaware of them. The challenge is to 'make' the connections. There is no formula for being grounded. It means different things to different people, but it usually involves a feeling of safety to be and express who we are. For some people it involves a concept of connection to land, whether it be rural, suburban or inner-city; for others there may be a connection to the mountains, bush or rivers of a particular country. Others may find grounding in an ancestral homeland, or simply in knowing where their ancestors are from. Some may feel grounded in the presence of family and friends, or in that place called home. One may feel grounded in a variety of places.

People often find that they only realise where they feel grounded when they live elsewhere, and/or when their own culture, values, world view or way of life come into question. For others, who have always known where they felt grounded, meeting new people, encountering different ways of living or confronting painful life-changing experiences can challenge them to discover a new source of grounding. Grounding for some is a constantly evolving dynamic.

Feeling grounded may mean retaining a strong connection with childhood roots. Australian historian Henry Reynolds offers a personal insight:

> I cannot remember a time when I didn't feel at home in Tasmania. It has little to do with the will or the intellect. You either feel you belong or you don't. And once that sense is there it can't be given up, willed away or reasoned out of existence. Almost thirty years of writing revisionist history changed my views about many things, but never touched my sense of where I had come from, where I belonged . . .[2]

Valuing Your Own Story

In Treaty education workshops, knowing your own story and feeling grounded in your own identity is the starting point for exploring New

Zealand's colonial history and understanding its current impact. Michael King captures this crucial truth: 'The key to redressing imbalances and reconciling past misunderstandings is knowledge; the first step towards knowledge is self-knowledge.'[3] New information about colonial history can invoke pain and discomfort in participants. For this reason this information is best presented in a way that enables people to make sense of it within the framework of their own life experience. In this process, the stories Pakeha have of their ancestors—where they came from, why they left their homeland, what happened when they arrived here—are pivotal.

Stories enable workshop participants to make meaning of their ancestors' journey to New Zealand and how that has shaped their own lives. These stories become metaphors for the body of knowledge transmitted in the workshop. As participants explore the process of colonisation, they realise that many of the laws that drove their European ancestors from their homelands were subsequently adapted and imposed on indigenous peoples in colonised countries such as New Zealand. This knowledge enables them to make connections between their countries of ancestral origin and New Zealand.

The story of each human being is unique, yet simultaneously embraces universal emotions found in the larger story of humanity. Writer Michelanne Forster believes that stories enable us to cross time, space and cultures. Stories can give a sense of connection, fulfilling the human need to alleviate isolation and the feeling that you are the only one experiencing this.[4] Understanding our own story gives us some clues on how to align ourselves with people of other cultures and the universal story. When we see the commonality in the human struggle, what to do with the new information becomes the next challenge.

Stories Bring History Alive

The Importance of Story

Listening to stories from history is one part of the healing process for countries facing their colonial past. The telling of stories is not an end in itself, but contributes to our understanding of where the healing needs to occur and what needs to be done. Stories enable us to acknowledge, honour and remember the past, and to begin to determine what is needed in the future to create more peaceful relationships within and between individuals, communities and nations.

However, every storyteller must retain the right to tell their stories to whomever they choose and in their own time. It is, after all, their story. Pakeha do not have the right to *know* the stories of Maori unless Maori choose to tell them. While a power imbalance remains in the relationship between Maori and Pakeha, there can be no equal relationship between the colonised and colonisers. Yet, when storytelling is greeted with deep listening, healing can begin for the colonised and understanding is awakened in the coloniser. When Pakeha *hear* the stories of indigenous peoples directly or through another, the new awareness can have a powerful impact.

Chris Sidoti, the human rights commissioner for Australia, shared his experience of listening to the stories of the Stolen Generations in 1997.[5] 'Stolen children' were Aboriginal children forcibly taken from their natural communities in the face of extreme resistance, and 'adopted' out to European families. They were often referred to as the 'children of the bleaching'. It is now recognised that they were kidnapped by the state and that the purpose was to wipe out Aboriginal culture. On New Zealand television Sidoti commented:

> The one that perhaps struck me most as an individual was the story of children who were taken from school. This was not an isolated story; it happened regularly. The children were farewelled by their parents, would go off to school for the day and never return. And I spoke to people who are my age [mid-forties] telling stories of how they went to school one day when five or six or seven, and how they never saw their parents again. I sat listening to those stories. I imagined how I would've felt had I been in their shoes 40 years ago, going off to school and never coming home to my parents. I try to imagine what it'd be like to lose my children. The thing about this issue is that it is something that must touch the heart of everybody who listens to it. If we were only prepared to listen to the experience, we couldn't help but be moved to respond with the utmost compassion.[6]

Sidoti tells us that many Australians are hearing these stories for the first time. By telling this history through story, Sidoti brings the issue alive in a way that is accessible and manageable for the listener. This is extremely powerful, for, as Michelanne Forster suggests, the paradox of human nature is that while people have an openness to change, they also have the desire to stay safe and resist change. Stories such as the Stolen Generations address the hunger to know more without the listener or reader having to undergo the experience themselves.[7]

In listening to stories such as those of the Stolen Generations, I recall an expression from the Philippines about the culture of silence: 'If you really want to know us, listen to what we are not allowed to say.' Chris Sidoti highlighted this aspect:

> We were very upset that we heard from very few mothers who had lost their children. There are still women alive and men alive whose children were taken away, yet it seems the hurt was so great that they couldn't even appear before our inquiry. The evidence we received from them had to be obtained in other ways.[8]

The silence says it all.

Stories of a country's colonial past have the most impact when delivered in a learning environment that enables listeners to place the new information in an historical framework. People can then explore their reactions and discuss what is being presented. Careful timing in the delivery of particular stories can enable people to accept views that may be different from their own.

In my experience there is a discernible link between being grounded, valuing your own story and understanding stories from our history. When these factors coalesce Pakeha are enabled to listen compassionately to the issues, stories and challenges being raised by indigenous peoples. When we have a firm sense of identity, connection and belonging, we are less likely to become daunted and personally threatened by the new information communicated through stories. Our fears are less likely to dominate our responses and we are more open to hearing what others are saying.

My Story

My understanding of the importance of knowing our own story developed as I uncovered my own. Ireland is my ancestral homeland.

New Zealand is my homeland. I remember well my first overseas visit. My reaction mirrored that of New Zealand historian Michael King, who wrote of the effect of his first year away from New Zealand: 'I felt more, not less a New Zealander. I became more deeply conscious of my roots in my own country because I had experienced their absence. I missed physical things, like empty land and seascapes, driftwood fires, bush, New Zealand birdsong.'[9]

Yet I feel strongly connected to Ireland for different reasons. Ireland is where my identity and roots began. I am convinced that my commitment to social justice is deeply connected to my Irish ancestral roots. Being involved in social change triggered me to find out who I was and make meaning of my own story. Large numbers of Irish were not only colonised in their own country but also driven out by the conditions and systems created by colonisation. One of my ancestors, Timothy Keary, was active as a United Irishman in the Irish rebellion of 1798. The penal laws had not yet been officially repealed and most Irish had an 'inferior identity'.[10] Many were landless in their own country by the end of the eighteenth century. This was not primarily a religious struggle but a class struggle, as many Catholic gentry were equally active in putting disturbances down.[11]

In a later generation Keary's great-nephew Patrick was jailed in the land wars of south-east Galway. The resistance was driven by 'a seething rage against the unjust land tenure system, which made the small and usually poverty-stricken tenant little more than a serf subject to the whims of his master'.[12] The conflict in east Galway in 1886 hit the world headlines, focusing on the town of Woodford, the home of my ancestors and family to this day. The struggle highlighted 'the ruthlessness and power of an obstinate and callous absentee landlord against his exasperated and determined tenantry'.[13] The campaign was regarded as enormously successful. In 1870 only 3 per cent of the tenants owned the land they lived on, but by 1916 this figure had increased to 65 per cent. The Woodford Heritage group report described this campaign as 'surely the greatest revolution in Irish history'.[14] I had to agree, especially after reading a letter written by Patrick Keary to his sister, recording his experience in a Galway jail in 1888:

You will be surprised to hear that notwithstanding my months of confinement, I have not been in better health for the last seven years than I am in at present. Nobody knows how much hardship they can endure until they are compelled to go through with it, whether they like it or not. Of course I felt the bread and water, and the plank bed for the first few days very keenly, though I never pretended to it, but I never for one moment lost my courage or cheerfulness, and those are the two great ingredients to pull a fellow through in prison life; besides I felt the proud consciousness that the crime for which I was being punished, was such as need never bring the blush of shame to my children's face, nor a pang of remorse to my own heart.[15]

Patrick's description of his release from jail has the hallmarks of Christ entering Jerusalem:

Raymond came to meet me in Galway, and his face was the first I saw on my entrance to the outside world, after leaving the prison gate. Father Willy [Roche] was with him and my journey from that home was one continued ovation. At Athenry and Loughrea cheers for Patrick Keary and Woodford were heard everywhere, and there was not a house on the side of the road from Loughrea to Woodford that had not a candle in every pane, with bonfires, music and torches at every cross roads. But the entry into Woodford was something awful. Crowds came out with the band, the town was illuminated, and then they all stopped outside the house I had to go to, that now historic window of the parlour upstairs and I made a flaming speech.[16]

Patrick's struggle for justice in Ireland and Te Whiti's resistance at Parihaka both had a profound influence on my decision to spend time in jail in 1981. If more Pakeha New Zealanders of Irish descent knew their collective histories, they may find themselves becoming natural allies with the Maori struggle in New Zealand.

My great-great-grandfather Thomas Sweeney was found guilty of 'felonious assault on a habitation between sunrise and sunset' and was sentenced to hang by the English colonial authorities in Tipperary on 1 April 1823. He had been found with one of the 'rural guerrilla groups engaged in a struggle against the payments of tithes by poor farmers and [who] also struck at certain landlords or their agents'.[17] The hanging sentence was subsequently commuted to transportation for life. Thomas and his cohorts were transported on the prison ship *Isabella*, which arrived in Sydney about nine months later, where they 'survived an outbreak of fever as well as the plottings of a group of desperadoes who were looking to stage a mutiny'.[18] After serving 12 years he was given a 'ticket of leave'.

I am interested in Australian colonial history partly because of this ancestral connection to that country. Thomas Sweeney stayed in Australia after his release, eventually working as a coastal trader. His descendants spread out throughout New Zealand and Australia and one of Sweeney's children, Kate, married a later Timothy Keary and came to the West Coast of the South Island for the gold in the early 1860s. The West Coast is where my New Zealand roots begin.

Thomas Sweeney's actions drove him out of his country of origin, yet he inevitably became a beneficiary of the dispossession of Aboriginal peoples in Australia. Sweeney's story highlights how difficult, if not impossible, it is to be concerned about the plight of another people when struggling for your own survival. The colonisers offered an alternative to being oppressed. The oppressors had power, money, possessions, land and choice. It follows that joining the oppressor became the goal of most people. This is one explanation why the Irish have often become allies of the coloniser. Frederick Douglass, in Ignatiev, speaking of the Irish in America in 1853, summed it up by stating: 'The Irish, who at home readily sympathise with the oppressed everywhere, are instantly taught when they step upon our soil to hate and despise the Negro . . . the Irish American will one day find out his mistake.'[19]

When racism and racial inferiority are perpetrated against people, sooner or later it is likely they will internalise the values of the racist. The outcome is often a hatred of self and a hatred of your own kind. If you are told something often and in a situation in which you are vulnerable, you are more likely to end up believing it. It appears some Irish succumbed to the tide of racial insults inflicted on them and in turn inflicted them on others. In New Zealand the Irish as a group did not join the Maori struggle against colonisation. Instead, it would appear that having being oppressed in their own country, many focused on establishing a route out of oppression towards their own liberation. This often meant joining the oppressors.

Taking Personal Responsibility

In understanding my own story and learning about the history of colonisation as a systemic process, I was able to maintain my integrity and not be manipulated by guilt that might be imposed on me by others. I am not responsible for what my ancestors did. I am also not responsible for what I was not taught in my formal education. However, as a Pakeha I undoubtedly benefited from the actions of my ancestors and from the forces of colonisation. I am therefore responsible for my own learning and commitment to change in the present.

The Treaty of Waitangi enabled European settlers to settle in this country peacefully. Hapu who signed the Treaty of Waitangi with the British Crown granted settlers this right. The Treaty therefore legitimises the presence of all other cultures in New Zealand. Pakeha people have a right to be here, but that right carries an obligation to honour the promises that enabled settlement to occur. The historical fact is, however, that by the time the settlers became the majority all promises to Maori had been discarded. The failure to keep this agreement, regarded by Maori as a sacred covenant, and the subsequent imposition of a colonial system, lies at the heart of the contemporary Treaty debate. To recognise that European colonisation had a devastating impact on Maori peoples is not to attack our ancestors. Rather, it is to acknowledge the fact of an imposed system that was based on legal fiction and contrary to the sacred promises made to the indigenous peoples. This system benefited most European settlers at the expense of the indigenous peoples.

Guilt has no place in the Treaty debate. The challenge is personal responsibility. 'Responsibility', says Jorge Rosner, 'literally means "the ability to respond". You only respond when you are fully aware of your behaviour and your choices, then, on the basis of your awareness, you can freely choose what to do.'[20] We cannot act on what we do not know. However, we now live in an environment where the impact and outcomes of New Zealand's colonial past are evident. We can and need to take responsibility for our own learning about it. We can reflect on our own behaviour and attitudes and freely choose whether we need to make changes in our personal and professional lives or in our thoughts and actions regarding the issues confronting New Zealand today.

We can take responsibility by being open to change in our places of work, by exercising a willingness to find and accept new ways of functioning that recognise and honour cultural diversity. My American colleague Joe Barndt adds this challenge:

> It is incorrect to assume that our institutions act without personal accountability, and that we, therefore, have no responsibility for their actions. It is not true that if we disagree we can simply disassociate ourselves by disclaiming responsibility. When we believe this, we are not only deceiving ourselves but are also voluntarily decreasing our power to bring about change. It is theoretically impossible for a democratic society to function on any level without the acceptance and agreement of the majority . . . when any of a thousand decisions are made that affect our daily lives, our silent and passive acceptance is interpreted as agreement.[21]

Making meaning of my own story in relation to the work I do has been pivotal in my ability to respond to the impact of New Zealand's colonial past. Reflecting on what I have read, learned and experienced through meeting a wide variety of people, travelling all over the world, taking part in political events and being part of a family has enabled me to understand the benefits of co-responsibility for others in many areas of my life. My childhood and life experience have conditioned in me a certain set of values that endorses co-responsibility for those around me, sharing resources, giving others the benefit of doubt, and being hospitable to people of all cultures and from all walks of life. Participating in different communities has nurtured these values. I have experienced the benefits of belonging and being part of something bigger than me.

Everyone benefits from living in a society that takes collective responsibility for healing the past. As well as culture, we are united in what it means to be human. We have internal struggles and conflicting desires that are part of the universal human experience. The challenge in increasing our self-knowledge is to find common ground in our story with people of all cultures and to celebrate the differences. Celebrating difference is the exact opposite to assimilation.

Overcoming Amnesia

Adoptions, forced removals and reconstructed families may contribute to the loss of ancestral information, preventing some people from learning parts of their own stories. Yet the challenge for those who can uncover their ancestry is to reclaim their own history and their own heritage. Not only will they confront their own pain and uncertainty, but they will also liberate themselves and in doing so help to liberate others. The alternative is to continue to chase the violent and superficial world that not only kills the human spirit but also encourages people to maintain amnesia about their own history. It is in the process of rediscovering our own roots that Pakeha people can move towards an authentic relationship with the indigenous world, based on shared values of relationship to the land and to the human spirit.

Many Maori are also reclaiming their stories. Maori lawyer Moana Jackson sums up the challenge:

> The pain will end . . . because as Maori, we are now seeking to reclaim the validity of our own institutions, the specifics of our own faith and the truths of our own history. That process will not only nourish once more the Maori soul, it will also eventually undermine the conceptual framework of the Pakeha word and the oppression which has flowed from it. It will thus be a redemption of the hopes expressed so long ago in the first remembered wisdom of our word.[22]

In the past, majority cultures have denied or ignored the terrible damage inflicted on indigenous peoples. Imposing solutions compounded the damage. If indigenous peoples are going to develop on their own terms, majority cultures have to change. This is our challenge. It is not about guilt—it is about responsibility. In New Zealand, some Maori call it 'creating the space'. I understand it as going on an exciting journey.

NINE

Respecting Identities: A Parallel Approach

The air was thick with tension. A group of Maori and Pakeha had come together to learn about the Treaty of Waitangi. Someone was crying; others were shouting. By morning tea some had left the workshop, disgusted at the behaviour of other participants. This may have been the day I witnessed a Pakeha fundamentalist Christian attacking Maori spirituality, or a Pakeha lecturing Maori on their laziness and unwillingness to help themselves. Or was it the day when outright hostility flew across the room towards a group of Maori participants? Or when some Maori participants had to be restrained when they came dangerously close to physical violence? Or perhaps it was the day of a stormy departure by a group of Maori who couldn't stand the racism of some Pakeha participants and were appalled at their ignorance.

These scenarios are not uncommon when Maori and Pakeha come together at a beginner's level to learn about the Treaty of Waitangi and colonial history. Individuals tend to adopt roles. 'Angry Maori' attack the Pakeha system. 'Defensive Pakeha' respond that Maori have not taken the opportunities available to all. Maori who want to be accepted try to smooth all the issues over. 'Pleasant Pakeha', who want to help, try to make everyone feel comfortable. 'Assertive Maori' challenge individual Pakeha. 'Inarticulate Pakeha' feel caught between a rock and a hard place. 'Shy Maori', who have learned to get along, become invisible. 'Verbal Pakeha', who just keep talking and talking and talking. There are Maori who want Pakeha to learn Maori language; Maori who don't want Pakeha to learn Maori language; Pakeha who feel they should learn about Maori language and culture but often don't know how; Pakeha who feel Maori are getting everything; Maori who know they are not. The roles are endless.

In the volatility of a culturally mixed environment, each party can easily resort to blaming. Pakeha are often seen as privileged, while Maori find themselves having to represent everything Maori. In a predominantly Pakeha setting the dominant culture usually prevails, while in a Maori setting many Pakeha become over-sensitive and inarticulate. Invariably the outcome is that Maori and Pakeha become increasingly entrenched in their roles, reducing any likelihood of a meeting point between the two groups.

Years of experience in Treaty education have taught me that culturally mixed workshops at an introductory level do not work. The lessons are clear. Introductory workshops for Pakeha led by Maori are ineffective and de-colonisation workshops led by Pakeha for Maori are inappropriate. They fail to provide a culturally safe environment for either Maori or Pakeha to begin exploring issues. All New Zealanders need a safe space in a non-confrontational environment to reflect on their own identity issues and, from that basis, begin the process of understanding colonisation. These lessons continue to inform my approach to Treaty education, which is supported by many Maori and Pakeha colleagues.

A Parallel Workshop Approach

I operate what are called parallel workshops. This approach grew out of my own experience leading many workshops and extensive dialogue with my professional colleague Irihapeti Ramsden (Rangitane, Ngai Tahu), members of Kai Tahu, and a network of Maori throughout New Zealand. In the parallel workshop approach Maori are invited to attend a de-colonisation workshop facilitated by a skilled Maori workshop leader. Pakeha and people of other cultures are invited to attend a parallel Treaty workshop facilitated by a skilled Pakeha workshop leader.

In the de-colonisation workshop for Maori, participants are brought together in a culturally safe environment and given an opportunity to explore their diverse realities and their own cultural journeys, the effect that colonisation has had on successive generations of Maori peoples, and what it means to be Maori today. This approach recognises the need for Maori to have the opportunity to disconnect themselves from the majority Pakeha culture in order to explore their issues in an appropriate environment.

In a Pakeha workshop participants are also brought together in a safe, non-confrontational environment, where they can explore together their own cultural journeys, investigate New Zealand's colonial history, and examine issues of personal, institutional and cultural racism from a Pakeha perspective. Pakeha attend a workshop that engages them in an anti-racism, de-colonisation process with a focus on the Treaty.

Pakeha have a vast ancestral history connected to greater Europe, which is used throughout the workshop to inform their understanding of the New Zealand experience. This ancestral history may include the highland clearances of Scotland, the enclosure laws of England, the penal laws of Ireland or a variety of wars and revolutions on the continent of Europe and beyond. Pakeha have a rich mix of ancestry and personal experience in New Zealand that affects their contemporary cultural functioning. In order for colonisation to make sense, Pakeha need to integrate historical information with knowledge of their own story. Part of that process involves exploring what it means to grow up in a society dominated by institutions that reflect the values of the dominant group. To do this work successfully requires a supportive, safe and culturally familiar environment.

Early on, Irihapeti Ramsden and I recognised that parallel Treaty workshops could work to celebrate, promote and strengthen the cultural diversity within, among and between Maori and Pakeha. All cultures are constantly evolving and changing. Cultural diversity is affirmed when differences in language, values, customs and practices are acknowledged and valued. Cultural diversity challenges the idea of assimilation grounded in much of western education philosophy, which makes minorities invisible and ensures that minority differences are suppressed. A recognition of cultural diversity is central to a progressive educational process.

Parallel workshops also acknowledge that Maori and Pakeha have had different experiences in the colonisation process, the origins of which lie in the power dynamic between 'the colonised' and 'the coloniser'. Maori live daily with the devastating impact of colonisation on their whole way of life. Pakeha know only the dominance of their cultural values and ways in everyday New Zealand life. Effective Treaty education must recognise that Maori and Pakeha are positioned differently and thus have different learning needs.

Maori and Pakeha are not homogeneous groups. Class and gender play an active role in determining how some, regardless of cultural background, benefit from the system. Mason Durie notes that

> [a]lthough Maori collectively are over-represented in lower socio-economic groupings, there is nonetheless considerable variation between individuals. The Maori/non-Maori gap is wide but there is also an emerging gap between Maori who are employed and well qualified and those who are unemployed with poor prospects of employment.[1]

A parallel workshop approach is better able to recognise and make meaning of differences among Maori, and the differences among Pakeha and other New Zealanders.

For those who have a mixed heritage and feel strongly connected to both cultures, choosing which workshop to attend can create a dilemma. We empower people to make their own choice, encouraging them to attend the workshop that will enable them to feel connected to and comfortable with those around them, or alternatively to do the work they most need to do, which may involve stepping into the unknown. Mason Durie again:

> People and groups are best able to articulate their own positions, values and beliefs. Imposed stereotypes create misleading impressions that certain individuals will automatically wish to move in particular ethnic or cultural directions when in fact they may have quite different inclinations.[2]

While the policy of parallel workshops has been in place for several years, some Maori do continue to attend Pakeha workshops. This happens either because they have been told to attend, or because they believe that none of these issues will affect them. Many later share with me that the workshop was not safe or enjoyable for them and that they wished they had opted to go to a Maori workshop instead. It is not uncommon for Maori people to decide to leave a mixed workshop after listening to Pakeha for as little as half a day. Pakeha often have the same negative reaction to a marae visit. They often choose not to verbalise their reaction for fear of being labelled racist. Although there are individual exceptions, the policy within our organisation of separating Maori and Pakeha for an introductory Treaty workshop remains firm as confirmed by the following additional reasons.

Fear and Self-censorship

Much Treaty debate is conducted in an environment of considerable fear. When Maori and Pakeha gather together to explore Treaty issues, either out of fear or cultural sensitivity, both parties tend to edit what they are saying. Self-censorship impacts on the learning process, often negatively affecting the outcomes achieved. In a culturally safe, familiar and comfortable environment participants can express any view and ask any question, no matter how awkward or politically incorrect.

Honouring the Pain, Not Adding to It

A significant amount of our colonial history and many of the deeds of our ancestors are pain-filled. One of the outcomes of colonialism is that most New Zealanders have grown up in a monocultural, racist colonial society, absorbing many of the cultural stereotypes permeating that environment. One workshop exercise explores negative attitudes about Maori, inviting participants to identify and reflect on common stereotypes in order to gain insight. Negative stereotypes may include that Maori are lazy, drunken, happy-go-lucky, poor parents and uneducated. These stereotypes must be worked through—identified, confronted, understood and let go—if transformational learning is to occur. Clearly, this needs to happen in an environment that is safe for everyone. For Maori to sit and listen to Pakeha discussing negative stereotypes is very painful. Parallel workshops enable Pakeha to discuss these stereotypes freely.

Intimidation of Maori Participants

When Maori people participate in a Pakeha workshop the group tend to treat the Maori participants as if they are an authority on all things Maori. This is not only culturally unsafe, it can also leave Maori participants feeling embarrassed and shamed. Many Maori have lost contact with significant aspects of their culture and history through colonisation and assimilation processes. Yet Maori participants in this workshop setting are often stuck with the responsibility for all that is happening in the Maori world. No one Maori person is able to speak for the whole Maori world. The outcome is that such individuals find themselves feeling intimidated, marginalised and silenced.

I was in a workshop recently where this happened. A Maori staff member came to the Pakeha workshop as the only Maori participant. Pakeha participants were very friendly and hospitable, but their capacity to express their views was immediately limited and they began to defer to him, ask him questions about being Maori to which he had no answer, and unconsciously blame him for inappropriate Maori behaviour in the community. During the break I took the Maori man aside and asked how he was finding the workshop. He told me that he was feeling embarrassed because although he was Maori he did not know anything about *being Maori*. He wanted to stay, but chose to sit back from the circle and participate less within the group.

Participant Support for Parallel Workshops

In 1995 Ruth Millar of the Christchurch College of Education undertook research exploring students' perceptions on the topic of parallel workshops.[3] Millar's findings supported the parallel workshop approach. Students were asked their views on the need for parallel workshops for Maori and Pakeha students, both before and after attending a Treaty education workshop. Before attending, 16 per cent believed that parallel workshops were needed. After attending the workshop, however, 90 per cent of the students supported the concept, for a variety of reasons.

One participant, who identified as Maori and attended a workshop for Pakeha through a misunderstanding, said:

> Prior to the workshops I thought it [the parallel workshop idea] was racist. I didn't like it at all . . . I thought I'd be all right because of Dad's Scottish side . . . and that I'd be open to that just as much as the Maori side. But it was really hard . . . I just thought that everyone had the same views as me, but they don't . . . if you've got any Maori in you, I think you should go to the Maori one because . . . it's just part of you . . .

Other students (whose cultural backgrounds were not identified) offered the following views:

> My initial reaction was . . . I wish they didn't have to be [separate]. We've all got to get on . . . we may as well do things together . . . And also that it would be very valuable to hear a different perspective . . . [The facilitator] emphasised the fact that it was a first step in a series of activities . . . where the first one was separate so that everyone could say everything they wanted to say and then people should come together. And I do feel that makes sense to me.

> Beforehand I saw the workshops as a forum for discussion and I felt there was no reason at all for it to be separate. However, speaking to [the facilitator] during the course . . . I do see there's a place where people can be safe and say whatever they feel like. Maybe in a different situation they wouldn't be quite so frank.

> I think a workshop that first identifies and celebrates *everyone*'s cultural background (in different groups if necessary) is important. I would also like to experience some form of combining the different groups, bringing the groups together in some form of meeting at the end.

> I'd just like to re-emphasise the value I found in the focus on our own Pakeha background, celebrating this and moving on to Treaty issues from this base.

Although I feel separate workshops are necessary, some coming together at some stage would be valuable in learning more about each other and other cultures.

The separation of Maoris from Pakehas—this was completely necessary. Good decision, guys.[4]

Other research on a similar theme supports these findings.[5] Alison Jones, a lecturer of a feminist theory in education course at the University of Auckland, divided her class of 90 students, who were mostly women, into two groups. Maori and Pacific Island students formed one group and Pakeha students formed another group. Students were asked to keep a journal of their experience throughout the course. In their journals the Pakeha students expressed hostility at being separated, while Maori and Pacific Island students were uniformly pleased with the course division.[6]

The following extracts are taken from some of the students' journals.

Pakeha Students Speak:

I would have thought it would be interesting for all the students to be able to share their unique cultural perspectives with each other. I know I would have found that valuable. I am sometimes quite ignorant and intolerant of other viewpoints, so wider input would have been educational.

It does not seem right. Could we not learn from each other? Wouldn't it be valuable to share our differences in experience? . . . it is different reading about it in books, or having it taught by teachers. It is better to hear it straight from the women who are having the experience. It is easier to relate to.

Nothing can be changed unless 'we' know and are aware of what needs to be changed. Behind closed doors doesn't help the process of change.

I wonder if by separating us that is going to reinforce that emphasis on being different, rather than learning to live with one another's differences . . .

When will I ever get to learn how Maori and Pacific Islanders perceive the world (since we are supposed to be so different) when we are continually separated?

As part of the European 'mainstream' [I found] the experience of being classified as 'other' to Maori . . . a learning experience. The feeling of exclusion, of being left over, is not pleasant . . .

Maori and Pacific Island Students Speak:

Not realising that we would be split up into the cultural groups, I prepared myself to argue any point I felt at odds with, with anybody not of a brown skin tone, to enlighten them upon the cultural ideals, values and beliefs that didn't correspond to their own. It was with audible relief that I realised we were dividing into cultural groups, brown and white.

This is the first time I have had a [course] which has been streamed with Maori and Pacific Islanders in one and non-Maori in the other. I cannot begin to describe how much more I enjoyed coming to classes . . .

What was even more pleasing for me was the fact that we were going to be split up for classes. I don't know why but I always feel a lot more confident when I am among other Pacific Islanders.

I felt validated or even vindicated. Being in a class of Maori and Pacific Island students, I stopped feeling like I was 'the other'. Instead I felt as though I had moved towards the centre and stepped into the centre where white people normally reside. It felt good.

In the lecture room I witnessed an interesting sense of power-shift once it was suggested that Maori and Pacific Islanders would form their own group. Once the dominant Pakeha group had lost their 'marker', things Pakeha seemed to suddenly lose their advantage. As Maori knowledge was being affirmed as being important, a comment from one of the students next to me was, 'It's all right for the Maori students. They have all the information.' Suddenly there was a reversal of what counts as knowledge and who was having it.

The different streams also allow Maori and Pacific Island women to identify the issues of feminism amongst their own, as too often the discussions are taken over by . . . Pakeha women.

> . . . the pivotal focus on my culture broadened my horizons to question, argue and debate . . . I am sure that it would not have been the same if I had been in a regular class with Pakeha women.[7]

In the Auckland University research Jones found that 'Many Pakeha students saw their separation from their classmates as a lost opportunity to "learn" . . . [learning] is seen as having direct speaking access to the other . . .'[8]. She continues:

> . . . a threat to the dominant group at the very point of their power in education . . . A sense of exclusion and outrage marks the refusal of the already privileged to accept that some knowledges and relationships might not be available to them/us . . . All knowledge is available to the individual who reasonably seeks it—such is an important assumption of the liberal western education system . . . But the accessibility of all knowledge to all people is not a view shared by indigenous peoples such as Maori for whom access to certain knowledge must be actively granted. Knowledge comes with particular responsibilities and powers and therefore is not necessarily made available to those who simply 'want to know'.[9]

Western educational philosophy promotes the belief that we are entitled to access to all the knowledge we want to learn. Without any analysis of colonisation, Pakeha tend to believe that 'we' have the right to demand indigenous knowledge. Yet if knowledge is power we may well ask: why would Maori want to share their unique knowledge in a system that has never shared any power with them and has rendered them institutionally powerless?

In indigenous cultures, knowledge belongs to a community and carries with it responsibility back to that community. In the liberal individualistic world view of the dominant western education system people who acquire the knowledge often want it purely for their own advantage in a system where their values dominate. At worst, it is used to disadvantage the giver of the knowledge.

Accountability and Integrity

In the parallel workshop process the issue of accountability is profoundly important. Sincerity of purpose on its own is not adequate. People with sincere purpose have carried out some of the worst atrocities in history against indigenous peoples, for example some of the Christian missionaries discussed in Chapter 3.

While I work independently, I maintain a relationship with a network of Kai Tahu people and other Maori and Pakeha throughout New Zealand who support our Treaty work. Professional Maori colleagues help to ensure that the reading material supplied to workshop participants is suitable. While no one Maori person can speak for all, these relationships enable me to discuss issues that may arise, and gain support and guidance. In the end, I accept full responsibility for the path I choose.

There is now a vast body of writing and research by Maori academics and Maori media, such as radio's *Mana News*, *Mana* magazine and *Tu Mai* magazine. Te Puni Kokiri—the Ministry for Maori Development—also publishes a range of information resources. Collectively, these resources enable me to keep up to date on a variety of Maori perspectives on Treaty issues so that the workshop process maintains integrity. I can also refer participants to articles and books, enabling them to draw their own conclusions.

Parallel Workshop Adaptability

While I was in the US in 1992 I outlined to many African American anti-racism trainers the concept of European people dealing with 'white' racism. It seemed to be a new idea for many of them and it created considerable interest because their experience was that 'black' on 'white' anti-racism work had limited success. One of the trainers told me that white people, no matter how well trained and how well intentioned, will always miss a lot of racism in themselves and in the people around them. I agreed. Although white people can do a great deal, there are limits on what they can do within the framework of their own culture.

One organisation I visited in the States actively sought to enrol people of a range of cultures in workshops. These workshops were regarded as a microcosm of American society and reflected the interaction between cultures, with the aim of 'undoing racism'. This approach constitutes the second stage of our anti-racism work in New Zealand. That is, after Maori and Pakeha each have their own workshops, we follow up with mixed workshops facilitated under Maori and Pakeha co-leadership. My American experience taught me that there is a place for both models, and reinforced for me the strengths and limitations of each.

The New Zealand parallel workshop model is very adaptable. It could be used in almost any multicultural country as a multi-parallel workshop system. That is, each cultural group would initially work with its own to come to an understanding of that culture's history and what that means in their relationship with indigenous peoples and other minorities. In the process, they could potentially discover commonality of purpose and develop solidarity. Although this model was specifically designed to address relationships between the Treaty partners in New Zealand, it could be adapted to examine all forms of oppression and exclusion.

The Success of Parallel Treaty Workshops

The system of parallel Treaty education has been functioning for more than 15 years. During this time we have been accused of apartheid, exacerbating racial tensions, driving the cultures apart and furthering racism. The accusations come almost exclusively from people who have never attended a Treaty workshop. In contrast, tens of thousands of New Zealanders have now attended parallel Treaty education workshops and overwhelmingly support that approach. It is a unique approach to confronting colonisation. It offers such a rich experience that many want to repeat it and take it to a further stage. Parallel workshops enable people to become open to new perspectives. It is after an introductory parallel Treaty workshop— and not before—that mixed workshops are more likely to be effective. When the groundwork has been done, then participants are more ready and able to enter a combined learning experience.

Feedback following workshops suggests that parallel Treaty education workshops do contribute to visible attitudinal changes in individuals and teams, and to policy and other organisational changes. For example, from 1990 the Christchurch College of Education provided Treaty workshops for all its primary teaching students. In 1997 the Primary Programme decided to discontinue the workshops for budget reasons. However, during the year staff voted unanimously to reintroduce them. They had discovered that the treatment of cultural issues in class and the attitudes of the students towards Maori were so negative that it adversely affected other aspects of their training. In 1998 the workshops were reinstated.

Today I am still asked why, as a Pakeha with no Maori ancestry, I am engaged in this work. There is an assumption that because Maori are pressing for change, they are responsible for teaching Pakeha about the Treaty and colonial history. Why do we insist on making Maori responsible for Pakeha ignorance? In the process of healing history, both parties have to change. I believe this necessitates that Pakeha initially work with Pakeha and Maori work with Maori, in exploring what they need to learn and what roles they each have to change.

New Zealand as a nation is in a process of radically changing the relationship between Maori and Pakeha. As Helen Clark noted in a speech to the Pacific Vision Conference in July 1999: 'New Zealand will be a stronger nation if we can all contribute to it knowing of our respective cultures and backgrounds and bringing our unique contributions to New Zealand life.'[10] Parallel workshops offer one way to explore and understand the Treaty obligations between Maori and the Crown, valuing our own cultural backgrounds in the process and providing a strong foundation from which to examine the range of choices that face New Zealand as we discover together the constitutional issues involved in honouring the Treaty of Waitangi.

TEN

White Privilege:
The Hidden Benefits

Robert Consedine

Koukourarata (Port Levy), Banks Peninsula, 2003
The environment is spectacular and the silence begins to calm my
grieving heart. Standing at the top of the urupa, I view the harbour
before me in all its colours as the setting sun creates a canvas of
contrasting light across the water and into the valleys. In the ground
at my feet, slightly higher up the hill than her ancestors, the Tikao
and Manawatu whanau, Irihapeti Ramsden (Ngai Tahu/Rangitane),
my friend, colleague, mentor and fellow traveller on the journey, lay
in her final resting place. The clay, flowers and flax weavings lay
scattered across the grass like a rich quilt celebrating a life lived to
the full. As I stood there the memories of an earlier journey with
Irihapeti, to this place Koukourarata, flooded back in the balmy
warmth of the late afternoon sun.

After passing Onawe, where Ngati Toa chief Te Rauparaha
massacred many Ngai Tahu in the 1830s, and visiting the marae at
Onuku, near Akaroa, where her ancestor, Tikao of Pigeon Bay and
Iwikau of Puari, had signed the Treaty of Waitangi, Irihapeti decided
to show me her land at Koukourarata. 'We'll take the short-cut. Just

turn right at Little River. It's not far,' she announced. For the next terrifying 20 kilometres we lurched our way on a steep, narrow shingle road, around a winding cliff face, over the top of the hill and down the other side into the spectacular beauty of the harbour. As I struggled to keep my old car on the road, Irihapeti laughed, completely oblivious to the fact of my 'near-death' experience, as she gave me a running commentary on the history of her people in this place.

Banks Peninsula had been 'purchased' by the Crown in three blocks. Between 1849 and 1856 negotiations occurred at Port Cooper, Port Levy and Akaroa. Commitments were made about Maori reserves and natural resources. Most of these promises, however, were not kept, and as a result of these Crown acts most Ngai Tahu of Banks Peninsula were driven off the land and lost their turangawaewae.[1] Irihapeti's anger about the plight and place of her people and other indigenous peoples was never far below the surface. She had endured ridicule, like most prophetic people, in her struggle to develop her lasting legacy of cultural safety.[2] As is the lot of many indigenous peoples, some of the criticism included the added sting of racism. Yet the levelling influence of a mischievous sense of humour prevented her from ever becoming bitter—whatever the provocation.

Standing on top of the urupa that day, looking out over the land and sea, caused me to reflect, once again, on my connections to this country, the differences in the life journeys of myself and my friend Irihapeti. Although she never raised the subject directly in the many years we worked together, I became increasingly aware of the many privileges I enjoyed as a white middle-class male as we travelled and worked together throughout New Zealand.

What I took for granted, she fought for daily. This was evident in a range of different ways: the way people deferred to me in conversation; the appointments I could secure for both of us (often only after vouching for her competence and political reliability) that would not have been readily available to her alone; the patronising way she was 'tolerated' in some groups; the way I almost never had to think about 'being Pakeha' in the way she had to think about 'being Maori'; and the fact that I could worry about racism without being seen as 'self-interested'. I could express alternative views and not be seen as speaking for all Pakeha; did not have to educate my children to be aware of how systemic racism may impact on their lives; was not singled out as a failure or a success because of my culture; and had always been free to criticise the government of the day without being seen as a demanding Pakeha seeking more benefits for my own people. I could have an argument with a colleague, or be late for a meeting, without these 'failings' being attributed to my culture. Never once did I have to carry the cultural stereotypes of laziness, violence, trouble-making, poor parenting and living by 'Maori time'.

My experience with Irihapeti, and increasing knowledge of New Zealand's colonial history, made me more aware of the immense benefits I had simply inherited by virtue of belonging to the majority culture. I live in a system which, despite significant limitations, largely reflects my cultural values. But while I have a love of and pride in my Irish Catholic Pakeha culture and history, it stands alongside my awareness of the privileges I have inherited as a result of the dispossession of Maori.

What is White Privilege?

White privilege is based on a set of assumptions about what is regarded as neutral, normal and universally available. Says James Baldwin: 'The biggest problem with white privilege is the invisibility it maintains to those who benefit from it most. The inability to recognize that many of the advantages whites hold are a direct result of the disadvantages of other people . . .'[3] In New Zealand white privilege evolved in colonial times where structures were put in place that were designed to meet the needs of Pakeha settlers. Immigration, assimilation and integration policies directly benefited Pakeha and marginalised Maori, yet these systemic structural benefits remain 'invisible' to most Pakeha.

Reading 'The Invisible Knapsack', an article exploring the concept of white privilege by international researcher Peggy McIntosh, expanded my awareness. In it McIntosh identifies 46 'white privileges' as 'an invisible package of unearned assets, which I can count on cashing in each day, but about which I was "meant" to remain oblivious. White privilege is like an invisible weightless knapsack of special provisions, maps, passports, codebooks, visas, codes, tools and blank checks.'[4] McIntosh says she was taught to see racism only in 'individual acts of meanness, not in invisible systems conferring dominance on my group'.[5] It is crucial, if we are to further this debate, to understand the origins of the invisible systems of institutional racism and policies from which Pakeha have benefited.

Maori Land: The Historical Foundation of Settler Wealth

In the nineteenth century there was nothing unusual about the dispossession of aboriginal peoples by European powers. Despite solemn commitments by the British at Waitangi and some legal protection, what happened in New Zealand was normal for the times. Theodore Allen, an independent scholar, discusses the way land was 'acquired' from indigenous peoples globally through colonisation. His conclusions apply equally to the New Zealand colonial story. Allen talks about colonial society as 'a society organised on the basis of the segmentation of land and other natural resources under private, heritable individual titles, [underpinned by] a corresponding set of laws and customs, acted out under the direction of the ruling class'. This society, Allen argues, 'brings under its colonial authority people of societies organised on principles of collective, tribal tenure of land and other natural resources, and having their respective corresponding sets of laws and customs'.[6]

After assuming sovereignty in New Zealand, Britain brought Maori under its colonial authority. That meant British governors imposed a legal process intended to deny, ignore and de-legitimise the tribal and kinship system that underlay traditional Maori society, making Maori structures and systems illegal. Maori were 'stripped of their tribal and kinship identity . . . rendered institutionally naked to their enemies, completely deprived of the shield of social identity . . . [and] made strangers in their own native land'.[7] As in all colonised countries, the colonised people (Maori) were unilaterally assigned a place in the new system defined by the coloniser (the British).

In 1840 all land and resources were recognised by the Crown as being owned by Maori hapu, under Maori customary tenure. There had been pre-Treaty 'sales', but these were thoroughly investigated.

The 'Chief Protector of Aborigines', George Clarke, who had been appointed on 6 April 1840, returned some land to the Crown—but not to the Maori owners. Because Clarke was also responsible for purchasing Maori land on behalf of the Crown he had a clear conflict of interest. In 1842 he asked to be relieved of his land-purchasing role, and this was agreed to.[8]

Fraudulent land deals had started well before the Native Land Courts were set up in the 1860s, despite the explicit royal instructions from the Marquis of Normanby that 'the acquisition of land by the Crown for the future settlement of British subjects must be confined to such districts as the natives can alienate, without distress or serious inconvenience to themselves'.[9] The 'Right of Pre-emption', which made the Crown the sold land agent, was included in the Treaty in order that the Crown could protect Maori from land sharks. Maori were not allowed to sell directly to settlers.

But in the event the Crown became the biggest land shark of all. The Waitangi Tribunal's 81 claim reports and 29 research reports detail widespread and systemic theft and fraud by Crown agents, to the ultimate benefit of the government and British settlers.[10] And yet all the transactions by the Crown in the following examples are still considered legal sales, so the land involved cannot be reclaimed:

- In 1840, the centre of Auckland city (3000 acres) was bought from local Maori for cash and goods worth £341. Within nine months a mere 44 acres was resold for £24,275.

- In 1845, 16,000 acres of Ngati Whatua land were retained by the Crown without compensation.

- In 1850, in suburban Auckland, 700 acres, 'after prolonged and wearisome interviews' were bought for £5000 and one-third of this was then sold immediately for £32,000. The whole block eventually realised £100,000.[11]

- From 1844 through to the 1860s, 34 million acres of land passed from Ngai Tahu to the Crown for a total of £8750. In effect the Crown paid six one-hundredths of one penny for each acre purchased.

- In North Canterbury, 'two years prior to concluding the purchase of 1,140,000 acres from Ngai Tahu for £500, the government actually sold a block of land containing 30,000 acres for £15,000, which on a per-acre equivalent was 1142 times more than Ngai Tahu was paid two years later. It was also more than the Crown paid for all Ngai Tahu's 34.5 million acres'.[12]

Historian Jim McAloon describes another government strategy that contravened the Treaty of Waitangi. This policy forbade Maori to lease land to settlers directly. 'This edict proved essential in the purchase of the Wairarapa and Hawke's Bay, for it threatened Ngati Kahungunu income and left them with little choice but to sell in order to raise capital, despite the obviously low price'.[13]

Legislation passed to alienate Maori land proliferated. From 1865–90, some 360 Acts of Parliament were passed that affected Maori land. Another 199 Acts came into force in the period 1891–1908.[14] In fact the entire infrastructure of New Zealand was initially paid for by Maori, as their land was alienated and sold to settlers by the Crown at staggering profits. Gaining possession of New Zealand had cost the British government a derisory £3365/18s, with 'gifts for Maori' valued at an additional £562/1/5.[15]

However, there was nothing unique about this process. It happened in most colonised countries, to a greater or lesser degree, where colonisers imposed a political structure that furthered their own interests. In New Zealand it was done through a legal process that overrode and disregarded Treaty of Waitangi guarantees and Maori common-law rights. One such right was the right to exclusive possession and use of lands. This was further entrenched in an 1847 court judgement that said: 'It cannot be too solemnly asserted that [Native Title] is entitled to be respected, that it cannot be extinguished (at least in times of peace) otherwise than by the free consent of the Native occupiers . . .'[16] In the event, however, Maori rights were discarded as the needs of land-hungry settlers took precedence.[17]

The true value of the overwhelming transfer of wealth from Maori to settler society over the past 165 years is impossible to calculate.

When Ngai Tahu accepted $170 million in 1998 as a full and final settlement of their claim, their chief negotiator, Sir Tipene O'Regan, stated that the full value of their South Island claim was about $16 billion.[18] O'Regan observed that 'this level of generosity to Pakeha society has never been acknowledged'.[19]

Native Land Courts

The Native Land Acts, which created the Native Land Courts of the early 1860s, were supposed to 'acknowledge Maori rights as British subjects by recognising their legal right to all their land and allowing them to do what they chose with it, including getting full market value if they sold it'.[20] In practice, however, the Native Land Courts became a vehicle for further Maori dispossession. A leading Maori scholar, Sir Hugh Kawharu, has called the courts a 'veritable engine of destruction for any tribe's tenure of land, anywhere'.[21] Historian Bryan D. Gilling notes that the courts have been 'the subject of sustained condemnation by historians as the central instrument of colonial oppression, depriving Maori of their lands peacefully and with a minimum of inconvenient fuss'.[22]

There were some legislative mechanisms put in place to protect Maori, but in practice the courts had enormous power over Maori in respect of their property rights. Argues Alan Ward, 'If the court failed to interpret custom correctly, and found for the wrong claimants, or for insufficient claimants, some Maori would be dispossessed'.[23] The notorious 10-owner rule required hapu to name 10 owners for blocks of land of less than 5000 acres. This rule—a gift for speculators—became the source of all manner of difficulties for Maori, since those 10 owners were legally required to be absolute owners, not trustees for the tribe.[24]

The entire process naturally undermined the Maori communal lifestyle and destabilised tribal structures. As Ward concludes, '[S]ettler politicians placed well-nigh insuperable obstacles in the path of well-founded Maori enterprise'.[25] Legal historian David Williams also asserts that the policies behind the Native Land Acts, along with other methods of promoting land purchasing from Maori, 'were implemented by the Crown without sufficient (or any) regard to the guarantees of the Treaty of Waitangi'.[26] A conclusion from Williams's study of the period 1865–1909, when 18 million acres were 'alienated' through the courts in the North Island, is that the work of the Native Land Courts amounted to 'judicial confiscation . . . the Native Land Courts were not truly an independent body, but actually an agent of the central government fulfilling its policy, and thus its actions were essentially actions of the Crown'. Further, the Native Land Acts, Williams argues, were 'an all-out effort to relinquish Maori of title to their lands in the interests of European settlement . . . the entire project of colonisation was a forward-looking enterprise and could have contemplated and did contemplate the outcome'.[27]

Government Policies: White Privilege the Outcome

Although downstream economic benefits to Pakeha were obviously not evenly spread, new settlers arrived in a country that was governed by, and for the benefit of, primarily Anglo-Celtic immigrants. Maori became increasingly marginalised (see Chapter 4) in a process that was systemic. It was an English, largely male landowning Parliament that spawned New Zealand's criminal justice system, land courts, education and health systems. Maori were systematically excluded from any influence or decision-making. Hundreds of laws were passed without any reference to a Maori view, let alone Maori authority. It was not all deliberate. Ward notes that 'though altruistically conceived, amalgamation policies could, in doctrinaire hands, become as oppressive as settler self-interest'.[28] The outcome, to paraphrase Palestinian-born Professor of English Edward W. Said, was that Maori were reconstituted as a people requiring a British presence.[29]

The idea of power-sharing with Maori, as guaranteed in the Treaty of Waitangi, was anathema to most settlers. The so-called guarantee to Maori (in Article Two of the Treaty) of tino rangatiratanga—unqualified exercise of authority—was denied time and again. Maori were expected to discard their traditional way of life, including their language, as the new settler government proceeded to pass an overwhelming number of policies that ensured British 'rule' was normalised. Maori were denied ordinary citizenship rights that Pakeha took for granted.

The Old Age Pension

The introduction of the old age pension in 1898 highlights the ways Maori have been denied a range of welfare benefits to which they were legally entitled. Despite the equal opportunity underpinning the Act, Deputy Registrars were instructed to make Maori access to pensions extremely difficult. A decision was made to refer all Maori claims for pensions to the Native Land Court, which then had to place them in front of a magistrate, effectively slowing the process.

A wide range of mechanisms was used against Maori, including removing a significant number of Maori from the pension rolls. For those Maori who managed to stay on the roll the most common discriminatory policy was to reduce their pension to two-thirds of the amount paid to Europeans.[30] In 1904 a decision made by New Plymouth magistrate Thomas Hutchinson to pay a reduced rate of pension (£12 rather than £18) to a Maori pensioner 'set a precedent for an unofficial policy which lasted over 40 years'.[31] From 1925 the maximum Maori pension rate was £32.6s per annum, or 71 per cent of the maximum of £45/10s. In 1927 many Maori pensions were below £20, less than half the rate paid to Pakeha. While officials were targeting Maori with these administrative mechanisms designed to block their entitlement to pensions, 'Maori pensioners were starving.'[32]

The raising of Maori pensions was not automatic after the Pensions Amendment Act 1936, as it was for Pakeha. McClure notes that 'when [Prime Minister] Savage requested statistics on Maori pension rates in 1937, they showed that the department still held in nearly all cases to an arbitrary level for Maori which was one-fifth lower than Pakeha pensions: 2,213 out of 2,380 Maori received the lower rate of age pension, and 429 out of 474 widows were denied a full pension'.[33] Reduced pensions were paid to Maori until at least 1945.[34] (It is worth noting that the 1898 Pensions Act specifically excluded Asian residents from any pension.[35])

McClure also notes the irony that 'the extreme poverty of Maori communities became the rationale for different treatment. In critical Pakeha eyes, Maori poverty was a sign of lower expectations rather than greater need, and by the 1920s living in a pa had become a reason to disbar Maori from full pension entitlement'.[36]

Even after the law removed the possibility of discrimination after World War II, it continued until the late 1940s.[37]

Other Social Welfare Benefits

Social security benefits followed the same discriminatory pattern. Maori were promised that the Social Security Act 1938 would mean a fresh start of new rights and entitlement. Yet a loophole was provided by section 72 (2). 'In the first few years of administering social security, Social Security Department officers used this to continue their earlier pattern of clear-cut discrepancy between Maori and Pakeha payments by disbursing Maori benefits at a consistently lower rate. In the early 1940s leaders in Rotorua and Ratana communities complained that not one Maori in their district was receiving full payment'.[38]

McClure notes that the high level of family benefit payments in the 1940s brought scrutiny of Maori rights. 'Family benefit made a huge difference to the spending capacities of Maori communities and meant that Maori children were better fed and dressed than they had been previously'.[39] However, the Treasury remained particularly 'concerned at the cost of raising Maori to equal pensions'.[40] White privilege continued to be maintained at Maori expense.

World War I and World War II

After World War I Pakeha soldiers went into a ballot for land for resettlement, but returned Maori soldiers did not. Apirana Ngata thought it might be seen as 'improper [for] the Crown to earmark land for Maori soldiers when it was popularly supposed that Maori had sufficient land of their own'. Provision for Maori was therefore made out of Maori tribal lands.[41] A clause in the Native Land Adjustment Act 1916 enabled Maori to either sell land to the Crown or set their own land aside for soldiers who had been discharged.[42]

During World War II the Maori War Effort Organisation,

approved by Cabinet on 3 June 1942, operated with relative autonomy in profoundly Maori ways. Custom and tradition were central to the functioning of this voluntary organisation, which involved all tribes. While its primary purpose was military (recruitment for the Maori Battalion), it also came to have a welfare function. Some 315 tribal committees were formed, co-ordinated by 41 executive committees.[43] The popularity and the heroism of the Maori Battalion began to have a positive impact on Pakeha attitudes to Maori. But despite this, it was not until the late 1940s that 'equal levels of age, widows' and invalids' benefits were accorded to Maori beneficiaries, and this was achieved in small stages as Maori protests made dents in the government's policy'.[44]

The Maori Social and Economic Advancement Act (1945), which was designed to promote the well-being of Maori communities, was seen by some as 'an attempt to deflect a move towards rangatiratanga implicit in the success of the [Maori] War Effort Organisation', which had ceased to exist in April 1944'.[45] Historian Claudia Orange concludes that the government was only willing to accept Maori leadership in a war crisis.[46] The Act, not surprisingly, had limited success. The tribal committees, argues Orange, 'were in an ambiguous position—neither completely independent nor wholly a part of government', autonomous up to a point and simultaneously firmly under government control.[47] The committees operating under the Act were confused over their responsibilities and lacked direction. Ngata apparently considered the Act a 'botch'.[48]

Orange concludes that under the first Labour government 'Maori [were] concerned for the right to act autonomously, the Pakeha [were] concerned about the "mismanagement" of Maori affairs. The capacity to make political gain out of Maori policy and practice, often to the detriment of Maori welfare, [was] also evident'.[49] In the new millennium that conflict persists.

White Privilege 'Normalised'

The dispossession of Maori land as well as the impact of the Native Land Courts and of successive social welfare policies demonstrates how the colonial infrastructure excluded Maori and guaranteed 'white privilege'. Every institutional aspect of the new society was imported and implanted, and the wealth owned by Maori was systemically transferred to the new settlers.[50] White privilege was further reinforced through a long-term policy to ensure that only 'suitable' British and other European immigrants, with a few exceptions, immigrated to New Zealand until the early 1970s. The emerging majority British culture guaranteed that the New Zealand Parliament governed primarily in the interests of settlers.[51] This 'white' immigration policy only changed with a labour shortage in the early 1970s.[52]

The full impact of these major policies has taken generations to emerge and intensify. The 1907 Suppression of Tohunga Act (discussed in Chapter 3) and assimilation policies that required Maori to abandon their culture and become English (discussed in Chapters 6 and 8) were other examples of policies that discriminated against Maori.[53]

Public works legislation theoretically applied to all citizens, but there is overwhelming evidence that Maori were targeted disproportionately for public works schemes.[54] The British government provided no money to develop the infrastructure of New Zealand, but private British investors lent money to the New Zealand government, especially from the 1870s onwards. By that time investor confidence was maintained by portraying New Zealand as a 'New Britain'. Former Treaty Negotiations Minister Sir Douglas Graham has noted that wealth accrued primarily from 'buying land on the cheap from Maori and selling it at a profit to settlers'.[55]

Although some individual settlers had mutually beneficial relationships with Maori, most people's attitudes were shaped by the beliefs of the time, which portrayed Europeans and European practices as superior and 'normal'. Maori were expected to learn the Pakeha way of life; Pakeha certainly did not expect to learn the Maori way of life. Cultural misunderstanding was naturally rife. For example, the Muriwhenua land report notes that 'transactions posited as land sales by one race were contracts for long-term social relationships for the other'.[56] Maori had no word for sale and differences in understanding were endemic.[57]

Colonial policy aimed to keep 'white' countries and peoples together, connected through the mechanism of the British Empire and more recently the Commonwealth. Loyalty to the 'home country' was nurtured in a variety of ways, including royal visits and a variety of educational exchanges, such as Rhodes scholarships. Rugby and cricket were a conscious part of the colonial relationship. The belief that everything important came from greater Europe and that Europeans were 'brighter, better and bolder' than everyone else was an assumption that permeated society, and particularly the education system.[58]

Maori as 'The Other'

In this colonial climate emerged the idea of Maori as 'the other'. In essence this was a way of thinking that meant Maori and Maori culture were seen as being 'less than' and 'inferior to' everyone and everything European. Settler thinking was that Maori were lazy, immoral, degraded and dirty, and suffered from 'natural depravity'. This thinking created a rationale that made white supremacy inevitable, particularly as British settlers became the majority.[59]

The notion of Maori as 'the other' remains deeply embedded in the unconscious of Pakeha New Zealand. Otago University lecturer Brendan Hokowhitu sums up the phenomenon thus: 'Racially based traits imposed on Maori . . . were the antithesis of those qualities desired by Europeans . . . representing Maori as physical, unintelligent and savage; a process that continues unabated'.[60] The savage was represented as 'immoral and sinful, ruled by mythical ritual, and burdened by an encumbering collective', while the 'civilizers' were 'virtuous, secular, liberated in thought and autonomous'.[61] However, while Maori and tikanga Maori (Maori culture) were viewed as abnormal and inferior, the dominant culture approved of aspects of Maori culture that were in accord with colonial thinking. Consequently, kapahaka and ka mate as well as Maori success in war and sport were praised, and cited as further evidence of Maori as the savage other.

Irihapeti Ramsden's thinking about Maori as 'the other' was prophetic. 'If you think Maori have experienced racism when we are poor, powerless and marginalised, you wait and see what happens when we begin to become more powerful and successful. While we remain in our colonised state, know "our" place and remain "the other", it will be less evident. But, watch the climate change when we begin to threaten the privileges of the dominant culture and their normality, which Pakeha take for granted and assume is "their" right. Then we will really experience the deep ugly underbelly of racism that exists in this country.'

We didn't have long to wait.

Despite the political, social and legal advances of the last 20 years, Pakeha amnesia concerning our colonial history remains. The public uproar against the Labour government's Closing the Gaps policy in 2000, designed to target poverty among Maori and Pacific Islanders, revealed a significant level of confusion and racism in the majority culture.[62] Many New Zealanders still do not want to face the ugly side of our colonial history. Others claim that colonialism happened so long ago that there are no contemporary outcomes. Still others argue that colonisation was for the *benefit* of Maori.

Another method of muddying the waters is the contention that we are all indigenous.[63] Maori studies lecturer Rawiri Taonui describes this assertion as 'unreasonable where it infringes upon Maori identity, denies history and ignores international law'.[64] It would seem the *winners* and beneficiaries of New Zealand's colonial history are reluctant to look back, let alone through the cultural mirror, and recognise the level of Pakeha privilege. This is the shadow, painful side of New Zealand's colonial history.

The source of Pakeha privilege remains embedded in the functioning of our institutions. The following are examples of the fact that our democratic system still functions on the assumption that the Pakeha way of doing things is 'normal', and fails to include Te Ao Maori—the Maori world view.

Town and Environmental Planning

In 1976–78 the occupation of Bastion Point (see Chapter Five), overlooking Auckland harbour, highlighted Maori exclusion from town and environmental planning. This despite the fact that the

Treaty provided a basis for the evolution of a dual environmental planning tradition. In a video history, *Bastion Point: The Untold Story*, protest leader Joe Hawke describes how Ngati Whatua had been unable to get permits to rebuild and refurbish buildings, install running water, sewerage and electricity on this piece of prime real estate. The resultant downgraded state of the land became part of the rationale for its brutal clearance by the Muldoon government in 1978.[65]

Environmental and planning expert Hirini Matunga argues that both the Maori and the English texts of the Treaty explicitly affirmed 'the highest degree of Maori authority over their natural resources'.[66] He further notes that 'the colonial discourse of exclusion has created an environmental planning system devoid of even minimal recognition of rangatiratanga'.[67] This exclusion was consolidated through 'adoption of planning law which simply excluded iwi from regulatory planning'.[68] The Town Planning Act 1926 made no reference to rangatiratanga, Maori people or Treaty promises. Matunga further notes that it took until 1977 for a revised Town and Country Planning Act to acknowledge the 'uniqueness of the relationship between Maori and their environment', although the Act 'still did not acknowledge the existence of a parallel Maori planning framework'.[69]

In the 1990s resource management law reform addressed the need for the restoration of rangatiratanga, including recognition of Maori rights of self-government, restoration of tino rangatiratanga over natural resources, recognition of Maori ownership of resources such as water, seabed and coastal habitat, protection of and access to resources, and provision for Maori involvement in resource decision-making processes. However, eight years on, Matunga concluded 'that the Maori Treaty partner [is still] on the outside, looking in on a passing parade of environment decision and policy processes' from which they are excluded.[70]

Conservation: A Recent Pakeha Discovery?

What are modern conservationist values? How have they come to be in opposition to Maori rights?[71] The colonisation of plants and animals was driven by the same imperative as the colonisation of the 'natives'. New Zealand scientist and historian Ross Galbreath records that the 'British colonists arriving in New Zealand came armed with the expectation that all the native life—plants, animals and people alike—would inevitably be supplanted and displaced'.[72] He further contends that 'ideas concerning the native people on the one hand, and native plants and animals on the other, were closely connected'.[73]

It was expressions of alarm from Britain and the subsequent promotion of protection ideas that prompted some small policy changes, including colonial laws, from the late nineteenth and early twentieth century. This initiated the preservation of some native bush, flora and fauna.[74] But it took mass protests from the 1960s to see the government act to 'conserve, protect and preserve the eco-systems that . . . give this country its unique character'.[75]

When Pakeha did discover conservation, around 1900, this was pretty much at the expense of Maori traditional use. Bird protection laws made no exceptions for traditional harvest.[76] Distinguished doctor, anthropologist and Maori leader Sir Peter Buck summed up the contradiction in 1910. 'There is no greater menace to the animal life of this country . . . than the so-called sporting proclivities of the white man . . . the attitude taken up by the Maori race in this country in that respect was totally different. The Maori never killed for sport, he killed for the pot'.[77] The modern conservation movement could learn much from studying this history.

Foreshore and Seabed: 'The Latest Pakeha Land Grab'

At a meeting one evening with concerned local residents, our local MP attempted to explain the Labour government's response to the foreshore and seabed controversy. A group of about 60 vocal Pakeha had arrived and the atmosphere was electric. Some were so angry they refused to allow the MP to explain the government's policy. The anger was palpable: 'Those bloody Maori are getting everything'; 'More privileges for Maori'; 'Haven't they got enough?'; 'Now we can't even go to the beach'—it was a litany of fear and prejudice.

The Court of Appeal in June 2003 decided in the case brought by

Ngati Apa, Ngati Koata and others in Marlborough that 'the Maori Land Court has jurisdiction to determine the status of the foreshore and seabed'. [78] It has this jurisdiction under Te Ture Whenua Maori Act 1993. The case was designed to protect commercial rights to coastal space. The judgement further noted that 'the transfer of sovereignty did not affect customary property. They are interests preserved by the common law [of England] until extinguished in accordance with the [new] law . . . the legislation relied on in the High Court does not extinguish any Maori Customary property in seabed or foreshore'.[79]

The Court of Appeal also decided that the 1963 ruling *In Re the Ninety Mile Beach* (where the High Court and Court of Appeal ruled that Maori ownership had been extinguished) 'was wrong in law and should not be followed . . . as it had followed the discredited authority of *Wi Parata v. Bishop of Wellington* (1877)'.[80] Maori customary title to the foreshore, if any, the court found, 'has not been extinguished by any general enactment' and it rejected 'the ingenious Crown argument that the reference to "land" in Te Ture Whenua/Maori Land Act 1992 . . . excludes the foreshore and seabed'.[81]

This Court of Appeal decision therefore affirms that Maori held *customary property rights to land* at the time of Pakeha settlement. It confirms that those rights were *not* dependent on or derived from the Treaty of Waitangi or Crown recognition. Furthermore, these customary rights continue to exist after the Crown assumed sovereignty. The Court of Appeal noted that 'native property over land is entitled to be respected and cannot be extinguished, "at least in times of peace" otherwise than by the consent of the owners'.[82]

Despite the limited nature of the decision, public fear and confusion, mainly created by politicians and the media, was widespread. Subsequently, all major political parties broadly supported the Labour government's proposed seabed and foreshore legislation, which aims to place the foreshore and seabed in Crown ownership. All parties thus committed to extinguishing Maori property rights.[83] Little wonder many Maori leaders labelled it confiscation, and more than 20,000 Maori from all walks of life, supported by many Pakeha, marched on Parliament in 2004 in the biggest hikoi in the country's history.[84]

According to figures sourced from Land Information New Zealand, about one-third—some 5866 kilometres of foreshore—is in private hands, with Maori owning almost 2000 kilometres of it.[85] In addition, 47 kilometres of seabed and 670 kilometres of eroded coast is also in private hands. Irrespective of ownership, most of the privately owned coastline has no public access. Furthermore, there is no such thing as an uninterrupted Queen's Chain—only 187 kilometres of privately owned coastline has public access.[86] A report from the 2003 Land Access Ministerial Reference Group states that '70% of what would be regarded as the Queen's Chain is in public ownership. The remaining 30% is in private ownership'.[87]

The obvious question is: why is it possible for nearly one-third of our coastline to be in private ownership already, with virtually no public access and hardly a murmur of political, media or public concern until the issue of potential Maori ownership emerges?

The government's declaration that all remaining foreshore and seabed ownership would be vested in the Crown, with Maori getting access where some vague ancestral connection could be established, prompted an immediate claim by Maori to the Waitangi Tribunal. After six days of sittings in January 2004 the tribunal—an independent body with power to recommend only—condemned the policy of cutting off Maori access to the courts and taking away recognised property rights.[88] It further stated that the Crown's proposed legislation was 'failing to treat Maori and non-Maori citizens equally. The only private property rights abolished by the policy are those of Maori. All other classes of rights are protected by the policy'.[89]

The current position of the mainstream political parties is to confiscate Maori citizenship rights only. These are the rights guaranteed in Article Three of the Treaty of Waitangi to all New Zealand citizens. No Pakeha—non-Maori—rights are being touched. This is highly discriminatory. On 18 November 2004 this legislation was passed by a Labour government, with the support of NZ First. Will future generations look back and ask how a government in the new millennium, with the vast knowledge, expertise and resources at its disposal, could repeat the shameful land confiscations of its colonial forebears? Will they discover that Pakeha privilege was, once again, guaranteed at the expense of Maori legal rights? Or will they look back and celebrate a government and a political system that had the maturity and the courage to do what was right and just—and legal?

'Democracy: The Tyranny of the Majority'

The right for Maori to exercise full authority—tino rangatiratanga, as guaranteed in Article Two of the Treaty—has always been marginalised. However, the extent of Maori exclusion from political power in the majority system may well be driving some of the current political struggle. The nation state has failed to provide Maori with the same citizenship rights (as in Article Three) as other New Zealanders.

In New Zealand, democracy was *designed* to exclude Maori from political power, and there is no more obvious example than in the restriction of Maori to four parliamentary seats right up until 1996. In 1867 Maori were thus considerably under-represented: some 50,000 were given four seats, whereas some 250,000 Europeans had 72 seats.[90] A Maori MP had to represent 12,500 constituents, while a non-Maori (European) MP had only 3472 constituents to look after. There is overwhelming evidence that Maori, representing Maori interests, cannot get elected at any level of the system in a First Past the Post (FPP) system.

This fundamental issue emerged at the time of the Royal Commission on the Electoral System in 1986.[91] The commission considered the FPP system 'unfair, inequitable, and unrepresentative of the general population'.[92] It noted that FPP 'favours the election of middle-class, middle-aged Pakeha (upper-income) males'.[93]

In 1996 the introduction of the Mixed Member Proportional (MMP) Representation system enabled Maori to gain representation in Parliament proportional to their population size for the first time.[94] Without Maori seats in Parliament and ministerial appointments to health boards allowed for in legislation, Maori would be left very marginal in all areas of governance.[95] In the current political climate these special mechanisms are wrongly being called privileges.

This is borne out by the following statistics: (Note that Maori make up approximately 14.7 per cent of the population.)

Parliamentary election 2002: 120 MPs (16.6 per cent Maori)[96]

- 2 Maori elected in general seats
- 7 Maori elected in Maori seats
- 11 Maori entered from party list seats

Local government elections 2001 (FPP)[97]

- 1083 councillors elected
- 52 Maori elected (4.8 per cent)
- No Maori mayors

District health board elections 2001 (FPP and ministerial appointments)[98]

- 147 candidates elected onto 21 boards (7 per board)
- 5 Maori elected (3.4 per cent). There were 120 Maori candidates
- 51 additional Maori (plus 33 non-Maori) board members appointed by Minister of Health.

In May 1993 a national gathering of Maori was convened by the Electoral Law Committee to canvass views on electoral reform. It was the culmination of 20 regional hui convened by the Maori Congress, Maori Council and Maori Women's Welfare League. The overwhelming consensus of the gathering at Turangawaewae Marae, Ngaruawahia, was that the government had obligations under the Treaty of Waitangi to ensure 'fair and effective representation for Maori', and that the Maori seats should therefore be retained.[99]

Comedian Mike King summed it up succinctly when he delivered a message to what he called 'all those worshippers of the democratic system': 'I have this to say: democracy only works when you are the majority. As soon as you become the minority, it's a pretty stink system . . . just ask Maori'.[100]

Conclusion

New Zealand, through its colonial history, has been designed primarily to benefit Pakeha. Maori were required to fit into Pakeha culture and systems. All our basic institutions functioned on the assumption that being Pakeha was 'normal' and that there was only one way to make decisions, one way to deliver justice, health and education, one approach to conservation, and only one law and language that mattered. Assimilation was predicated on the assumption that Maori tikanga was irrelevant if Maori were to succeed: everything had to be done the 'white way'. The result is that the infrastructure of New Zealand society is structured to deliver white privilege. Only the exotic features of Maori culture were encouraged, where they benefited the country in areas such as tourism and sport.

The legacy is the exclusion of an enormously rich indigenous culture—the marginalisation of an entire way of life.

The outcome has been highly destructive for Maori people. Even recently, in a report entitled *Decades of Disparity: Ethnic Mortality Trends in New Zealand 1980–1999*, the Deputy Director-General of Public Health, Don Matheson, notes that in all countries 'indigenous people tend to have poorer health'.[101] Dr Tony Blakely, one of the report's authors, notes that in the 30 years after World War II 'Maori life expectancy improved considerably, but during the 1980s and 1990s the life expectancy at birth widened between Maori and non-Maori, showing a ten-year life expectancy gap'.[102] Matheson concludes that 'inequalities in access to and decisions over resources are the primary cause of health inequalities . . . These structural inequalities may explain more of ethnic inequalities than is often recognised . . . personal discrimination or institutional bias makes an important contribution to ethnic inequalities in New Zealand'.[103]

The appalling record of intergenerational discrimination against Maori needs to be considered alongside the contemporary assertions of Maori privilege.[104]

In the mid-1980s New Zealand began to move towards being a more Treaty-based, bicultural society—one that began to recognise the existence of Maori culture in its structures. It has been a painfully slow change for Maori, and an extremely rich experience for those Pakeha who faced their fears and had the courage to begin the bicultural journey. Tragically, in 2004, white supremacy has reasserted itself in all its ugliness, as the major political parties compete to take New Zealand back to a time when Maori 'knew their place' and white was right. But it won't happen, can't happen, because Maori, after 165 years of marginalisation, are better equipped than ever to confront the racism of the political system and find a way forward, drawing on their own strength and the inspiration of their tipuna.

In 1996 Justice E. T. Durie, chairman of the Waitangi Tribunal, defined the basis of right relationship in a challenging and insightful lecture entitled, 'Will the Settlers Settle?' He said that successful settlement in another country 'requires an appropriate respect for the pre-existing law and people, and if recognition is chary or tardy cultural conciliation will be delayed. As a test for cultural conciliation I am using mutual comprehension and respect'.[105]

This is the challenge still faced by most Pakeha 165 years after the signing of the Treaty of Waitangi.

ELEVEN

Healing Our History

Christchurch, 4 August 1993

It was another ordinary day. I was leaving my house on my way to a funeral when a policeman walked up our driveway. He told me that my eldest daughter, Suzanne, had been in an accident and invited me to go back inside the house. Suzanne's sisters, Joanna and Bernadette, were inside. We waited in silence for the policeman to make a phone call to find out the outcome.

In that moment, Suzanne's grandmother rang from Dunedin. She had heard on the radio that there had been an accident at Outward Bound and wanted to know if it was Suzanne. 'We're unsure at this stage. I'll ring you back.' She didn't believe me. She knew. We stood in the kitchen as the policeman made his call.

'I'm very sorry. Your daughter Suzanne has been killed. She fell down a bluff and died instantly.' The policeman told us that Suzanne's body had to be recovered from a remote valley in the Marlborough Sounds, where she had died 26 hours earlier. I went numb. I thought of Trish, Suzanne's mother. She was at work, counselling clients on the other side of town. I called my brother Michael and he went immediately to tell her and bring her home.

When Trish arrived, she, Joanna, Bernadette and I held on to each other. The few who had already gathered around us stood aside, allowing us to begin to realise the full impact of our loss. I thought of Suzanne: her energy, zest and love of life. To know that I would never again see her burst through the door and have her give me a hug while chattering away, smiling from ear to ear, was too painful to imagine. How would I ever come to terms with her death?

Within a few hours the house was bursting with people. Sister Pauline O'Regan, my brother Noel and sister-in-law Veronica set out for Blenheim, driving through the night, to bring Suzanne's body home. They returned late afternoon the following day. I felt numb with pain and grief as I helped carry her body inside. How could this have happened?

The house remained in a state of controlled chaos for nearly a week as our family and friends came and went at all hours of the day and night, sitting with Suzanne's body, cooking, caring and being with us. The spoken words, the unspoken words, the hugs, the endless cups of tea and bowls of soup all helped. After a visit to Te Rangimarie Marae and a magnificent liturgy led by Father Kevin Burns in our local parish, Trish and I, supported by our extended family and many friends, buried Suzanne on the day of our twenty-fourth wedding anniversary. She was 22.

Various journalists approached us over the next few days. I told them that the information we had suggested that Suzanne's death was a 'chance accident'. I thought she had died helping a member of her group, and no, I had no safety concerns about the course. My view changed within a couple of weeks, however, when my family and I met with the rest of the group at Outward Bound in Anakiwa and heard their stories. There we were shattered by the realisation that Suzanne's death had been an accident waiting to happen, and had been preventable.

As I left Anakiwa that day, questions continued to race through my mind. I wanted answers. How could my daughter be sitting at her office desk on a Thursday afternoon and by the following Tuesday be lost in the bush on a mountain without an instructor, cold and utterly disoriented, falling to her death? When Suzanne accepted an invitation to go to Outward Bound, she was not told that she might be placed in a situation of mortal danger.

'It was an accident,' said Outward Bound emphatically. They

denied any responsibility and were reluctant to talk to our family. We soon discovered that Outward Bound was a sacred cow of New Zealand society; even our local paper apparently did not want to 'upset' them. Unfazed by this, I discussed my concerns with the editor of the *Nelson Evening Mail*, David Mitchell, who had covered such accidents before. He sent journalist David Manning to pursue the story, despite a threat of legal action.[1]

We persisted with our demand that Outward Bound take responsibility for Suzanne's death, inviting Cate Brett, an award-winning journalist for the magazine *North and South*, to listen to our story. She carried out her own investigation and wrote a cover story, 'Death by Adventure', placing Outward Bound under public scrutiny.[2] Brett found that some of our criticisms were 'echoed by a handful of very experienced and well-respected outdoor experts'.[3]

Finally, after a difficult year of publicly calling Outward Bound to account, our family and key members of their organisation met face to face in an intense nine-hour meeting to discuss the issues. For the first time our family felt heard. We presented a detailed written account of our grievances and received answers to some of our questions. Towards the end we discussed how the outcome of the meeting would be presented and agreed to a joint statement for media release.[4]

The joint statement symbolised the culmination of a process during which we had a chance to air our feelings and concerns and Outward Bound had acknowledged its part in the events surrounding Suzanne's death. Further, they had identified a need for safety measures and systems (subsequently implemented) to prevent this kind of accident happening again. The institution that we held responsible for the death of our daughter at last had a human face. The process enabled us to continue integrating what had happened, begin to be with Suzanne differently, and continue the healing process. That was our next big challenge: to forgive and to embrace Suzanne in a profoundly new way.

Forgiveness: The Path to a New Relationship

In order to move on we knew we had to forgive. First, Trish and I had to forgive ourselves for not stopping Suzanne from going to Outward Bound. Second, we had to forgive Outward Bound for their carelessness, insensitivity and incompetence. Finally, we had to forgive God for a lack of divine intervention at a critical moment, and for giving Trish and me the task of raising our beautiful daughter for 22 years and then taking her from us. We are often asked what it is like to lose a child. The experience taught us that for those who have experienced it, no words are necessary, and for those who haven't, few words are possible.

To forgive in situations where we feel 'wronged' is one of the biggest challenges humans face. Knowing when to hang on and when to let go is an internal conflict for us all. As Stephanie Dowrick has said: 'To forgive may be an act of supreme love and gentleness, but it is also tough. It demands that at least one party face the truth—and learn something of value from it.'[5] Our family went through a range of emotions from shock, trauma, disbelief, devastation and sadness to rage and anger at losing Suzanne in the way that we did. Moving through the intensity of our emotions took time as we processed what had happened and let the reality set in.

Yet we were determined to work towards freeing ourselves from a lifetime of what *not* forgiving would mean.

> Forgiveness is one of the really difficult things in life. The logic of receiving hurt seems to run counter in the direction of never forgetting the hurt or the hurter. When you forgive, some deeper, divine generosity takes you over. When you can forgive, then you are free. When you cannot forgive you are a prisoner of the hurt done to you.[6]

Striving for forgiveness was for our own sakes and vital for our healing. We did not want bitterness to destroy our lives—our family, friendships, relationships and health. If the circumstances of Suzanne's death had been different, with an individual more clearly culpable, it may have been even more difficult, if not impossible, for our family to contemplate forgiveness. However, we would still have had to find a way to live without Suzanne's physical presence in our lives. In acknowledging this fact, we began slowly to regain peace in ourselves and learned to relate to Suzanne in a new way.

Healing History

History cannot be changed, but sometimes it can be healed. History must be healed if humankind is to survive. It has been estimated that 160 million people were killed in twentieth-century wars. Is this it? Is the human race doomed to a never-ending cycle of war and violence? What is the place of forgiveness and healing?

Part of Suzanne's legacy to those who knew her was her clear understanding and vision of the indigenous peoples of New Zealand and of who she was in relation to them. This understanding contributed to her interest in the implications of the Treaty of Waitangi. As a journalist for Radio New Zealand in Wanganui she was committed to learning correct Maori language pronunciation, creating an holistic relationship with local tangata whenua and deepening her understanding of the Treaty. Suzanne's death challenged me to make more meaning of the work I do for justice. My disbelief, anger, rage and sadness, coupled with my energy and vision, led to an expanded understanding of my own journey and the human journey. My commitment to supporting the struggles of indigenous and other marginalised peoples everywhere deepened.

Our family's experience after Suzanne's death is a microcosm of what people can and may need to do in order to forgive and heal themselves, their history, their relationships, their communities and societies. Suzanne's story enabled me to recognise that forgiveness at any level, personal or political, requires a range of personal and possibly communal processes. A person deciding whether or not to forgive another person, institution or government for an injustice needs to go through a series of steps.

Maori and other indigenous peoples all over the world are confronting governments in colonial societies to force them to honour treaties. As the new millennium evolves, the challenge is to expand and deepen our understanding of what is required to heal our history. Nothing will change until historical grievances are recognised and confronted. Equally challenging is the need to honour the original agreements made with indigenous peoples, which in New Zealand means honouring the power-sharing agreement guaranteed under the Treaty of Waitangi. If governments do not take responsibility for the injustices of history, then they simply perpetuate the conflict. While some governments have responded with new policies, most continue to avoid issues of authority and power.

Acknowledging the Pain of History

Healing needs to occur at many levels. The start of the process is to acknowledge the history, damage and pain caused by colonisation. To recognise at an official level that what happened actually happened. Official acknowledgement is vital and its impact cannot be underestimated. It means that the histories of indigenous peoples are recognised. Their experience is taken seriously. Proper recognition of wrongdoing paves the way for the beginnings of transformation, setting the scene for further steps towards reconciliation and healing.

The Truth and Reconciliation Commission was set up in South Africa by Nelson Mandela to expose many of the atrocities committed under the apartheid system. The work of the commission has enabled South Africa to move towards an entirely new way of functioning. Under the previous regime, the stories of victims of apartheid were largely repressed. The commission provided an opportunity for the victims of apartheid to tell their stories publicly and to achieve a certain catharsis. The commission dealt with politically motivated crimes and amnesty for the perpetrators requiring full disclosure of the truth. Finding out the whole truth may have assisted families of the victims to begin to find closure. Confronting the perpetrator, telling and hearing the truth, even if painful, offers the possibility of assisting the process of healing and letting go.

The commission was inevitably riddled with inconsistencies, contradictions and uncorroborated statements. A key compromise in the process has been that the perpetrators of heinous crime can escape criminal conviction and evade taking personal responsibility in return for a full admission of their wrongdoing. Nigerian Nobel laureate Wole Soyinka has observed that 'there is little evidence of remorse at these public confessionals'.[7] Soyinka argues that without remorse perpetrators faced with the same circumstances again may commit the same crimes.

The commission nonetheless offered a prophetic process in a world needing an alternative to revenge and the continued cycle of violence in history. South Africa can begin the journey to closure because an unjust system is changing. The commission has heard from 21,300 victims, who have collectively recounted 9980 killings.[8] In the political climate the commission represents a remarkable effort that may help to avoid civil war and a level of revenge akin to that played out in the last decade in Eastern Europe.

Offering a Genuine Apology

After acknowledgement, a genuine apology is the next step in accepting personal or collective responsibility for wrongdoing. A genuine apology is an expression of remorse and regret. It implies a commitment to change, ensuring that the wrongdoing does not occur again.

Governments around the world are apologising for historical injustices. In 1997 US President Bill Clinton apologised to 400 indigent African Americans for the syphilis experiments undertaken in the 1930s. This public-relations exercise was useful as it raised the level of debate concerning unethical research; however, it is tempered by the fact that unethical medical experiments continue, not only on US citizens but, more damningly, on the poorest citizens in other more economically dependent countries.[9] That same year British Prime Minister Tony Blair publicly accepted British responsibility for the Irish potato famines during the previous century. However, it was ironic that while Blair was apologising for one famine, he was promoting another, as his government was supporting a trade boycott against Iraq, which was reported by Unicef to have starved more than 500,000 children. Other examples include the official apologies with compensation by the Japanese government to Korean women who were used as prostitutes during the Second World War, and those to Jews by the German and Swiss governments for the criminality of the holocaust.

Apologies are not always appropriate. In November 2000 Clinton became the first US president to visit Vietnam since the Vietnam War. He didn't insult the Vietnamese people by apologising. How could he? This war created havoc in the world and in the lives of millions of people, for which the immediate victims and world economies are still paying. The fact that one of the main architects of the war, Robert McNamara, has recently admitted that the war was a terrible mistake is of scant help to the 58,000 Americans and over 3 million Vietnamese who died and the millions who continue to suffer.[10]

Demands that the US government apologise for slavery and make reparations to the black community are also growing. Slavery was a crime against humanity which left a contemporary legacy of racism and grinding poverty for most African Americans. It is not just an economic issue: the rebuilding of self-esteem and healing the legacy of psychic and social scars is a staggering challenge facing African American people.[11]

Apologies without changed behaviour lack credibility and become another political tool, which risks devaluing their meaning. For President Clinton to apologise to the Guatemalan people for the US government's overthrowing of the democratically elected Guatemalan government in 1954,[12] while it continues to interfere with and sometimes overthrow democratically elected governments inhospitable to US capital and foreign policy objectives, is hardly credible and smacks of blatant self-interest.[13]

Yet the continued level of destruction inflicted on the world by the US and British governments alone raises questions about the credibility of any acknowledgements, apologies and reparations.

9/11—A Day We Will Never Forget

On 11 September 2001, three passenger planes ploughed into buildings in New York and Washington, killing over 3000 people. There was righteous outrage throughout the US and other western countries. It was an obscene and unconscionable act of terrorism. In this enormous tragedy 'we' could identify with the victims: they were 'us'. The perpetrators were 'the other'.

The media—the mass perpetuators of ignorance—went to work to ensure that we would share the outrage. Film stars, political leaders, church leaders and other celebrities trekked to the site of the tragedy in New York. Memorial services were held in many parts of the world. The war on terrorism was geared up and the message was clear: 'we' in the West were the innocent; and 'they', people who were different and whom we didn't know or understand, were the guilty.

Consequently Iraq was invaded and Iraqi civilians have continued to be slaughtered, despite having no proven connection to this horrifying act. The horrendous number of deaths is hardly noticed by the western media. We hear little about Iraqi civilian deaths and as a consequence remain more unaffected by them. The Iraqi dead have never been officially counted—only American and British.[14] Why? Because Iraqis are not 'us'. They are 'the other'.

An understanding of British and US foreign policy sheds some light on how a tragedy of this magnitude had the potential to happen. Former US State Department officer William Blum has detailed American interventions and killing in 55 countries since the Second World War. He calls it an American holocaust that has brought death and misery to millions of people.[15] American Politics Professor Robert Elias states that 'from 1945 to 2000, the USA attempted to overthrow more than 40 foreign governments, usually successfully, and crushed more than 30 populist movements struggling against dictatorships'.[16] His analysis puts the number of deaths conservatively at about 12 million.

The notion of 'the other' has dehumanised the innocent. It removes 'us' from 'them'. In 1968 the British government secretly and illegally removed the entire population of 1500 Illois people from Diego Garcia in the Indian Ocean. This was done to provide for a US military base allowing for interventions in the Middle East. It was barely reported. They were 'the other'.[17] In 1984 an American multinational was responsible for a gas leak at its plant in Bhopal, India. America still refuses to extradite the chairman of the company, Warren Anderson, to be held accountable. Some 16,000 people were killed, but their deaths were apparently irrelevant.[18] They were 'the other'. In 1996 when Madeleine Albright, American Ambassador to the United Nations, was asked about the half-million deaths of Iraqi children caused by the sanctions she replied that it had been worth it.[19] Their deaths were an unfortunate statistic. They were 'the other'.

The rationale for these slaughters and dehumanisation is in the name of democracy. Yet the real purpose can be seen as making the world safe for capitalism and to capture and exploit the world's wealth. After Saudi Arabia, Iraq contains the world's second-largest oil reserves at 11 per cent, and therefore remains vital to western interests.[20] In addition, there is overwhelming evidence that American and British state-sponsored terrorism against a variety of Third World peoples is by far the most serious type of terrorism in the world today.[21] Acknowledgement, apologies and reparations become meaningless in the face of blatant indifference to human rights. There is a famous quote from the Chinese writer Moh-tze, who said that to kill one person is murder, to kill thousands is foreign policy. America and Britain will inevitably reap what they sow.

New Zealand—Apologies

In 1996 in New Zealand Queen Elizabeth became the first British monarch to make an official apology. In the presence of the Maori Queen, Te Arikinui Dame Te Atairangikaahu, she signed into New Zealand law a bill in which the Crown apologised to Tainui, the people of Waikato, for sending imperial forces into their land in the 1860s and for the subsequent devastation and injustice. Since then an official apology from the Crown has accompanied all settlements with Maori, totalling 15 by September 2003.

Although controversial, apologies have been a feature of the current government's 'political package', as part of the process of acknowledging the suffering in the history of some minority groups. In February 2002 Prime Minister Helen Clark formally apologised to the Chinese people in New Zealand for the discrimination they suffered from the late nineteenth century until after the Second World War.[22] This discrimination began with the Chinese Immigrants Act (1881), which set an expensive poll tax of £10 per person on Chinese immigrants entering New Zealand. Fifteen years later this was raised to £100 pounds, imposing great hardship on Chinese immigrants.

In June 2002 Helen Clark apologised to the Samoan people in a speech broadcast live from Apia to hundreds of Samoans at emotional gatherings at venues in Auckland, Wellington and Christchurch. The apology was directly connected to New Zealand's treatment of Samoans during colonial times more than 70 years ago.[23] Later that month she offered a formal public apology to New Zealand's gay and lesbian community for its mistreatment at the hands of government. She described the history of discrimination and criminalisation against gay people as appalling.[24]

These apologies are important as they formally acknowledge our history of discrimination and signal a seismic change in the behaviour and attitude of the Crown.

Making Reparation

Reparation must follow apology. Reparations

> can deepen the power of an apology, by showing sincerity of remorse and a desire to make things different in the future . . . apologies are most believable when they're accompanied by reparations, and reparations are least offensive when they really are about apology.[25]

In New Zealand various of forms of reparation to Maori are possible, including cultural redress, for example enhanced status and responsibilities for kaitiaki of resources, dual place names and mahinga kai, financial compensation, restoration of land, and provision for representation on local decision-making bodies critical to tribal interest.

The Ngai Tahu claim offers an example of the settlement process at work in New Zealand. Ngai Tahu registered their claim with the Waitangi Tribunal in 1987, giving rise to investigation by the Crown and the claimants. The tribunal, representing a cross-section of New Zealand society, heard the claim and subsequently reported its findings and recommendations. The Crown publicly acknowledged the history in the proposed deed of settlement and agreed to offer an official apology to Ngai Tahu. It further proposed a settlement package amounting to $170 million, including land, name changes to mountains, rivers and lakes, and representation on various government boards within the Ngai Tahu rohe.

The settlement was signed in 1998, 150 years and 19 commissions of inquiry after Ngai Tahu first lodged a claim with the Crown. Whether or not this represents a full and final settlement is a matter for future generations.

Notwithstanding the token nature of the settlement (less than 2 per cent), this is a major success story. Te Runanga o Ngai Tahu is the 18-member tribal council that governs Ngai Tahu, with members being elected from each local runanga or tribal council. Ngai Tahu Holdings Group of Companies has had a significant increase in net asset worth, from $139,000 in 1990 to $276 million in 2002, inclusive of the $170 million Treaty of Waitangi settlement. Total tribal assets are valued at $372 million. Ngai Tahu Property Ltd's core business operations are grouped within five 'pillars' of business activity: equities, property, seafood, tourism and tribal services. It has grown its asset base from $5.6 million in 1994 to $170 million in 2003 and is now one of the largest property companies (and the largest private property owner) in the South Island.[26]

Critics of the current settlement process highlight a significant flaw: the party representing the perpetrator is also the party deciding on redress. Many Maori are critical of the government playing the thief, the Crown prosecutor and the judge. It is true that the Crown controls the agencies involved in investigating claims and negotiating settlements. It holds all the cards. In practice the offers to Maori are largely non-negotiable. Ideally, there needs to be an independent body to finalise redress.

Commitment to a New Relationship

Real change in the relationship between indigenous peoples and governments requires vision and political courage. It involves structural change incorporating treaty and common-law rights, because restorative processes are pointless if governments continue their colonial behaviour.

Some governments around the world are at a very early stage of addressing the damage inflicted on indigenous peoples historically. This involves their negotiating an electoral minefield of entrenched bureaucracies and an unsympathetic majority population. Yet, there is a growing recognition that grievances are likely to fester and haunt colonial governments unless underlying injustices are dealt with properly and real change occurs. By working together in collaboration both parties may achieve acceptable solutions to current challenges. An effective process of reconciliation will enable a society to move forward in its personal and collective development, recognising the unique status of indigenous peoples and respecting the cultural diversity of other citizens.

Case Studies

The following case studies show how Australia, British Columbia and New Zealand are dealing with indigenous rights issues. These case studies demonstrate varying commitments to developing a new relationship with indigenous peoples.

Australia: Back to the Future

In May 1982 three Murray Islanders and members of the Merriam people, Eddie Mabo, David Passi and James Rice, initiated proceedings against the state of Queensland. They claimed that since time immemorial the Merriam people had occupied the Murray Islands in settled communities with their own social and political organisation.[27] The Australian High Court delivered its decision in this case, known as the Mabo decision, in 1992. The court confirmed that Aboriginal peoples had common-law rights (native title) pre-dating and continuing after European settlement. The ruling in the Mabo case rejected the colonial fiction of *terra nullius* (empty land), the basis on which the British had declared sovereignty over Australia in 1788. The ruling did not deny British sovereignty but, notwithstanding its limitations, it has had substantial long-term implications.[28]

Four years later, in another case the courts decided by a narrow majority in favour of the Wik people of northern Queensland. The Wik people claimed title to pastoral land leased to European farmers in 1915. The court decided that pastoral leases and native title could coexist. The Wik judgment went further than the Mabo decision. But when Parliament later enshrined the Mabo decision in the

Native Title Act 1993 it excluded pastoral leases from native title claims.[29] The effect was to arbitrarily exclude 40 per cent of Australia from the protection of native title.

The reactionary Native Title Amendment Act 1998 nullified many of the gains made in the Mabo and Wik decisions. The Aboriginal and Torres Strait Islander Commission, in analysing the impact of the Amendment Act, argued that native title-holders now have less say on exploration in their traditional country and on the management of parks, forests and other activities in their traditional country, including offshore fishing and mining. Not only can primary production activities continue without negotiating with native title-holders, but it is also easier for state governments to extinguish native title and compulsorily acquire land. Aboriginal peoples are required to prove traditional and physical connection to disputed land and to present a case in a claim hearing. The legislation enables native title to be extinguished before the courts have considered claims.[30] In short, Aboriginal rights were marginalised and the pastoralists and miners won again. The anti-Aboriginal rights rhetoric of the extremely right-wing One Nation Party, for whom a million people voted, carried the day. As Henry Reynolds observes: 'The aristocratic gentlemen who ran the colonial office in the 1840s were willing to concede more to indigenous Australians than the leaders of modern Australia'.[31]

The Australian government's stand on the issue of native title is symptomatic of a country divided over how to respond to its colonial past. It would seem that the courts are more able to take a more robust stand in interpreting law than can government, which is at the mercy of public opinion. One hopeful sign of a growing national awareness was 250,000 Australians walking across Sydney Harbour Bridge on 'Sorry Day' in 1998, demanding that the government take responsibility for its part in the historical injustices and reverse its decision not to apologise to the Aboriginal peoples.

Australian writer/critic Robert Hughes, author of the magnificent epic *The Fatal Shore*, which traces the fate of 160,000 convict men, women and children to Botany Bay, concluded in his latest television series that the government is the problem:

> Until we have a government that is prepared to give ground, what hope can there be for reconciliation? Is our past condemned to be our future? The present Australian government likes to speak of the violence and terrible history of black and white in Australia as being a blemish on our past. It is not a blemish. It is a deep, infected and suppurating wound and no one knows when it is going to heal.[32]

Any hope of reconciliation is now doubly threatened by the growing strength of the denialist movement promoted by Prime Minister John Howard. Australian historian Dirk Moses defines denialists as those who 'offer preposterous counter-explanations or redefine words and contexts to render harmless the charge of genocide'.[33] Howard adopted the denialist expression coined by historian Geoffrey Blainey, which rejected the black-armband view of Australian history.[34] On semantic grounds the Howard government denied the existence of any stolen generations and treated the claim of genocide in the Bringing Them Home report as absurd. A formal government apology and any compensation was refused.[35]

Howard has worked to make Australians 'comfortable and relaxed' about the destruction of Aboriginal society in the colonial settlement of Australia. Anthropologist W. E. H. Stanner called it 'The Great Australian Silence'. The whole tragic and complex story of the massacres carried out by settlers, which included an estimated 20,000 killings on the frontier between the 1780s and the late 1920s, has been reduced to what one historian called 'a melancholy footnote' and another a mere 'codicil'.[36]

The denialist movement reflects an international trend. In Japan conservative imperialists 'deny the national past contains much to be regretted'.[37] In Germany Holocaust denial is widespread. In 1993 Deborah Lipstadt's Denying the Holocaust: The Growing Assault on Truth and Memory highlights the 'malicious motivation and the pervasive contempt for truth that lie behind the various guises and tactics' of the denialist movement.[38] In Turkey the state itself is denialist concerning the slaughter of over a million Armenians in 1915.[39]

British Columbia, Canada: The Healing Journey Begins

Canada's Constitution Act in 1982 recognised and affirmed existing aboriginal rights, including 'any rights or freedoms recognised by the Royal Proclamation of 7 October 1763 and any rights or freedoms now existing by way of land-claim agreements or [which] may be so required'.[40] This means that aboriginal rights are constitutionally protected and entrenched and therefore, it would appear, more secure in Canada than in Australia and New Zealand.

The 1997 claim by Delgamuukw and two nations of indigenous peoples, the Gitksan and Wet'suwet'en, for 58,000 square kilometres of north-western British Columbia resulted after two appeals in one of the most significant Supreme Court rulings in Canadian history. Different Canadian states have different stances on aboriginal title and the Court ruled that 'a provincial law of general application cannot extinguish aboriginal rights'.[41] This ruling reaffirmed aboriginal rights that had been variously disregarded.

The British Columbia Treaty Commission had allocated approximately $255 million in negotiation support funding to more than 50 First Nations—$204 million in the form of loans and $51 million in the form of contributions. As at 18 December 2003, after 10 years the BC Treaty process had five First Nations in or near final agreement and 40 in Agreement in Principle negotiations. Three First Nations were still negotiating a framework agreement and five First Nations had yet to complete the 'readiness to negotiate' process. 'In all, 53 First Nations were negotiating around 42 Treaty tables. Some 114 of the 197 Indian Act bands in British Columbia are in the Treaty process (plus eight from the Yukon), while 83 BC bands have chosen not to become involved in treaty negotiations'.[42]

While the appearance of progress exists, underneath the surface there is simmering anger against the provincial government of British Columbia that no claims have actually been settled after 10 years. Speaking at a rally in May 2004, Grand Chief Edward John, a member of the First Nations summit taskgroup, expressed 'our complete disappointment with the federal and provincial governments' continued denial of the existence of aboriginal peoples, aboriginal title and aboriginal rights'.[43] In December 2003, 63 tribal groups initiated lawsuits claiming title to their territory. They are also instigating constitutional challenges opposed to corporate takeovers against a government that has staked its future on supporting resource-extraction companies. Ongoing political action is planned.

In British Columbia, as in Australia and New Zealand, public education about indigenous rights is largely non-existent. This enables governments, largely controlled by corporate backers and supported by the corporate media, to manipulate public opinion against the rights of indigenous people everywhere.

The biggest settlement to date in British Columbia is the Nisga'a Treaty. This was the sixteenth settlement in British Columbia history and the first negotiated in modern times. The settlement includes approximately 2000 square kilometres of land, parks, water, forests, fisheries and wildlife, as well as self-governance extending to authority over the local administration of justice and taxation.

Critics argue, however, that such settlements could become a double-edged sword, allowing the government to evade responsibilities for indigenous peoples under the guise of granting independence and autonomy to tribes. In Canada this has been called 'getting out of the Native business'.[44] It is seen by some as the government's way of increasingly handing over social and economic problems to the tribal peoples and progressively limiting their access to resources.

Other critics argue that the settlements process itself is fundamentally flawed—based on the mistaken premise that Canada owns the land it is situated on. By engaging in the settlement process Native peoples are obliged to accept the Crown's sovereignty over Canada, a premise that many continue to reject. Taiaiake Alfred, raised in Kahnawake Mohawk territory and now director of the Indigenous Governance Program at the University of Victoria, writes: 'Indigenous peoples have been obliged to go along with the historically false idea that they must make a claim against the state in order to gain ownership of lands that they have always possessed'.[45]

The British Columbia government's share of the overall cost of the treaty process to date is estimated at C$2 billion, plus rural Crown land with a notional value of C$2.8 to C$3.5 billion. But independent studies have projected that up to 17,000 new jobs will be created as result of treaty settlements and that for every dollar spent the government is projected to gain three dollars in return.[46] On the surface these projections have all the hallmarks of a win–win process, but it is still controversial and public misunderstanding is a continuing difficulty. As in Australia and New Zealand, the public education process in Canada leaves much to be desired.

New Zealand: Restoring Right Relationships

In New Zealand, Maori customary and common-law rights over land and water (upheld in the Treaty of Waitangi) were recognised by the courts in 1847 and 1872, but subsequently disregarded until a High Court ruling in 1986.[47] In *Te Weehi v. Regional Fisheries Officer* Justice Williamson upheld an appeal by Tom Te Weehi, who was earlier convicted of taking undersized paua. Te Weehi had sought protection of his customary fishing rights under Section 88(2) of the Fisheries Act 1983. The High Court accepted Te Weehi's argument, upholding native title, particularly the rights of traditional societies to natural resources in their territory. Justice Williamson, drawing on Canadian law, considered that the Crown in acquiring sovereignty over a territory has an obligation to uphold the customary and common-law rights of earlier inhabitants. He held that these rights continue unless extinguished by law, purchase or some specific action.[48] This new ruling would inform later claims.

In 1992 the Crown settled a Treaty claim relating to fisheries, which came to be known as the Sealord deal. The Crown bought a half share in Sealords Products, a major commercial fishing company owning 26 per cent of all fishing quota, for $150 million, and gave it to Maori. Brierley Investments Ltd purchased the other half share. In addition, the Crown agreed to give Maori 20 per cent of each new species of fish brought into the quota scheme. Maori in return agreed to cease litigation in respect of commercial fisheries, which meant the Waitangi Tribunal no longer had jurisdiction over any Treaty claims made in respect of fishing or fisheries.[49]

Although Maori negotiators appeared to favour the Sealord deal, many Maori had reservations. At a number of hui held throughout the country in September 1992, concern was expressed that abandoning Treaty claims was more than any deal was worth. But the negotiators, recognising that the government held all the cards, took all that was on offer, subsequently enabling many Maori to take up commercial fishing and a wide range of educational opportunities. By 1996 Te Ohu Kaimoana (the Treaty of Waitangi Fisheries Commission) had become the major stakeholder in New Zealand's fishing industry with assets totalling $507.4 million. Sealord had 630 employees, and 50 iwi were operating their own fishing businesses, including in some cases processing and marketing their own products.[50]

The Sealord deal was significant because it overrode Treaty rights. Article Two of the Treaty of Waitangi guarantees Maori tino rangatiratanga over and undisturbed possession of their fisheries and at no time in the previous 160 years had Maori negotiated away *any* let alone all of their fishing rights.[51] Historian Paul Moon, in his analysis of the Sealord settlement, argues that the government avoided the implications of the Treaty of Waitangi by adopting a new stance: 'They relied in this case on extinguishing iwi (tribal) rights to commercial fisheries under the Treaty in return for a one-off payment to be made to a pan-tribal body to acquire a portion of the fishing quota'.[52] This change in the philosophical approach to the Treaty, which rested in offering an alternative to, rather than a fulfilment of, the promises, became morally acceptable to the community including many Maori.

Twelve years after the 1992 'full and final' Sealord settlement was signed, the Maori Fisheries Bill was finally passed in September 2004. The settlement has had a turbulent history. The key issues were: 'whether quota should be based on an iwi's population or a tribe's coastline; entitlements for "urban Maori" who are disassociated from their iwi authorities; those who want the entire settlement to be distributed out and those who want the assets to be consolidated into a central organisation'.[53]

After successive legal challenges, what the Court of Appeal

described as an unprecedented level of consultation and about 50 submissions to the select committee, the allocation model recommended in 2003—supported by 91.3 per cent of iwi representing 96.7 per cent of iwi-affiliated Maori—was incorporated into the legislation. The final allocation model covers all the Maori fisheries assets estimated to be worth about $750 million, increased threefold during the last decade as follows:

- Nearly half of the settlement assets, estimated at approximately $350 million, in the form of all quota and cash will be transferred directly to mandated iwi organisations.

- The iwi that are likely to receive the largest parcel of assets represent a mixture of coastal and populous iwi. They are Ngai Tahu, Ngati Kahungunu, Ngapuhi, Ngati Porou, Chathams iwi and Waikato.

- There is an allocation formula for inshore and deep-water quota that takes account of coastline and population.

- Half of the settlement assets in the form of all company shares will be held in a new Maori fishing entity called Aotearoa Fisheries Limited (AFL), in which each recognised iwi organisation will receive a minimum allocation package of cash, quota and income shares.

- Three Maori trusts, including urban Maori, will get small allocations for associated activities.[54]

When the 1992 claim was being settled I was visiting leaders of the Wampanoag, Micmac, Maliseet, Penobscot, Chippewa, Tewa and Jemez Pueblo nations in North America. Many expressed the view that treaties should never be extinguished for economic gain. They believed that this had been a fundamental error in some of the historical negotiations between their tribes and the US government. They conceded that when treaties were surrendered or eliminated, the tribes often had no choice. But the decision was always a dilemma. If your people are starving, do you hold on to a treaty right or take the cash? Indigenous peoples in the United States and New

Zealand may well consider that building a strong economic base in this generation may lay a sound basis for greater self-determination in the next.

Committing to a New Relationship

If the world is to create new ways of functioning and new relationships, then all countries have to address and redress their history. If we courageously confront our history and work to resolve the enormous rupture that colonisation has created, all people will benefit. In doing so we must be careful not to solve one injustice by creating another. The majority culture's single greatest challenge is to listen to indigenous peoples as they articulate and take charge of their own solutions to their own problems and their own lives. In this process, forgiveness may become possible.

I remain inspired by the words of Martin Luther King Jr, who said:

> Forgiveness does not mean ignoring what has been done or putting a false label on an evil act. It means, rather, that the evil act no longer remains as a barrier to the relationship. Forgiveness is a catalyst creating the atmosphere necessary for a fresh start and a new beginning . . .[55]

In order to move past historical injustices, evil acts and wrongdoing need to be recognised as evil. When governments acknowledge past wrongs, apologise and negotiate an acceptable reparation, a commitment to a new, just, fair and equitable relationship with indigenous peoples becomes more feasible.

As I continue to overcome challenges in my work as a Treaty educator, I also remain inspired by the gift of my daughter Suzanne and what I learned from her life and death. Suzanne shared my passion, awareness, motivation and commitment to working towards social justice. She hoped for peaceful relationship between Maori and Pakeha in the future. This hope was poignantly captured in a letter Suzanne wrote (when she was 19) for a time-capsule recently opened by our family: 'By the year 2000, the New Zealand government and people *must* have moved and be honouring Te Tiriti O Waitangi.' While this process has begun, there is still a long road ahead.

Around the world, a need for restoration and healing is becoming increasingly apparent as all cultures deepen their understanding of history. How to achieve collective ways of functioning that benefit all cultures living alongside each other remains a challenge. Humankind is in a constant state of creation. The journey is the key. That, and a willingness to commit to what Saul Alinksy called a 'blurred vision as to what the outcome might mean'. History cannot be changed, yet it can be healed over time and provide lessons for future generations. Everyone will benefit as we rediscover the richness that exists in a society that honours the agreements made by its ancestors, and respects the cultural diversity of all its citizens.

TWELVE

The Paradox of Hope

Panmunjom: The Border between South and North Korea, 1984

It was midnight as we sped through the dark, deserted streets of Pyongyang towards the railway station. As guests of the government of the Democratic Peoples' Republic of Korea (North Korea) we, in our small fleet of cars, had right of way through lights and intersections. After being whisked through a side entrance to the station we boarded a carriage with covered windows, shut off from the rest of the train, and left for Panmunjom. The secrecy made me curious and I asked many questions. While our courteous Korean hosts were resolutely polite, they had a capacity for deflection that was impossible to penetrate. As the train left the station I felt as if I were in the 1950s spy thriller *The Third Man*. Any minute I expected to hear the Harry Lime theme and to see the magnetically flamboyant Orson Welles standing in the shadows.

It was a seven-hour rail journey to the infamous border between North and South Korea, which was established in 1953 at the armistice ending the Korean War. The two sides had been in a state of war ever since. At Panmunjom officers of the North Korean Army met and briefed us on the political significance of what we were about to see. We were then taken to the actual border by jeep.

The serenity of the demilitarised zone was deceptive. High fences, barbed and razor wire enclosed both sides of the border, with more than a thousand guard-posts, watchtowers and reinforced bunkers on either side. All civilian activity was banned, except for one tightly controlled village on each side. In the Second World War barracks a thick white painted line on the floor in the middle of the building designated the border. The American Military Police photographed every move we made and we were warned not to cross the border-line.

The border symbolised a dangerous flashpoint between two seemingly incompatible systems: one side oppressed by the totalitarian world of communism; the other exploited by corporate capitalism, backed by the military industrial complex of the United States of America. Backing these positions are two of the world's largest military powers, 1.1 million North Koreans against 660,000 South Koreans with 37,000 US troops in support.[1] Both sides remained deeply embedded in their own myths. Truth had long departed the scene as they traded in propaganda, which had deepened an already distorted view of reality. Did either side really know why they were there, let alone what they wanted?

A Growing Awareness

I am reminded of my experience at the South and North Korean border when I reflect on the myth-making that happens in New Zealand today. The entrenched relationship between Maori and the government has historically been played out according to set roles developed and refined over generations. Each has become locked into a way of relating to each other, which can prevent the relationship from evolving.

Investigative journalist John Pilger warns us not to think in terms of living in an information age. Rather, he says, we live in a media age in which information is repetitive, safe and limited by invisible boundaries. He argues that refusing to accept the platitudes, clichés and stories of the spin doctors and PR people is the duty of all journalists.[2] In this respect New Zealand journalists and the media who employ them have a way to go. The insidious purpose of spin doctors, now routinely employed by governments, is to alter the truth. A critically aware population needs to continually be reading between the lines.

Although successive New Zealand governments have constantly reiterated rigidly held positions about the absolute authority of the Crown, political reality and court rulings have, since the mid-1980s, signalled change.[3] There is a growing awareness and consensus among some of New Zealand's leading public figures—Maori and Pakeha—about the sequence and meaning of what actually happened in 1840.

The core of the debate, as outlined by Ranginui Walker, is that the 512 Maori who signed the Maori text of the Treaty at Waitangi understood, in Article Two, that they were confirming their own sovereign rights—their rangatiratanga—in return for limited cession of governance (kawanatanga).[4] Walker further writes that the chiefs understood kawanatanga, in Article One, to mean 'the establishment of a system of government to provide laws that would control British settlers and bring peace among warring tribes'.[5] Kawanatanga is a subordinate power to rangatiratanga.[6]

Senior law lecturer Richard Boast concludes: 'The notion that at one stroke or, rather, a short succession of strokes, Maori signed their sovereignty away in 1840 is pure legal fiction.'[7] Moana Jackson further argues that any Treaty arrangement should be about the sharing of power.[8] But what Maori got was absolute indivisible sovereignty exercised by and for Pakeha. From the moment of proclamation in May 1840 the exercise of power by the British Crown exceeded anything conceded in the Treaty and to that extent it constituted a revolutionary takeover.[9]

At least two former National Party cabinet ministers have indicated they see it in this way. Simon Upton has stated that 'the New Zealand Parliament effected a revolutionary seizure of power'.[10] And Jane Kelsey quotes former Minister of Treaty Negotiations Sir Douglas Graham as saying: '. . . unflinching in its assertion of European supremacy . . . the English Crown had seized power by revolution and that power had since prevailed'.[11]

British colonisation of New Zealand is a legal fact, but it lacks legitimacy.[12] As the claims process develops, the New Zealand government and people will have to respond to the legitimate reassertion of Maori authority because Maori will never give up their fundamental human, common-law and Treaty right to live *as* Maori. As Chief Justice E. T. Durie has pointed out: '. . . the Crown, in 1835, had formally acknowledged the sovereign rights and capabilities of Maori . . . In accepting the authority of the Crown in 1840 Maori did not envisage any diminution of their own.'[13] History tells us that Maori will continue to demand recognition and respect for their unique status as Treaty partner and acceptance of their common-law and Treaty rights.

The Treaty debate is about the future of political and social relationships in this country. The challenge is to create structures where authority can be shared by Maori and the Crown in a way that will enable all New Zealanders to live and prosper together. This challenge will not go away. If we ignore it, the problem has the potential to intensify as the gaps between Maori and other New Zealanders widen, new Treaty claims arise and Maori seek their rightful place in New Zealand society.

The Complication of Globalisation

The debate is taking place in a country undergoing rapid social, economic and political change, while trying to maintain itself in an increasingly globalised world. The threat to New Zealand's survival as a nation cannot be understated. The World Trade Organisation, the International Monetary Fund and other multinational or private corporate interests now compete with, and in some cases control either directly or indirectly, nation state economies around the globe. 'National economies are interlocked, commercial banking and business ownership (controlled by some 750 global corporations) transcend economic borders, international trade is integrated and financial markets around the world are connected through instant computer link-up.'[14] To put it another way: 'The top 200 corporations collectively have sales in excess of combined economies of 182 of the 191 countries in the world.'[15]

Despite their political posturing the policies of such organisations are based on the relentless accumulation of private wealth and are aimed at maximising returns to shareholders. Such organisations have little concern for the social, cultural, economic and environmental goals of a nation. The global free market increases the likelihood that economic power will subsume political power and weaken democracy. It is not inevitable. It is a political project that is predicted to increase global instability and the misery of millions as the competition for scarce resources intensifies, except where targeted support may facilitate further economic activities and gains.[16]

This international economic turmoil has the power to undermine the social cohesion and confidence in New Zealand's future. The Labour government's Closing the Gaps policy aimed at addressing Maori inequalities has created a public backlash because in this climate of economic unease the policy has created a false perception that Maori are receiving special privileges to which they are not entitled. Part of this perception can be attributed to the fact that many other New Zealanders are struggling economically.

It is clear that New Zealand's economic reforms in the 1980s were disastrous for many New Zealanders. Official data confirm that the lowest income groups suffered real loss of spending power between 1984 and 1996, while the top 10 per cent captured all the gains from the reforms.[17] It is also clear that Maori were disproportionately affected because many of the low-skilled manufacturing jobs that disappeared during the reforms were held by Maori workers. During the first three years, for example, Maori employment fell by a staggering 25 per cent, imposing an enormous economic cost on Maori families and communities.[18] New Zealanders now know the outcome of that massive government 'welfare handout' to the rich during 1987–99. It was carried out under the cover of a privatisation programme. The 'big lie' was that it was the only way. Economist Bryan Gaynor sums up the colossal handouts to the wealthy, when 40 state-owned commercial assets were sold for $19.1 billion. In 1999 they had an estimated value of $35.7 billion, $16.6 billion above their original sale price.[19] This is wealth that should belong to New Zealanders. The remainder of the government's commercial assets have a book value of $4.6 billion.

The privatisation programme has been a huge windfall for

overseas investors. The justification was to lower the total debt and public-sector overseas debt. The outcome was a modest reduction of $15.4 billion (from $68.8 billion to $53.4 billion). In the 10 years 1989–99 New Zealand's overseas debt had risen from $46 billion to $102 billion.[20] Gaynor concludes that 'the massive transfer of wealth to foreigners, which has had a negative impact on the economy, has been facilitated by the Government's sale procedure policy'.[21]

This is not an argument against all the reforms of the 1980s, but the 'selling' of New Zealand assets to domestic and wealthy overseas investors was 'theft' from the working people of New Zealand, who had paid for them over generations. It was a programme completely bereft of imagination and original thinking by governments slavishly following the International Monetary Fund prescription.

This recent history needs to be contrasted alongside the minimal amount budgeted for settling legitimate Treaty claims ($1 billion over the 10 years 1995–2005, amounting to 3 per cent of all appropriations for one single year). It also makes government pleas of poverty to Maori completely hypocritical.[22] The criticism by politicians and the media of the amount spent on Maori programmes is completely two-faced.

New Zealand—the easiest country in the world to do business, according to the World Bank—is a country that is sharply divided in many other ways.[23] In 2004 a staggering 300,000 children (30 per cent) live in poverty (1991: 16 per cent). All policies have consequences. In the early 1990s we had benefit cuts, the abolition of the family benefit and market housing rentals imposed on our poorest and most vulnerable citizens. In 1993 we had the onset of an epidemic of meningococcal disease directly related to these cuts.[24] This is a disease of poverty. Overcrowded housing is named as a significant factor. Maori and Pacific people are vastly more affected than Pakeha. Notified cases 1993–99, on average per 10,000 population, were Maori 40, Pacific 73, Pakeha 13. Tuberculosis is another disease of poverty. Notified figures per 100,000 population are Maori 510, Pacific 212, Pakeha 23.[25]

This poverty is occurring in the same country where 187 Pakeha individuals and families have a combined net worth of more than

$22 billion and are 'experiencing an explosion of wealth in a time of exceptional prosperity'.[26] Contrast this with the entire Maori asset base, currently $9 billion in value.[27] The Retirement Commission figures indicate that 20 per cent of the population now hold about 60 per cent of the country's wealth.[28] The good news is that unemployment nationally is down to 4 per cent, with Maori unemployment down to 8.8 per cent, the lowest in 18 years.[29]

The Hui Taumata of 2005, 20 years after the first gathering, will have much to celebrate. Examples would include the rapid growth of kohanga reo, kura kaupapa and wananga, 23 Maori radio stations and Maori television, the fact that Maori generate 2.3 per cent of the country's exports and make up 17 per cent of industry trainees, that 240 Maori health providers are contracted to 21 district health boards, $680 million in Treaty claims have been settled, and there are 17,000 Maori self-employed or employers. With a focus on improving economic pathways for all Maori, the 2021 population statistics capture the focus. Maori are expected to number 749,000 (17 per cent) of the population, and their average age will be 27–28 per cent under 14, compared with an average age of 43 for non-Maori. Some 468,000 Maori will be of working age.[30]

Despite this, racism continues to appear in many guises. Reports are endemic.

- (2000) Many senior male psychiatrists of more than 10 years' experience believe Maori are naturally inclined to psychiatric illness, despite the fact that there is no evidence to back the biological-genetic theory.[31]

- (2000) An Otago University study shows that despite having similar jobs and qualifications Maori were paid 9–14 per cent less than non-Maori.[32]

- (2001) Maori receive fewer health services than they are entitled to because a disproportionate amount of the health dollar is spent on Pakeha.[33]

- (2004) Three former police officers reported regular racial attacks against Maori during the 1990s.[34]

The crunch issue for the Crown–Maori relationship is this. Special programmes to assist Maori, however well intentioned, are no substitute for effective power-sharing. Whatarangi Winiata sums up the contradiction when he says that 'evidence over the last 135 years screams out the proposition that it is not possible for people of one culture to formulate and implement policies for people of another culture and get it right . . . wave after wave of Crown designed and implemented policies have not produced the goods'.[35] Winiata notes that:

> A huge amount of money is spent on Maori every year . . . the Maori partner has little to say about how much the appropriations should be, what the policies should be, how policies are to be implemented and how policies and their managers are to be evaluated . . . [b]ut this partner [Maori] gets the blame for poor performance.[36]

He believes that the only 'long-term relief for Maori from the present circumstances will not come from more Pakeha-inspired policies but from constitutional change which ensures that the two partners can grow within their respective cultures and value systems and can make decisions together as full partners mindful of each other's concerns and preferences'.[37]

It is in this climate of economic uncertainty that all New Zealanders will need to come to terms with the implications of the Treaty relationship.

What Does Power-sharing Mean?

Recent governments in New Zealand have steered clear of establishing an official policy on the Treaty of Waitangi, beyond a Treaty settlement policy. However, changes to constitutional arrangements are inevitable as New Zealand grapples with its unique and evolving identity as a nation. Courageous leadership is needed by the Crown to chart a new course *with* Maori to ensure that the Treaty partnership can come to mean more than the settlement of historical claims. New ways of shared governance are inevitable. Maori are not alone; a significant number of Pakeha support their claims and want justice for all New Zealanders.

The sovereignty sought by Maori does not have to be in

opposition to the Crown. To date, various constitutional propositions and models have been suggested for discussion, which open up a range of possibilities for the future. Mason Durie has identified some of the major options.

First, Te Pihopatanga o Aotearoa model, which involves a reconfiguration of Parliament to include a tikanga Maori house, a tikanga Pakeha house, and a Treaty of Waitangi house with senatorial responsibilities. Second, a Maori regional model, which includes delivery of services at a regional level with the potential of a national structure based on regional representation. Third, a national Maori assembly, including representation from iwi and Maori communities and in which all Maori policy units in the state sector including Te Puni Kokiri would be retained as assembly staff. Fourth, a Maori policy commission, which would promote and propose Maori policy to government, taking over responsibility for Maori policy and the resources of Te Puni Kokiri. And fifth, the New Zealand Maori Council model based on marae and Maori communities.[38] These and other options need to be further considered by Maori communities and examined in the context of informed public debate. 'If there is one single unifying desire for Maori people, it is for self-determination. No longer are Maori content to let others decide policies for them or to have key decisions made on their behalf. The essence of tino rangatiratanga is that policies for Maori should be made by Maori, at all levels'.[39]

Mason Durie identifies another key challenge for Maori: 'At present the exercise of tino rangatiratanga at national and international levels is handicapped because there is no body politic which can represent all Maori interests at constitutional levels'.[40] Current support among Maori for such a body would appear to be significant. The absence of structures to guarantee tino rangatiratanga also prevents the nation from moving forwards and will continue to enable the Crown to avoid those Treaty responsibilities it does not wish to address.

It is worth remembering that historically some indigenous people had flourishing participatory democratic systems well ahead of most people in Europe. Benjamin Franklin and many of the colonists of

North America were not only influenced by Native American ideas of democracy and confederation, but also saw the Iroquois Confederacy as a model on which to build the United States system of government.

> In fact Indian democracies were working democracies that Europeans admired greatly from the first contacts. Many European theorists compared the Iroquois to the Romans, the Greeks and the Celts in the areas of mutual rights, statecraft, oratory and public consensus . . . which provided a viable alternative to the prevailing ideas in European society . . . the Iroquois Confederacy was a functioning constitution in an established society.[41]

The checks and balances, separation of powers, federalism and the consent of the governed incorporated into the American system were modelled on Iroquois Confederacy ideas and models.[42] We have much to learn from indigenous peoples—but we must work with them and not co-opt their knowledge.

New Zealanders have nothing to fear from the Treaty debate. Most Maori do not seek to engender guilt or lay blame for historical injustices at the feet of Pakeha living today. Instead, Maori seek justice and want to participate fully in a unified nation. This search for justice and inclusion is in the interests of all New Zealanders, the nation as a whole and our economy. New Zealand cannot move forward without the full participation of all its citizens.

Honouring the Treaty Will Benefit All New Zealanders

Many New Zealanders still do not see the Treaty as giving them access to a better future. Yet there are powerful economic, human rights and political reasons that should persuade them to support the Treaty being honoured. The cost of keeping disproportionate numbers of Maori in jail, the cost to the public health and education systems, and to the state generally in high Maori unemployment rates and other welfare dependency is a cost to us all. No one benefits from maintaining a situation where some New Zealanders are not able to contribute creatively in developing the nation. Given the authority and resources, most people have the capacity to create their own solutions.

The moral imperative is even greater. When we fail to fulfill our obligations and deny other people their legitimate human rights, we diminish our own humanity. Historically, it is unlikely that many slave owners saw benefits in liberating slaves, or men the benefits of women getting the vote, or European Americans in the United States supporting full civil rights for African Americans, or Protestants in the north of Ireland granting full civil rights to Catholics. Many people did not believe that society would benefit by changing the status quo. All of these advances occurred in the face of vigorous opposition. Yet few would not support these advances in human rights now. When we think of the Treaty debate in the context of this history, it offers hope that Treaty and indigenous rights will be fully honoured.

History verifies over and over again that the human spirit is capable of much more than self-interest. There is an innate fairness, generosity and grandeur in every human being that has the capacity to reach out and respond to the demands of justice and the common good. The task of every human being is to improve society. To do this we need to know our history.

There are powerful political arguments for moving the Treaty commitments towards an alliance between Maori and the Crown based on justice and right relationship. The constant demands through protests, occupations, expensive litigation and confrontation, apart from wasting creative energy, divides families, communities and the nation. It prevents people from focusing on some of the fundamental challenges facing the survival of New Zealand as a nation in a ruthless globalised economy.

Encouraging Informed Public Debate

Building an inclusive, unified and prosperous nation that honours its historical commitments requires a well-informed public. There is a danger that the Treaty debate in New Zealand may remain the exclusive domain of some government officials and politicians, academics and community educators, and some Maori. Witness the Building the Constitution Conference held in Parliament in April 2000.[43] Some excellent papers were presented, but who was there?

Leaders of the nation and others representing different interests perhaps, but a small selected gathering nonetheless, labelled in the media as an élite group. Such gatherings need to happen around the country with access for all New Zealanders.

Information which facilitates informed Treaty debate needs to go into the streets, the suburbs, and the small towns in the rural areas. It needs to occur in business communities, factories, offices and neighbourhoods. It needs to happen in schools, community organisations and rest homes. It needs to take place in sporting facilities, pubs, prisons and places of religious worship. It needs to happen within and among families and hapu. It needs to happen wherever New Zealanders gather. It needs to engage a variety of perspectives and involve as many New Zealanders as possible. Otherwise it will remain a debate reserved for a select few and continue to alienate a large section of the population who feel confused, excluded and angry about where they think the country seems to be heading.

Any significant power-sharing and changes to the constitutional arrangements in this country need the broad support of the population. In order for this to happen the Crown needs to be proactive in anticipating what information people require in order to participate in informed debate on the Treaty, our constitution and the future of our nation. If this does not happen, then as a nation we may further threaten race relations, and make social disruption inevitable. New Zealanders demonstrated their capacity for protest and social disruption during the 1981 anti-Springboks campaign. Families and communities were divided, laws were broken and some relationships ended. The potential for this kind of disruption still exists. The less informed the population, the more divisive the debate.

Good government seeks to ensure that the public is fully equipped to contribute to informed debate on issues affecting the nation. Many New Zealanders want the opportunity to learn about our country's colonial history in a respectful, engaging and comprehensible way. Reading a book may provide adequate information for some. Television documentaries will assist others. Modern school curricula will help to inform and prepare our children and young people. But also of great assistance to many adult learners is attendance at a culturally safe and interactive educational workshop. To this end there is an opportunity for the government to support and work in partnership with experienced Treaty educators to enhance the understanding of all New Zealanders on our colonial history and current issues in the Treaty debate. The challenge is for each of us to become better informed, to utilise easily accessible written material and websites and to take advantage of education opportunities be it in the local school, university or work situation.

Treaty education would offer New Zealanders an opportunity to develop an understanding of a national identity that is grounded in the partnership between Maori collectives, exercising tino rangatiratanga, and the Crown, representing all New Zealanders. A distinct national identity grounded in partnership honours and respects the special identity and status of Maori as tangata whenua as well as valuing the rich cultural diversity of Pakeha and other New Zealanders. A partnership approach is required to ensure the full participation of Maori and other citizens in New Zealand's society and economy. A partnership approach offers possibilities for creating alternative global economic networks, markets and practices aimed at enhancing the public and private good of nation states, all humanity and the environment on which we all depend. The Treaty partnership has the potential to develop a unique national identity in an increasingly diverse and complex world.

Conclusion

I have come to see the Treaty of Waitangi as an essential guide to building a unified, prosperous and peaceful nation. I place my best efforts in working practically towards restoring right relationship with indigenous peoples. This work involves valuing my own cultural identity, understanding the colonial history of this country, raising the awareness of and working with Pakeha, and standing alongside Maori and other indigenous peoples in their struggles for justice.

New Zealand novelist Patricia Grace of Ngati Toa, Ngati Raukawa and Te Ati Awa presents a compelling vision:

The Treaty allows for tolerance of different ways of operating, different ways of sovereignty. It allows the setting up of another system alongside its own system. It is a document that had everything in it that we need on which to base our modern society, a two-system society . . . it is a Treaty of allowance and tolerance that allows all of us to be here together. I think we need to understand the Treaty and embrace it, not be afraid of it, not get paranoid about a Maori rugby team having pride in a tino rangatiratanga flag, not be afraid of a dual system where there needs to be common sense more than anything else. We must be educated about our true history. We must understand as we stand at the beginning of this stony, rocky, mountainous, tangled path that gaps and discrepancies, in education, health, work and social status will not lessen until the yawning chasm in understanding of the Treaty is breached, until racism in all its forms is [ended] and the effects of colonisation are realised.[44]

I have spent my life searching for the elusive concept of social and transformational justice. My journey began in an Irish Catholic ghetto in the working-class Christchurch suburb of Addington in New Zealand. I was confronted with institutional disorder when I represented New Zealand at the World Congress of Catholic Laity in Rome. I was further politicised by my meetings with liberation movements and inspired by the turbulence of the 1960s and my involvement with the civil rights and anti-Vietnam War movements. As an international aid worker my visits to war zones in Vietnam and Bangladesh were a wake-up call to the evils of colonialism.

I have witnessed the struggle for human dignity in some of the most marginalised places in the world, from the ghettos of Chicago in the 1960s, to the slums of Calcutta in the 1970s, to New Orleans and Wabanaki Indian reservations in the 1990s. I have met members of many liberation movements including the Irish Republican Army, the Palestine Liberation Organisation, the African National Congress and various indigenous groups. I have viewed the world from the Berlin Wall and stared down the gun barrels of American GIs at Panmunjom on the Korean peninsula.

Learning about my country's colonial history has both enriched and challenged my life. This learning has helped me to understand Maori grievances and current Treaty issues in an historical context and encouraged me to hope for and consider new possibilities for a more united nation maintaining our uniqueness in a relentless global village. It has raised my awareness of the plight of indigenous peoples around the globe and strengthened my resolve to work in solidarity with them for justice.

For the past 20 years I have worked with a national network of Maori and Pakeha to create a programme that would enable New Zealanders to learn about and courageously confront our colonial history. The response from the people in our Treaty education workshops is inspiring. The commitment is growing. The way forward is grounded in our growing sense of national identity, which is fundamentally rooted in honouring Te Tiriti O Waitangi and our unique relationship with Maori.

I remember with gratitude the Sisters who taught me as a child to see my life in the light of eternity. They enabled me to view my journey as a continuum in relationship to my ancestors. The philosophy I absorbed has profoundly influenced me to make constructive choices in a world where hunger, war, racism, poverty, despair and hopelessness exist. Yet for me, the paradox of hope remains. I have always managed to maintain faith in my own humanity and a belief in the divine spark in every human being. This hope is constantly nurtured in my relationships with my family, community and a network of people throughout New Zealand and other parts of the world. Maintaining faith when you don't know the reality of suffering can be relatively straightforward. Maintaining faith when you do is the challenge.

APPENDIX I

A DECLARATION OF THE INDEPENDENCE OF NEW ZEALAND
(1835)

1. We the hereditary chiefs and heads of the tribes of the Northern parts of New Zealand, being assembled at Waitangi, in the Bay of Islands, on this 28th day of October 1835, declare the Independence of our country, which is hereby constituted and declared to be an Independent State, under the designation of the United Tribes of New Zealand.

2. All sovereign power and authority within the territories of the United Tribes of New Zealand is hereby declared to reside entirely and exclusively in the hereditary chiefs and heads of tribes in their collective capacity, who also declare that they will not permit any legislative authority separate from themselves in their collective capacity to exist, nor any function of government to be exercised within the said territories, unless by persons appointed by them, and acting under the authority of laws regularly enacted by them in Congress assembled.

3. The hereditary chiefs and heads of tribes agree to meet in Congress at Waitangi in the autumn of each year, for the purpose of framing laws for the dispensation of justice, the preservation of peace and good order, and the regulation of trade; and they cordially invite the Southern tribes to lay aside their private animosities and to consult the safety and welfare of our common country, by joining the Confederation of the United Tribes.

4. They also agree to send a copy of this Declaration to His Majesty the King of England, to thank him for his acknowledgement of their flag, and in return for the friendship and protection they have shown, and are prepared to show, to such of his subjects as have settled in their country, or resorted to its shores for the purposes of trade, they entreat that he will continue to be the parent of their infant State, and that he will become its Protector from all attempts upon its independence.

Agreed to unanimously on this 28th day of October, 1835, in the presence of His Britannic Majesty's Resident.

[Here follow the signatures or marks of thirty-five hereditary chiefs or Heads of tribes, which form a fair representation of the tribes of New Zealand from the North Cape to the latitude of the River Thames.]

English witnesses—

(signed)   Henry Williams, Missionary, C.M.S.
George Clarke, C.M.S.
James C. Clendon, Merchant.
Gilbert Mair, Merchant.

I certify that the above is correct copy of the Declaration of the Chiefs, according to the translation of Missionaries who have resided ten years and upwards in the country; and it is transmitted to his Most Gracious Majesty the King of England, at the unanimous request of the chiefs.

(signed)   JAMES BUSBY,
British Resident at New Zealand

He Wakaputanga o te Rangatiratanga o Nu Tirene

1. KO MATOU, ko nga tino Rangatira o nga iwi o NU TIRENE i raro mai o Haurake, kua oti nei te huihui i Waitangi, i Tokerau, i te ra 28 o Oketopa, 1835. Ka wakaputa i te Rangatiratanga o to matou wenua; a ka meatia ka wakaputaia e matou he Wenua Rangatira, kia huaina, 'Ko te Wakaminenga o nga Hapu o Nu Tirene'.

2. Ko te Kingitanga, ko te mana i te wenua o te wakaminenga o Nu Tirene, ka meatia nei kei nga tino Rangatira anake i to matou huihuinga; a ka mea hoki, e kore e tukua e matou te wakarite ture ki tetahi hunga ke atu, me tetahi Kawanatanga hoki kia meatia i te wenua o te wakaminenga o Nu Tirene, ko nga tangata anake e meatia nei e matou, e wakarite ana ki te ritenga o o matou ture e meatia nei e matou i to matou huihuinga.

3. Ko matou, ko nga tino Rangitira, ka mea nei, kia huihui ki te runanga ki Waitangi a te Ngahuru i tenei tau i tenei tau, ki te wakarite ture, kia tika ai te wakawakanga, kia mau pu te rongo, kia mutu te he, kia tika te hokohoko. A ka mea hoki ki nga tauiwi o runga, kia wakarerea te wawai, kia mahara ai ki te wakaoranga o to matou wenua, a kia uru ratou ki te wakaminenga o Nu Tirene.

4. Ka mea matou, kia tuhituhia he pukapuka, ki te ritenga o tenei o to matou wakaputanga nei; ki te Kingi o Ingarani, hei kawe atu i to matou aroha, nana hoki i wakaae ki te Kara mo matou. A no te mea ka atawai matou, ka tiaki i nga Pakeha e noho nei uta, e rere mai ana ki te hokohoko, koia ka mea ai matou ki te Kingi kia waiho hei Matua ki a matou i to matou tamarikitanga, kei wakakahoretia to matou Rangatiratanga.

Kua wakaaetia katoatia e matou i tenei ra, i te 28 o Oketopa 1835, ki te aroaro o te Rehirenete o te Kingi o Ingarani.

APPENDIX 2

TE TIRITI O WAITANGI 1840

Ko Wikitoria, te Kuini o Ingarani, i tana mahara atawai ki nga Rangatira me Nga Hapu o Nu Tirani, i tana hiahia hoki kia tohungia kia ratou o ratou rangatiratanga, me to ratou wenua, a kia mau tonu hoki te Rongo ki a ratou me te ata noho hoki, kua wakaaro ia he mea tika kia tukua mai tetahi Rangatira hei kai wakarite ki nga tangata Maori o Nu Tirani. Kia wakaaetia e nga Rangatira Maori te Kawanatanga o te Kuini, ki nga wahi katoa o te wenua nei me nga motu. Na te mea hoki he to komaha ke nga tangata o tona iwi kua noho ki tenei wenua, a e haere mai nei.

Na, ko te Kuini e hiahia ana kia wakaritea te Kawanatanga, kia kaua ai nga kino e puta mai ki te tangata Maori ki te pakeha e noho ture kore ana.

Na, kua pai te Kuini kia tukua a hau, a Wiremu Hopihona, he Kapitana i te Roiara Nawia, hei Kawana mo nga wahi katoa o Nu Tirani, e tukua aianei amua atu ki te Kuini; e mea atu ana ia ki nga Rangatira o te Wakaminenga o nga Hapu o Nu Tirani me, era Rangatira atu, enei ture ka korerotia nei.

Ko te Tuatahi

Ko nga Rangatira o te Wakaminenga, me nga Rangatira katoa hoki, kihai i uru ki taua Wakaminenga, ka tuku rawa atu ki te Kuini o Ingarani ake tonu atu te Kawanatanga katoa o o ratou wenua.

Ko te Tuarua

Ko te Kuini o Ingarani ka wakarite ka whakaae ki nga Rangatira ki nga Hapu, ki nga tangata katoa o Nu Tirani, te tino Rangatiratanga o o ratou wenua o ratou kainga me o ratou taonga katoa. Otiia ko nga Rangatira o te Wakaminenga, me nga Rangatira katoa atu, ka tuku ki te Kuini te hokonga o era wahi wenua e pai ai te tangata nona te wenua, ki te ritenga o te utu e wakaritea ai e ratou ko te kai hoko e meatia nei i te Kuini hei kai hoko mona.

Ko te Tuatoru

He wakaritenga mai hoki tenei mo te wakaaetanga ki te Kawanatanga o te Kuini. Ka tiakina e te Kuini o Ingarani nga tangata Maori katoa o Nu Tirani. Ka tukua ki a ratou nga tikanga katoa rite tahi ki ana mea ki nga tangata o Ingarani.

(Signed) WILLIAM HOBSON,
Consul and Lieutenant-Governor

Na, ko matou, ko nga Rangatira o te Wakaminenga o nga Hapu o Nu Tirani, ka huihui nei ki Waitangi. Ko matou hoki ko nga Rangatira o Nu Tirani, ka kite nei i te ritenga o enei kupu, ka tangohia, ka wakaaetia katoatia e matou. Koia ka tohungia ai o matou ingoa o matou tohu.

Ka meatia tenei ki Waitangi, i te ono o nga ra o Pepuere, i te tau kotahi mano, e waru rau, e wa tekau, o to tatou Ariki.

[Here follow the 512 signatures, dates, and locations]

THE TREATY OF WAITANGI:
A TRANSLATION OF THE MAORI TEXT*

VICTORIA, the Queen of England, in her concern to protect the chiefs and sub-tribes of New Zealand and in her desire to preserve their chieftainship and their lands to them and to maintain peace and good order considers it just to appoint an administrator, one who will negotiate with the people of New Zealand to the end that their chiefs will agree to the Queen's Government being established over all parts of this land and (adjoining) islands and also because there are many of her subjects already living on this land and others yet to come.

So the Queen desires to establish a government so that no evil will come to Maori and European living in a state of lawlessness.

So the Queen has appointed me, William Hobson a captain in the Royal Navy, to be Governor for all parts of New Zealand (both those) shortly to be received by the Queen and (those) to be received hereafter and presents to the chiefs of the Confederation chiefs of the sub-tribes of New Zealand and other chiefs these laws set out here.

The First

The Chiefs of the Confederation and all the chiefs who have not joined that Confederation give absolutely to the Queen of England forever the complete government over their land.

The Second

The Queen of England agrees to protect the Chiefs, the sub-tribes and all the people of New Zealand in the unqualified exercise of their chieftainship over their lands, villages and all their treasures. But on the other hand the Chiefs of the Confederation and all the Chiefs will sell land to the Queen at a price agreed to by the person owning it and by the person buying it (the latter being) appointed by the Queen as her purchase agent.

The Third

For this agreed arrangement therefore concerning the Government of the Queen, the Queen of England will protect all the ordinary people of New Zealand and will give them the same rights and duties of citizenship as the people of England.

(Signed)   WILLIAM HOBSON,
Consul and Lieutenant-Governor

So we, the Chiefs of the Confederation and the sub-tribes of New Zealand meeting here at Waitangi having seen the shape of these words which we accept and agree to record our names and marks thus.

Was done at Waitangi on the sixth day of February in the year of our Lord 1840

* I.H. Kawharu, *Waitangi: Maori and Pakeha Perspectives of the Treaty of Waitangi,* (I.H. Kawharu is Professor of Maori Studies University of Auckland: Ngati Whatua and Mahurehure.)

The Treaty of Waitangi: An English Version 1840

HER MAJESTY VICTORIA Queen of the United Kingdom of Great Britain and Ireland regarding with Her Royal Favour the Native Chiefs and Tribes of New Zealand and anxious to protect their just Rights and Property and to secure to them the enjoyment of Peace and Good Order has deemed it necessary in consequence of the great number of Her Majesty's Subjects who have already settled in New Zealand and the rapid extension of Emigration both from Europe and Australia which is still in progress to constitute and appoint a functionary properly authorised to treat with the Aborigines of New Zealand for the recognition of Her Majesty's Sovereign authority over the whole or any part of those islands—Her Majesty therefore being desirous to establish a settled form of Civil Government with a view to avert the evil consequences which must result from the absence of the necessary Laws and Institutions alike to the native population and to Her subjects, has been graciously pleased to empower and to authorise me William Hobson a Captain in Her Majesty's Royal Navy Consul and Lieutenant Governor of such parts of New Zealand as may be or hereafter shall be ceded to her Majesty to invite the confederated and independent Chiefs of New Zealand to concur in the following Articles and Conditions.

Article the First

The Chiefs of the Confederation of the United Tribes of New Zealand and the separate and independent Chiefs who have not become members of the Confederation cede to Her Majesty the Queen of England absolutely and without reservation all the rights and powers of Sovereignty which the said Confederation or Individual Chiefs respectively exercise or possess or may be supposed to exercise or to possess over their respective Territories as the sole Sovereigns thereof.

Article the Second

Her Majesty the Queen of England confirms and guarantees to the Chiefs and Tribes of New Zealand and to the respective families and individuals thereof the full, exclusive, and undisturbed possession of their Lands and Estates Forests Fisheries and other properties which they may collectively or individually possess so long as it is their wish and desire to retain the same in their possession; but the chiefs of the United Tribes and the individual Chiefs yield to Her Majesty the exclusive right of pre-emption over such lands as the proprietors thereof may be disposed to alienate—at such prices as may be agreed upon between the respective Proprietors and persons appointed by Her Majesty to treat with them in that behalf.

Article the Third

In consideration thereof Her Majesty the Queen of England extends to the Natives of New Zealand Her royal protection, and imparts to them all the Rights and Privileges of British Subjects.

WILLIAM HOBSON
Lieutenant Governor

Now, therefore We the Chiefs of the Confederation of the United Tribes of New Zealand being assembled in Congress at Victoria in Waitangi and We the Separate and Independent Chiefs of New Zealand claiming authority over the Tribes and Territories which are specified after our respective names, having been made fully to understand the Provisions of the foregoing Treaty, accept and enter into the same in the full spirit and meaning thereof: in witness of which we have attached our signatures or marks at the places and the dates respectively specified.

Done at Waitangi this Sixth day of February in the year of Our Lord one thousand eight hundred and forty.

APPENDIX 3

Journeys of Discovery: Stories

Ottawa, Canada, 1997

I was honoured with an invitation to facilitate a workshop in Canada with the Royal Canadian Mounted Police. It was the Mounties who centuries ago enforced colonial law on the First Nation Peoples of Canada, violating their historical treaties, dispossessing them of their land and their traditional way of life, including banning their language, and ceremonial and spiritual gatherings.

This history no doubt contributed to the RCMP decision to consider anti-racism training. The New Zealand process of parallel training, using action methods and integrating personal story, was described as the breakthrough they needed to intensify the work already started.

The response to my presentation was very positive. At the end, a retired Jewish professor, who had made very thoughtful contributions, rose to his feet. He could hardly contain his excitement, saying: 'I have been everywhere and I have heard everything. Because of that, I am not easily impressed, but I am deeply impressed at what I have heard this afternoon'.

Tens of thousands of New Zealanders have attended Treaty education workshops. The feedback has been overwhelmingly positive, encouraging other New Zealanders to attend. Here, four New Zealanders and two Canadians comment on their experience of Treaty workshops.

Paul Fitzharris

Assistant Commissioner, New Zealand Police, 2000

Some police were antagonistic to the idea of the workshop because they felt that they had been coerced into attendance. The programme was enjoyable and very soon some of those who were there under sufferance became considerably more relaxed. It became apparent that earlier entrenched views about the Treaty were turned around.

The big, most difficult issues were put out front from the very outset and members were able to discuss and debate these issues immediately and robustly. Everyone attending that and subsequent workshops learned something about New Zealand's colonial history, and in particular the meaning and implications of the Treaty of Waitangi.

Dr Lesley McTurk

General Manager Healthcare Delivery, Southern Cross Healthcare, 2000

I first had contact with Waitangi Associates in 1996 when I was chief executive of Mercy Hospital in Auckland, and they provided a series of Treaty workshops to staff and board members. The staff who participated came back with extremely positive feedback. The workshops affirmed the cultural identity of participants and offered them a good understanding of the historical and contemporary issues surrounding the Treaty of Waitangi. This perspective was enlightening for many and brought a new level of understanding and tolerance into the workplace about what are often sensitive issues.

Robert created an enjoyable and non-confrontational learning environment for all participants, by providing accurate information and presenting a range of viewpoints so that all participants could draw their own conclusions. This learning environment was especially valued in workshops where there were a range of participants with a variety of experience and prior knowledge.

Professor Bruce Ross
Director General, Ministry of Agriculture and Forestry, 2000
I have sponsored presentations by Waitangi Associates in two different organisations, and have attended four myself, both to show my support and to monitor what is going on. The response to the workshops has been almost universally enthusiastic, with people coming away feeling much better informed, not only about Maori attitudes and grievances, but about themselves. There is also an extraordinarily high commitment among attendees to work towards a better New Zealand society.

Helen Matthews
Staff Developer, Christchurch Polytechnic Institute of Technology, 2000
In the late 1980s I was invited to become a trainer for Project Waitangi and attended a training programme based at the Polytechnic. This was my first real experience of the Treaty workshop process. I experienced the importance of a respectful process as participants coped with painful and shocking new awareness.

The process used by Waitangi Associates to achieve awareness is just as important as the content of the workshops. The process remains respectful, affirming and challenging, yet staff consistently emerge keen to go further on their learning journey. Our challenge as individuals and as an institution is to ensure this learning continues.

Darlene Sanderson
Victoria, British Columbia, 2000
The workshop had a significant impact on me. The magnitude of the problems generated by colonisation fairly blew me away. Yet the workshop had taken away the threatening nature of cross-cultural learning, opening the mind to allow learning to occur, and enabling a transformation of the heart to take place. This was not a workshop of 'talking heads' and lectures, but a workshop where emotions play a part in learning. The workshop gave me hope that there is the potential for this transformation to take place for other peoples in other settings. At this point, I knew we needed this process back home in Canada!

Ronnie Joy Leah, PhD

'Honouring our Stories' Director, Circle of Learning, Calgary, Alberta, Canada, 2000

I met Robert Consedine during his 1996 Canadian tour, and with his encouragement I developed a Canadian version of the Treaty workshop. The challenge was to adapt the basic process to the Canadian setting, to consult with the local aboriginal community, and to incorporate relevant resources, videos and learning activities.

Honouring our Stories workshops begin with the premise: 'Before you can respect other cultures, you must first honour your own culture.' As I facilitate workshops for other people—honouring each person's culture—I simultaneously do my own work: honouring who I am and *why* I am. This process has changed my life in profound ways. It has enabled me to 'work from the heart': to accept other people as they are; to engage in a process of deep self-awareness; to let go of negative prejudices and misconceptions; to work towards change in ideas and actions. I find myself modelling the behaviour I wish to encourage in workshop participants.

At the beginning of a workshop, participants usually raise the same kinds of questions:

- Why can't Native people get on with it? Why can't they just forget the past? Why are they stuck in history?

- Why do they blame us for the past? We didn't steal their land. Why are they still angry at us?

- Why do they want special treatment? The rules should be the same for everyone. Isn't it fair to treat everyone the same?

By the end of a workshop, people have begun to answer their own questions. According to their written comments on the participant evaluations, people say they have gained: 'self-awareness . . . insight into my own history and feelings ... awareness about the importance of culture . . . new insights about aboriginal people . . . better understanding of Native culture ... more about First Nations history, challenges, perspectives . . .'

Conclusion

Thousands of New Zealanders have had a positive experience of attending Treaty education workshops, and leave feeling open and encouraged to learn more. Yet, I do not wish to paint an idealistic outcome of what Treaty workshops achieve. Participants have different levels of knowledge and different expectations of what they would like to learn. It is the task of the workshop leader to assess where the group is at in order to determine the content and processes needed for a particular workshop. Inevitably at times the workshop does not meet everyone's needs.

Treaty workshops are one way New Zealanders can become more informed about the current debate. Racism, fear and division will continue if majority cultures are not taught this information and given the space to process it. The positive feedback we have collected from all of the participants suggests that the unique combination of tools and techniques used does work.

APPENDIX: 4

United Nations Working Definition of Indigenous Peoples

The first part of the working definition adopted by the United Nations Working Group on Indigenous Populations in 1982 reads:

> *Indigenous populations are composed of the existing descendants of peoples who inhabited the present territory of a country wholly or partially at the time when persons of a different culture or ethnic origin arrived there from other parts of the world, overcame them, and by conquest, settlement or other means, reduced them to a non-dominant or colonial situation; who today live more in conformity with their particular social, economic and cultural customs and traditions than with the institutions of the country of which they now form a part, under a state structure which incorporates mainly the national, social and cultural characteristics of other segments of the population which are predominant.*

The second part of the definition addresses the situation of isolated and marginal populations:

> *Although they have not suffered conquest or colonisation, isolated or marginal groups existing in the country should also be regarded as covered by the notion of 'indigenous populations' for the following reasons:*
> a) *they are descendants of groups which were in the territory at the time when other groups of different cultures or ethnic origins arrived there;*
> b) *precisely because of their isolation from other segments of the country's population they have preserved almost intact the customs and traditions of their ancestors which are similar to those characteristics as indigenous; and*

c) they are, even if only formally, placed under a state structure which incorporates national, social and cultural characteristics alien to theirs.

Source: UN Economic and Social Council Commission on Human Rights, Preliminary Report on the Problem of Discrimination Against Indigenous Populations. UN Document E/CN.4/Sub.2L.566, Chapter 11. From Franke Wilmer (1993), *The Indigenous Voice in World Politics*, Sage Publications, California.

GLOSSARY

aboriginal — A generic term referring to people living on the land at the time of colonial settlement.

Aboriginal — Pertaining specifically to Australian Aborigines.

contra-proferentem — A principle that applies in international law in the case of any ambiguity. It means a provision should be interpreted against the party who drafts it and that an indigenous-language text takes precedence.

First Nations — The collective name for Canadian aboriginal Indian peoples.

hapu — Sub-tribe, descendants, a group of families.

hui — Meeting.

iwi — People, tribe(s).

indigenous peoples — Indigenous peoples are referred to in the plural to acknowledge their unique status and diverse nature of collective existence.

kaitiaki — Guardianship.

Kai Tahu/Ngai Tahu — The terms Kai Tahu and Ngai Tahu have been used interchangeably. This is to acknowledge that Ngai is pronounced Gai or Kai in the southern Maori dialect.

kawanatanga — Governance.

mahinga kai — Traditional food and other natural resources.

mana — Authority, prestige, sovereignty.

mana whenua — Title, customary rights over land, sovereignty over land.

Maori peoples	Some Maori prefer to identify as Maori; others prefer to identify in terms of their iwi, hapu and whanau and in terms of their status as indigenous peoples; others identify primarily as New Zealanders and/or some as a combination of the foregoing. While we respect the sensitivity of this issue for many, we refer most often to Maori or Maori peoples in the interests of brevity.
Pakeha	'Pakeha is a unique and indigenous word for the non-Maori settler of Aotearoa/New Zealand [and] implies an acceptance of Maori as a separate cultural entity . . . a relationship with Maori as a Treaty partner, a cultural identity for people of Northern European origin and a sense of uniquely belonging to Aotearoa/New Zealand.'*
pre-emption	Sole right of the Crown to purchase property.
rangatiratanga	Chieftainship, authority.
rohe	Tribal area.
tangata whenua	Person or people of a given place.
taonga	Treasures, cultural heritage.
terra nullius	Empty land.
tikanga	Custom(s).
tino rangatiratanga	The unqualified exercise of chieftainship, highest chieftainship.
whakapapa	Genealogy.
whanau	Extended family.
whanaungatanga	Kinship.
whenua	Land.

* Rose Black, 'Political Implications of the Name "Pakeha"' in *Living Justly in Aotearoa Newsletter*, October 2000, Issue Three, Catholic Justice and Peace Office, Auckland, p. 1.

NOTES

Please note: (1) Where an article appears in a book, details of the book appear in the 'Book' section of the Bibliography; in other instances, the article appears in the 'Articles' section. (2) Where a source is marked 'website' in the Notes, details of the source and the relevant website can be found at 'Websites' in the Bibliography.

Preface
1 Speeches and news releases can be accessed on the websites of both political parties:
New Zealand National Party
http://www.national.org.nz/;
New Zealand Labour Party
http://www.labour.org.nz/
2 Arundhati Roy, *Power Politics*, p. 137.

Introduction
1 For definitions of Maori and Pakeha, see glossary.
2 I am very grateful to Frances Hancock for developing my understanding of the term 'right relationship'. It is a theological term used to describe a relationship defined by justice, where every component is in balance.

Chapter 1
1 Lyndon Fraser, *To Tara via Holyhead*, p. 111.

Chapter 2
1 Bangladesh is one of the poorest countries in the world. Over 100 million people live in an area smaller than the South Island of New Zealand. The country was formed in 1971 from territories that previously formed the eastern part of Pakistan after the locals' demand for greater autonomy was rejected by the military Pakistani government. The ensuring civil war left over a million people dead and caused a massive exodus of refugees to India.
2 Dhaka is the capital of

Bangladesh. It is often referred to as 'the Bread Basket of the World' by the United Nations because of the level of extreme poverty.

3 J. M. Blaut, *The Colonizer's Model of the World*, p. 51.

4 Ibid., p. 206.

5 Kent McNeil, *Common Law Aboriginal Title*, p. 110.

6 Robin Neillands, *A Fighting Retreat: The British Empire 1947–1997*, p. 17.

7 Richard H. Bartlett, *The Mabo Decision*, p. 1X.

8 Maire and Conor Cruise O'Brien, *Ireland: A Concise History*, p. 55.

9 Line from the song 'Famine', by Sinead O'Connor.

10 Tim Pat Coogan, *The I.R.A.*, p. 404.

11 Peter Harbison, *Pre-Christian Ireland: From the First Settlers to the Early Celts*, p. 19.

12 Else Roesdahl, *The Vikings*, pp. 221–30.

13 For a full explanation of this process, see Theodore W. Allen, 'Social Control and the Intermediate Strata: Ireland' in *The Invention of the White Race: Racial Opposition and Control*, Vol. 1, p. 53.

14 Ibid., p. 59.

15 Maire and Conor Cruise O'Brien, op. cit., p. 61.

16 Theodore W. Allen, op. cit., p. 82.

17 Noel Ignatiev, *How the Irish Became White*, p. 35.

18 Maire and Conor Cruise O'Brien, op. cit., p. 78.

19 Ibid., p. 77.

20 Noel Ignatiev, op. cit., p. 35.

21 Thoeodore W. Allen, op. cit., p. 87.

22 Robert Kee, *The Laurel and the Ivy: The Story of Charles Stewart Parnell and Irish Nationalism*, p. 290.

23 For a description of the process see Theodore W. Allen, op. cit., p. 92.

24 John Coolahan, 'The Irish and Others in Irish Nineteenth-century Textbooks' in J. A. Mangan (ed.), *The Imperial Curriculum: Racial Images and Education in the British Colonial Experience*, p. 55.

25 Ibid.

26 Hazel Waters, 'The Great Famine and the Rise of Anti-Irish Racism', *Journal of Race and Class*, p. 98.

27 Tim Pat Coogan, *The Troubles: Ireland's Ordeal 1966–1996 and the Search for Peace*, p. 10.

28 Hazel Waters, op. cit., p. 98.

29 Maire and Conor Cruise O'Brien, op. cit., p. 105.

30 From a population of about 8.2 million in 1841, more than one million people died between 1842 and 1850. Over 1.8 million people emigrated from 1847–55 and 65,000 families were evicted by landlords between 1847 and 1851. See Cecil Woodham-Smith, *The Great Hunger*, p. 26, and Christine Kinealy, *This Great Calamity: The Irish Famine 1845–1852*, pp. 168, 298, 218.

31 Tim Pat Coogan, *The I.R.A.*, pp. 27–28.

32 For a detailed description of the creation of Northern Ireland, see Anthony Carty, *Was Ireland*

Conquered? International Law and the Irish Question, pp. 135–66.

33 Ibid., p. 136.

34 Ibid., p. 135.

35 Desmond Wilson, *Democracy Denied*, pp. 18–19.

36 Ibid., p. 31.

37 Tim Pat Coogan, *The Troubles*, p. 37.

38 Ibid., p. 38.

39 Ibid., p. 34.

40 Desmond Wilson, op. cit., p. 25.

41 Tim Pat Coogan, *The Troubles*, p. 25.

42 Tim Pat Coogan, *The I.R.A.*, p. 363.

43 Ibid., p. 371.

44 Philip Ferguson, 'Ireland: The End of National Liberation' in *New Zealand Monthly Review*, No. 353, 1996.

45 Fintan O'Toole, 'Are the Troubles Over?' in *The New York Review*, 5 October 2000, p. 12.

46 Cheryl Coull, *A Traveller's Guide to Aboriginal B.C.*, p. 1.

47 Frank Cassidy, 'Aboriginal Land Claims in British Columbia', in Ken Coates (ed.), *Aboriginal Land Claims in Canada: A Regional Perspective*, p. 11. Over 40 per cent of all native peoples in Canada today live within the boundaries of British Columbia. The decline in the indigenous population followed a similar pattern in New Zealand.

48 Olive Patricia Dickason, *Canada's First Nations: A History of Founding Peoples from Earliest Times*, p. 206.

49 Wilson Duff, *The Indian History of British Columbia, Vol. 1: The Impact of the White Man*, p. 45.

50 Ibid., p. 42.

51 Statistics Canada, *2001 Census: Analysis Series, Aboriginal Peoples of Canada: A Demographic Profile*.

52 Cheryl Coull, op. cit., p. 1.

53 Olive Patricia Dickason, op. cit., p. 13.

54 Ibid., p. 233. The British proclamation of 1763 applied only to Upper Canada. With the Act of Union of 1841 Upper Canada became Canada West and Lower Canada became Canada East. The Dominion of Canada was created in 1867.

55 Shin Imai, *The 1997 Annotated Indian Act*, p. 322.

56 Hamar Foster, 'Canada: Indian Administration from the Royal Proclamation of 1763 to Constitutionally Entrenched Aboriginal Rights' in Paul Havemann (ed.), *Indigenous People's Rights in Australia, Canada and New Zealand*, p. 355.

57 Caren Wickliffe, *Report on Indigenous Claims and the Process of Negotiation and Settlement in Countries with Jurisdictions and Populations Similar to New Zealand's*, report for the Office of the Parliamentary Commissioner for the Environment, p. 32.

58 Hamar Foster, op. cit., p. 355.

59 Robin Fisher, 'With or Without Treaty: Indian Land Claims in Western Canada' in William Renwick (ed.), *Sovereignty and Indigenous Rights: The Treaty of Waitangi in International Contexts*, p. 54.

60 Ibid.

61 Hamar Foster, op. cit., p. 360.

62 Paul Tennant, *Aboriginal Peoples and Politics: The Indian Land Question in British Columbia 1849–1989*, p. 37.

63 Ibid., p. 39.

64 Robin Fisher, op. cit., p. 55.

65 Ibid., pp. 55–56.

66 James S. Frideres, *Native Peoples in Canada: Contemporary Conflicts*, p. 53.

67 Frank Cassidy, op. cit., p. 13.

68 For a full discussion of the early enfranchisement issue, see Olive Patricia Dickason, op. cit., pp. 251–72.

69 Hamar Foster, op. cit., p. 364.

70 Caren Wickcliffe, op. cit., p. 33.

71 Hamar Foster, op. cit., p. 366.

72 Ibid., p. 367.

73 Paul Havemann (ed.), *Indigenous Peoples' Rights in Australia, Canada and New Zealand*, p. 45. This policy acknowledged the *Calder* finding and stated 'that claims based on aboriginal title where not superseded by law or extinguished by treaty could be considered for recognition and compensation'.

74 This information was summarised from the paper *Treaty Negotiations in British Columbia*, published by the Ministry of Aboriginal Affairs (British Columbia), website.

75 *Delgamuukw v. British Columbia*, Court of Appeal File, 1997, website.

76 *Aboriginal Poverty Law Manual*, pp. 3–4, website.

77 Glen Coulthard, *Colonization, Indian Policy, Suicide, and Aboriginal Peoples*, p. 2, website.

78 Native Title and the Trans

Tasman Experience Conference (Mabo) Papers, Sydney, 24–25 February 1994.

79 Henry Reynolds, *The Law of the Land*, p. 12.

80 Ibid., p. 7.

81 Richard H. Bartlett, *The Mabo Decision*, p. V.

82 Henry Reynolds op. cit., p. 8.

83 Henry Reynolds, *Frontier: Reports from the Edge of White Settlement*, p. 53.

84 Henry Reynolds, *Why Weren't We Told? A Personal Search for the Truth About our History*, p. 113.

85 Henry Reynolds, *The Law of the Land*, p. 19.

86 Ibid., p. 13.

87 Stewart Firth and Robert Darlington, 'Racial Stereotypes in the Australian Curriculum: The Case Study of New South Wales' in J. A. Mangan (ed.), *The Imperial Curriculum: Racial Images and Education in the British Colonial Experience*, pp. 82–83.

88 Henry Reynolds, *Why Weren't We Told?*, p. 94.

89 Colin Tatz, *Genocide in Australia*, AIATSIS Research Discussion Paper, No. 8, p. 10, website.

90 For a useful discussion on genocide in Australia with particular reference to Queensland, see Alison Palmer, *Colonial Genocide*.

91 Colin Tatz, op. cit., p. 2.

92 Ibid., p. 6.

93 Hal Wootten, *Eddie Mabo's Case and its Implications for Australia*, (Mabo) Papers. p. 2.

94 Colin Tatz, *With Intent to*

Destroy: Reflecting on Genocide, pp. 104–105.

95 The Mabo decision is discussed in Chapter 11.

96 Peter Read, *A Rape of the Soul So Profound* provides an insight into this tragedy.

97 M. Annette Jaimes, *The State of Native America: Genocide, Colonization and Resistance*, p. 7.

98 For a description of the population figures, see Oren Lyons et al. (eds), *Exiled in the Land of the Free*, p. 48.

99 Linda Tuhiwai Smith, *Decolonizing Methodologies: Research and Indigenous Peoples*, p. 1.

100 Zohl de Ishtar (ed.) *Pacific Women Speak Out for Independence and Denuclearisation*.

Chapter 3

1 Lee Cohen, *Miingignoti-Keteaoag Legal Issues*, website. For a copy of the Jay Treaty and case law, see Shin Imai, *The 1997 Annotated Indian Act*, pp. 318–20.

2 J. R. Miller, *Shingwauk's Vision: A History of Native Residential Schools*. Chapter 14 provides a chilling assessment of the residential school system, from which this information is drawn.

3 Ibid., p. 438.

4 Ibid., p. 9.

5 I am deeply indebted to Father Michael Stogre S. J. for his seminal work *That the World May Believe: The Development of Papal Social Thought on Aboriginal Rights*. This summary and interpretation of his work is entirely my own. Two other books that canvass these and related issues are *Slavery and the Catholic Church: The History of Catholic Teaching Concerning the Moral Legitimacy of the Institution of Slavery* by John Francis Maxwell, and *Popes, Lawyers and Infidels* by James Muldoon.

6 John Francis Maxwell, ibid., p. 56.

7 George E. Tinker, *Missionary Conquest: The Gospel and Native Cultural Genocide*, p. 19.

8 Bartolomé de Las Casas, *In Defense of Indians*. This was an extraordinary document for its time.

9 Michael Stogre, op. cit., pp. 82–84.

10 J. M. Blaut, *The Colonizer's Model of the World: Geographical Diffusionism and Eurocentric History*, p. 24.

11 Francis Paul Prucha, *The Great Father: The United States Government and the American Indians*, p. 519.

12 George E. Tinker, op. cit., p. 6.

13 Ibid., p. 4.

14 Ibid., p. 5.

15 Ibid., p. 7.

16 Paul Tennant, *Aboriginal Peoples and Politics: The Indian Land Question in British Columbia 1849–1989*, p. 7.

17 Ibid., pp. 51–52.

18 Raeburn Lange, *May the People Live: A History of Maori Health Development 1900–1920*, pp. 242–62.

19 Mason Durie, *Whaiora: Maori Health Development*, 2nd ed., p. 44.

20 Ibid., p. 45.

21 Anne Pattel-Gray, *Through*

Aboriginal Eyes: The Cry from the Wilderness, p. 79.

22 Colin Tatz, *Genocide in Australia*, AIATSIS Research Discussion Paper, No. 8, p. 19, website.

23 Synod of Catholic Bishops, *Justice in the World*, p. 6.

24 Michael Stogre, op. cit., p. 152.

25 Ibid.

26 Richard Pablo, 'Inculturation Defends Human, Cosmic Life'. *National Catholic Reporter*, 19 December 1997, website. For further study on the Catholic Church and inculturation, see an excellent critique by Ivan Illich, *The Church: Change and Development* and an inspiring vision in Vincent J. Donovan, *Christianity Rediscovered: An Epistle from the Mesai*.

27 Michael Stogre, op. cit., p. 254.

28 Ibid., p. 211.

29 The School of the Americas, often known as the School of Assassins, is located in Fort Benning in Florida and funded by the US government. This school trains military dictators in torture, death squads and other human rights atrocities, and is one of the primary bases for CIA covert operations. Every year more than 10,000 Americans demonstrate to have it closed. A well-documented analysis of the role of the School of the Americas in the training of Third World dictators can be found in Jack Nelson-Pallmeyer, *School of Assassins*.

30 *National Catholic Reporter*, 2 June 2000, website.

31 Vincent J. Donovan, *The Church in the Midst of Creation*, p. 4.

32 George E. Tinker, op. cit., p. 56.

33 *New York Review*, 25 May 2000, pp. 19–20. The original article can be obtained from Joseph Cardinal Ratzinger, International Theological Association, Vatican, website.

34 John Dominic Crossan, *Who Killed Jesus?*

35 Raul Hilberg, *The Destruction of the European Jews*, pp. 10–12.

36 Rabbi Leon Klenicki, Commentary on *The Holocaust Never to be Forgotten: Reflections on the Holy See's Document We Remember*, p. 29.

37 John Cornwell, *Hitler's Pope: The Secret History of Pius XII*; Michael Phayer, *The Catholic Church and the Holocaust: 1930–1965*; Maureen Fiedler and Linda Rabben (eds), *Rome Has Spoken: A Guide to Forgotten Papal Statements and How They Have Changed Through the Centuries*; James Carroll, *Constantine's Sword: The Church and the Jews: A History*; Henri de Lubac, *Christian Resistance to Anti-Semitism: Memories from 1940–1944*; David I. Kertzer, *The Popes Against the Jews: The Vatican's Role in the Rise of Modern Anti-Semitism*; Daniel Jonah Goldhagen, *A Moral Reckoning: The Role of the Catholic Church in the Holocaust and its Unfulfilled Duty of Repair*; Susan Zuccotti, *Under His Very Windows: The Vatican and the Holocaust in Italy*.

38 Elizabeth A. Johnson E. S. J., 'Galileo's Daughters' in

Commonweal, 19 November 1999, p. 18.

39 John Francis Maxwell, op. cit., p. 13.

40 Ibid., p. 10.

41 Michel Chossudovsky has written an excellent analysis of the current world economic system: *The Globalisation of Poverty: Impacts of IMF and World Bank Reforms*.

42 Richard Pablo, 'The South Will Judge the North: The Church Between Globalisation and Inculturation' in Gary MacEoin (ed.), *The Papacy and the People of God*, p. 134.

43 A contemporary analysis of the corruption within the Roman Catholic Vatican power structure comes from Pulitzer Prize-winning author Garry Wills in *Papal Sin: Structures of Deceit*. The thesis of this book is that every era of papal history has its own besetting vice. The medieval papacy was consumed by lust for political power, as the renaissance popes were consumed by avarice for riches. Today, Wills argues, the structural sin characteristic of the papacy is intellectual dishonesty.

44 *National Catholic Reporter*, 27 October 2000, website.

45 *Declaration of Vision: Toward The Next 500 Years*, p. 1, website.

46 Ibid., p. 1. See also Valerie Taliman, *Revoke the Inter Cetera Bull*, website.

47 Tony Castanha, *Address on the Revocation of the Papal Bull 'Inter Caetera'*, website.

48 Joan Chittister, *Called to Question: A Spiritual Memoir*, p. 174.

Chapter 4

1 Anne Salmond, *Two Worlds: First Meetings between Maori and Europeans 1642–1772*, p. 270.

2 Ibid., p. 48.

3 Ian Pool, *Te Iwi Maori: A New Zealand Population Past, Present and Projected*, p. 237.

4 Anne Salmond, op. cit., p. 122.

5 James Belich, *Making Peoples: A History of the New Zealanders*, pp. 116–21.

6 Mason Durie, *Te Mana, Te Kawanatanga: The Politics of Maori Self-Determination*, p. 151.

7 Ibid., p. 151.

8 Waitangi Tribunal, *Wai 22: Muriwhenua Fishing Report*, pp. 42–44.

9 Michael King, *God's Farthest Outpost: A History of Catholics in New Zealand*, p. 32. According to King, a Catholic Mass was led by a French Dominican Priest, Father Paul Antoine Leonard de Villefeix, chaplain on the French merchant ship *Saint Jean-Baptiste*, which anchored in Doubtless Bay on 17 December 1769.

10 Anne Salmond, *Between Worlds: Early Exchanges Between Maori and Europeans 1773–1815*, p. 407.

11 Dom Felice Vaggioli, *History of New Zealand and Its Inhabitants*, p. 111.

12 Neil Benfell, 'Martyr to the Cause' in Robert Glen (ed.), *Mission and Moko: The Church Missionary Society in New Zealand 1814–1882*, p. 106.

13 Paul Moon, *The Origins of the Treaty of Waitangi*, p. 35.

14 R. D. Crosby, *The Musket Wars: A History of Inter-Iwi Conflict 1805–45*, p. 17. These estimates were based on population decline over the period.

15 Ian Pool, op. cit., p. 44.

16 James Belich, op. cit., p. 157.

17 The information in this brief summary comes from Michael King, *Moriori*.

18 This pacifist tradition had been developed in the late sixteenth century to ensure the survival of a viable population.

19 Michael King, *Moriori*, p. 64.

20 Ibid., p. 135.

21 Ian Pool, op. cit., p. 238.

22 Peter Tremewan, 'The French Alternative to the Treaty of Waitangi' in *NZ Journal of History*, p. 100.

23 Claudia Orange, *The Treaty of Waitangi*, pp. 11–13. Maori had petitioned King William IV in 1831 to send a representative to New Zealand to control the behaviour of Europeans.

24 John O. Ross, 'Busby and the Declaration of Independence' in *NZ Journal of History*, p. 84.

25 Ibid., p. 83.

26 Mason Durie, *Te Mana, Te Kawanatanga*, p. 2.

27 Ibid., p. 53.

28 Text supplied by Te Whakakotahitanga o nga iwi o Aotearoa/ The Maori Congress and distributed by the Federation of WEAs in Aotearoa New Zealand in alliance with Network Waitangi Otautahi.

29 Ranginui Walker, *Ka Whawhai Tonu Matou: Struggle Without End*, p. 88.

30 Claudia Orange, op. cit., p. 24. '. . . factories could be set up along the lines of the early British trading factories in India. Initially, two or three sites could be purchased and placed under British jurisdiction; a treaty with the chiefs would confirm this.' Busby had already discarded this idea.

31 Ibid., p. 27.

32 Mason Durie, *Te Mana, Te Kawanatanga*, p. 176.

33 Paul Moon, 'Three Historical Interpretations of the Treaty of Waitangi' in *Electronic Journal of Australian and New Zealand History*.

34 Paul Moon, *Hobson: Governor of New Zealand 1840–1842*, p. 48.

35 Paul McHugh, *The Maori Magna Carta: New Zealand Law and the Treaty of Waitangi*, pp. 373–85.

36 M. P. K. Sorrenson, 'Treaties in British Colonial Policy: Precedents for Waitangi' in William Renwick (ed.), *Sovereignty and Indigenous Rights: The Treaty of Waitangi in International Contexts*, p. 29.

37 Claudia Orange, op. cit., pp. 60–64. Orange provides a detailed summary of assurances made to Maori.

38 James Belich, op. cit., p. 219. Belich writes that by the 1850s over 60 per cent of Maori counted themselves nominally as Christians.

39 Claudia Orange, op. cit., p. 53.

40 Peter Adams, *Fatal Necessity: British Intervention in New*

Zealand 1830–1847, p. 166.

41 P. G. McHugh, 'Constitutional
    Theory and Maori Claims' in
    I. H. Kawharu (ed.), *Waitangi:
    Maori and Pakeha Perspectives of
    the Treaty of Waitangi*, p. 37.

42 Paul Moon, 'Three Historical
    Interpretations' op.cit.

43 Claudia Orange, op. cit., p. 56.

44 Ibid., p. 62.

45 Ranginui Walker, op. cit., p. 97.

46 Claudia Orange, *An Illustrated
    History of the Treaty of Waitangi*,
    p. 36.

47 Ruth Ross, *The Treaty on the
    Ground* in *The Treaty of
    Waitangi: Its Origins and
    Significance*, p. 17.

48 Paul Moon, 'Three Historical
    Interpretations' op. cit. p. 4.

49 Paul Moon, *FitzRoy Governor in
    Crisis 1843–1845*, pp. 187–209.

50 Dean Cowie, 'To Do All the
    Good That I Can: Robert
    FitzRoy, Governor of New
    Zealand 1843–1845',
    unpublished thesis, p. 177.

51 Waitangi Tribunal, *Wai 45:
    Muriwhenua Land Report*,
    pp. 11–40. This report gives
    in-depth coverage of the
    different understandings of land
    ownership and land sales.

52 Waitangi Tribunal, *Wai 27: The
    Ngai Tahu Report, Vol. 1:
    Summary of Grievances, Findings
    and Recommendations*, p. 52.

53 Waitangi Tribunal, *National
    Overview*, Vol. I, p. 9.

54 Claudia Orange, *The Treaty of
    Waitangi*, pp. 142–43.

55 Ibid., pp. 159–84.

56 Richard Boast et al., *Maori Land
    Law*, p. 8.

57 Waitangi Tribunal, *National
    Overview*, Vol. 1, p. 9.

58 Peter Spiller, Jeremy Finn and
    Richard Boast, *A New Zealand
    Legal History*, p. 150.

59 Dom Felice Vaggioli, op. cit.,
    p. 285.

60 Royal Commission on Social
    Policy, *The Treaty of Waitangi
    and Social Policy*, Discussion
    Booklet, No. 7, pp. 10–11. For
    an overview of Maori
    parliaments, see Lindsay Cox,
    *Kotahitanga: The Search for
    Maori Political Unity*.

61 M. P. K. Sorrenson, *A History of
    Maori Representation in
    Parliament*, report of the Royal
    Commission on the Electoral
    System: Towards a Better
    Democracy, pp. 83–84.

62 Waitangi Tribunal, *National
    Overview*, Vol. 1, p. 8.

63 M. P. K. Sorrenson, 'Maori and
    Pakeha' in W. H. Oliver (ed.),
    *The Oxford History of New
    Zealand*, p. 171.

64 Judith Simon (ed.), *Nga Kura
    Maori: The Native Schools System
    1867–1969*, p. 17.

65 James Belich, op. cit., p. 268.

66 Richard Boast et al., op. cit.,
    p. 83.

67 Tom Brooking, '"Busting Up"
    the Greatest Estate of All:
    Liberal Maori Land Policy
    1891–1911' in *New Zealand
    Journal of History*, p. 78.

68 I acknowledge the generous
    assistance of historian Sean
    Brosnahan for access to his
    research on the Dunedin
    prisoners in a letter to
    Robert Consedine, 17 December
    2002; also Bill Dacker, *Te
    Mamae Me Te Aroha, The Pain*

and the Love: A History of Kai Tahu Whanui in Otago, 1844–1994.

69 Office of Treaty Settlements, Deed of Settlement of the Historical Claims of Ngaati Ruanui, p. 30. There are two books on Parihaka: Days of Darkness: Taranaki 1878–1884 by Hazel Riseborough, and Ask That Mountain: The Story of Parihaka by Dick Scott; also an excellent video production: The Ploughmen of Taranaki.

70 Ian Pool, op. cit., p. 61.

71 John Stenhouse, 'A Disappearing Race Before We Came Here' in NZ Journal of History, p. 126.

72 Ibid., p. 140.

73 Claudia Orange, The Treaty of Waitangi, p. 231.

74 Mason Durie, Te Mana, Te Kawanatanga, p. 95.

75 Ian Pool, op. cit., p. 153.

76 Augie Fleras and Paul Spoonley, Recalling Aotearoa: Indigenous Politics and Ethnic Relations in New Zealand, p. 115.

77 Andrew Armitage, Comparing the Policy of Aboriginal Assimilation: Australia, Canada and New Zealand, p. 164.

78 Ibid., p. 168.

79 Paul Monin, This is My Place: Hauraki Contested 1769–1875, p. 4.

80 Giselle Byrnes, The Waitangi Tribunal and New Zealand History, p. 113.

81 Vincent O'Malley, Agents of Autonomy: Maori Committees in the Nineteenth Century, p. 13.

82 I am grateful to historian Jim McAloon for his assistance and advice with the final section of this chapter. Note: the conclusions reached are solely those of the author.

Chapter 5

1 Richard Boast et al., Maori Land Law, p. 103.

2 Te Matakite o Aotearoa: The Maori Land March, television documentary.

3 Ranginui Walker, 'The Treaty of Waitangi: as the Focus of Maori Protest' in I. H. Kawharu (ed.), Waitangi: Maori and Pakeha Perspectives of the Treaty of Waitangi, p. 276.

4 New Zealand Herald, 7 February 2004, website.

5 The Foreshore and Seabed of New Zealand, Protecting Public Access and Customary Rights: Government Proposals for Consultation, p. 9.

6 Don Brash, Nationhood - Don Brash Speech Orewa Rotary Club, website.

7 Tariana Turia resigned as a Labour MP on 17 May 2004 in protest at the government's foreshore and seabed policy. Subsequently the Maori Party was formed on 7 July 2004, and Tariana Turia was elected leader. In a by-election she was returned to Parliament representing the Te Tai Hauauru electorate, winning 90 per cent of the vote, with a majority of 7059.

8 Ranginui Walker, Ka Whawhai Tonu Matou: Struggle Without End, p. 214.

9 Ibid.

10 Paul Temm, The Waitangi

Tribunal: The Conscience of the Nation, p. 62.

11 Ibid., p. 64.

12 Ranginui Walker, *Ka Whawhai Tonu Matou*, op. cit., p. 215.

13 Ibid., pp. 218–19.

14 Ibid., pp. 200–21 for a full description of the groups and people involved.

15 Ibid., p. 225.

16 Ian McGibbon, *The Path to Gallipoli: Defending New Zealand 1814–1915*, pp. 201–202.

17 Andrew Trlin, 'Changing Ethnic Residential Distribution and Segregation in Auckland' in Paul Spoonley et al. (eds), *Tauiwi: Racism and Ethnicity in New Zealand*, p. 172.

18 Marcia Stenson, *The Treaty: Every New Zealander's Guide to the Treaty of Waitangi*, pp. 24–25.

19 Paul Temm, op. cit., p. 3.

20 M. P. K. Sorrenson, 'Towards a Radical Reinterpretation of New Zealand History: The Role of the Waitangi Tribunal' in I. H. Kawharu (ed.), *Waitangi: Maori and Pakeha Perspectives of the Treaty of Waitangi*, p. 164.

21 Ibid., p. 166.

22 Waitangi Tribunal, *Wai 11: Te Reo Maori Report*, p. 9. From 1867 the Native Schools Act decreed that English should be the only language used in the education of Maori children.

23 The statistics on the threatened state of the Maori language speak for themselves. In 1913, 99 per cent of Maori children still spoke their own language. By 1960 the Hunn Report on assimilation (as if advancing a self-fulfilling prophecy) described the language as 'a relic of ancient Maori life' (p. 9). By the late 1990s fewer than 10 per cent of Maori spoke their own language fluently.

24 For a full report of the history of the claim, see Waitangi Tribunal, *Wai 9: The Orakei Claim Report*.

25 M. P. K. Sorrenson, op. cit., p. 173.

26 Ian Shearer, Waitangi Tribunal, Wellington, email to authors, 6 August 2004. For detailed information check the Waitangi Tribunal website.

27 This and the following information is drawn from the Office of Treaty Settlements, *Healing the Past: Building a Future: A Guide to Treaty of Waitangi Claims and Negotiations with the Crown* (Summary Edition).

28 Waitangi Tribunal, *Te Manutukutuku*, Haratua, 2004, p. 3.

29 Paul Moon, 'The Creation of the Sealord Deal' in *Journal of the Polynesian Society*, p. 150.

30 M. P. K. Sorrenson, op. cit., p. 171.

31 Richard Boast, 'Maori Land and the Treaty of Waitangi' in Richard Boast et al., *Maori Land Law*, p. 276.

32 M. P. K. Sorrenson, op. cit., p. 161.

33 Ibid., p. 162.

34 Jane Kelsey, 'From Flagpoles to Pine Trees' in Paul Spoonley et al., *Nga Patai: Racism and Ethnic Relations in Aotearoa/New Zealand*, p. 178.

35 Augie Fleras, 'Politicising

Indigeneity: Ethno-politics in White Settler Dominions' in Paul Havemann (ed.), *Indigenous Peoples' Rights in Australia, Canada and New Zealand*, p. 210.

36 New Zealand Institute of Economic Research, *Maori Economic Development: Te Ohanga Whanaketanga Maori*, 2003.

37 Colin James, 'Search on for Maori Economic Leaders', *New Zealand Herald*, 18 November 2003, website.

38 Bruce Jesson, *Only Their Purpose is Mad: The Money Men Take Over New Zealand*, p. 12.

39 Jane Kelsey, *A Question of Honour? Labour and the Treaty 1984–1989*, p. 45.

40 Department of Maori Studies, Massey University, *Te Kawenata o Waitangi: The Treaty of Waitangi in New Zealand Society*, p. 87.

41 Marcia Stenson, op. cit., pp. 21–22.

42 Ibid., pp. 22–23.

43 Te Puni Kokiri, *He Tirohanga O Kawa Ke Te Tiriti O Waitangi: A Guide to the Principles of the Treaty of Waitangi as Expressed by the Courts and the Waitangi Tribunal.*

44 Ibid., p. 85.

45 Philip A. Joseph, *Constitutional and Administrative Law in New Zealand*, pp. 59–60. The previous quotes are drawn from court rulings cited therein.

46 P. G. McHugh, 'From Sovereignty Talk to Settlement Time: The Constitutional Setting of Maori Claims in the 1990s' in Paul Havemann (ed.), op. cit., p. 447.

47 Ibid., p. 449.

48 Douglas Sanders, *State Practice and the United Nations Draft Declaration on the Rights of Indigenous Peoples*, conference paper.

49 Wira Gardiner, *Return to Sender: What Really Happened at the Fiscal Envelope Hui.*

50 Department of Maori Studies, Massey University, op. cit., p.47.

51 For an analysis of the commercial fisheries and Ngai Tahu settlements, see Chapter 11.

52 The 1992 Fisheries settlement of $150 million was costed over three years (1992/93, 1993/94, 1994/95). The fisheries settlement also included the transfer of 20 per cent of new fisheries quota, which has been given an indicative value of $20 million, for estimating a total dollar value of the settlement of $170 million. Office of Treaty Settlements, *Quarterly Report to 30 June 2004*, p. 11.

53 Ibid., p. 12.

54 The factual data in much of this section is drawn from the Te Kohanga Reo National Trust website.

55 Titoki Black, Phillip Marshall, Kathie Irwin, *Maori Language Nests in New Zealand: Te Kohanga Reo, 1982–2003*, p. 10.

56 See 1 July returns, Ministry of Education, website.

57 Titoki Black et al., op. cit.

58 Ibid., p. 16.

59 Ibid., p. 7.

60 Briefing for the incoming

Minister of Education, 1999, website.

61 Titoki Black et al., op. cit., p. 14. See also Ministry of Education, *Review of Regulation of Early Childhood Education: Implementing Pathways to the Future: Nga Huarahi Arataki*.

62 Ibid., p. 17.

63 Statistics New Zealand, *2001 Census Snapshot*.

64 Education Review Office, *The Performance of Kura Kaupapa Maori*, website.

65 Ranginui Walker, 'The Development of Maori Studies in Tertiary Education in Aotearoa/New Zealand', in Marie Peters (ed.), *After the Disciplines: The Emergence of Cultural Studies*, p. 188.

66 Ministry of Education, *New Zealand's Tertiary Education Sector Report – Profile and Trends 2002*, p. 81.

67 Ministry of Education, *Maori in Tertiary Education*, April 2004, website.

68 Tiakiwai and Teddy, op. cit., p. 5.

69 Ibid., p. 6.

70 Mason Durie, *A Framework for Considering Maori Educational Advancement*, 2001.

71 Tiakiwai and Teddy, op. cit., p. 6.

72 Department of Maori Studies, Massey University, op. cit., p. 103.

73 He Putahitanga Hou—Labour Party *Manifesto on Maori Development 1999*, p. 1, website.

74 New Zealand Public Health and Disability Act 2000.

75 Don Brash, op. cit., website; Trevor Mallard, *We Are All New Zealanders*, website.

76 Mason Durie, *Te Mana, Te Kawanatanga*, pp. 175–76.

Chapter 6

1 One internationally recognised definition of racism is the assumption that one culture has the right, power and authority to define 'normality'. This normality is reflected in the functioning of all dominant, compulsory structures, starting with Parliament and permeating the institutional life of the entire country. In New Zealand this means that the Pakeha (English) way was early defined as normal and underpinned by the legal system; by definition Maori cultural values and tikanga Maori (Maori custom) were excluded from the institutional life of the country.

2 Robert Consedine, 'Exiled in the Land of the Free', pp. 21–26.

3 Joseph Barndt, *Dismantling Racism: The Continuing Challenge to White America*, p. 81.

4 In this book we have applied institutional racism as a framework to understand why a sanitised account of New Zealand colonial history was used in schools. However, we acknowledge the truth of this statement given to us by Colin McGeorge: 'The early texts were certainly racist and the later ones give a sanitised account of Maori–Pakeha dealings, [yet] school books tend to give a sanitised account of everything. Official curricula and approved textbooks generally reflect what someone rather nicely called

"society's best opinion of itself"'.

5 World Council of Churches report, *Racism in Children's and School Textbooks*, p. 11.

6 Eve Coxon et al., *The Politics of Learning and Teaching in Aotearoa–New Zealand*, p. 50.

7 Ibid., p. 51.

8 Section 84(1) of the 1877 Act listed the subjects to be taught in state primary schools and it ended: 'But no child shall be compelled to be present at the teaching of history whose parents or guardians object thereto.' This provision was because it was thought Catholics and Protestants would inevitably disagree over certain aspects of history. This clause also appeared in the Education Act 1914 but had disappeared from the Education Act 1964.

9 Education Act 1877, pp. 14–15.

10 Marcia Stenson, 'History in New Zealand Schools' in *New Zealand Journal of History*, p. 168.

11 Ibid., p. 170.

12 John L. Ewing, *The Development of the New Zealand Primary School Curriculum 1877–1970*, p. 23.

13 Regulations for Inspection and Examination of Schools, supplement to New Zealand Gazette, 14 April 1904, *Parliamentary Papers*, p. 1086.

14 John L. Ewing, op. cit., p. 88.

15 Ibid., p. 143.

16 Marcia Stenson, 'History in New Zealand Schools', p. 171.

17 Ibid., p. 174.

18 Ibid., p. 173.

19 Colin McGeorge, 'Race, Empire and the Maori in the New Zealand Primary School Curriculum 1880–1940' in J. A. Mangan (ed.), *The Imperial Curriculum: Racial Images and Education in British Colonial Experience*, p. 64.

20 Ibid., p. 66.

21 Ibid., p. 67.

22 Collins School Series, *The New Zealand Graphic Reader Sixth Book*, p. 93.

23 Colin McGeorge, op. cit., p. 65.

24 Ibid., p. 67.

25 Ibid.

26 Ibid., p 69.

27 E. P. Malone, 'The New Zealand School Journal and the Imperial Ideology' in *New Zealand Journal of History*, p. 13.

28 Colin McGeorge, op. cit., p. 72.

29 E. P. Malone, op. cit., p. 15.

30 Education Department, *Syllabus of Instruction for Public Schools*, p. 31.

31 Ibid., pp. 33–34.

32 Ibid., p. 34.

33 Ibid., p. 35

34 Ibid., p. 32.

35 Marcia Stenson, 'History in New Zealand Schools', p. 175.

36 *The Post Primary School Curriculum*, report of the committee appointed by the Minister of Education in 1942, p. 23.

37 John L. Ewing, op. cit., p. 232.

38 The Primary School Curriculum Revised Syllabuses, May 1948, p. 86.

39 Colin McGeorge, 'What Was "Our Nation's Story"? New Zealand Primary School History Textbooks Between the Wars',

in *History of Education Review*,
p. 49.

40 Ibid., p. 46.

41 Whitcombe's Primary History
Series, *Our Nation's Story: A
Course of British History*, p. 23.

42 Ibid., p. 21.

43 Colin McGeorge, 'What Was
"Our Nation's Story"', p. 53.

44 Ibid.

45 Ibid.

46 Ibid.

47 K. C. McDonald (compiler),
*Our Country: A Brief Survey of
New Zealand History and Civics*,
p. 20.

48 Russell Bishop and Ted Glynn,
*Culture Counts: Changing Power
Relations in Education*, p. 16.

49 Andrew Armitage, *Comparing
the Policy of Aboriginal
Assimilation: Australia, Canada
and New Zealand*, p. 145.

50 Department of Education, *Social
Studies Syllabus Guidelines Forms
1–4*, p. 3.

51 Carol Mutch, 'New Zealand
Social Studies 1961–1995: A
View of Curriculum Change' in
*Children's Social and Economics
Education*, p. 8.

52 Department of Education,
*Suggestions for Teaching Social
Studies in the Primary School
Index Parts 1, 2, 3, 4*, p. 27.

53 New Zealand Educational
Institute, *A Teachers' Index of
Core Materials for Social Studies*,
p. 7.

54 Ibid., p. 163.

55 Dunedin Community Law
Centre, *An Introduction to the
Waitangi Tribunal with Reference
to the Ngai Tahu Land Claim*,
p. 49.

56 R. M. Ross, *Te Tiriti o Waitangi*,
Primary School Bulletin, p. 43.

57 Harold Miller, *The Maori and the
Missionary*, p. 3.

58 Ibid., p. 7.

59 New Zealand Educational
Institute, op. cit., p. 167.

60 Department of Education, *The
Curriculum Review: A Draft
Report Prepared by the Committee
to Review the Curriculum for
Schools*, p. 45.

61 Ministry of Education, *Social
Studies Forms 3 & 4: A
Handbook for Teachers*, p. 4.

62 Ibid., pp. 9–24.

63 Ministry of Education, *Social
Studies 14 Years On: An
Evaluation of the Handbook for
Teachers of Forms 3 & 4 Social
Studies*, pp. 5–6.

64 Ministry of Education, *Social
Studies in the New Zealand
Curriculum*, p. 23.

65 Ibid., p. 25, for a policy
statement.

66 The authors thank Myra
Kunowski at the Christchurch
College of Education, Te Whare
Whai Matauraka Ki Otautahi,
for this research.

67 Ministry of Education, *Social
Studies in the New Zealand
Curriculum*, op. cit., p. 25.

68 Ibid., p. 21.

69 Avril Bell and Vicki Carpenter,
'Education's Role in
(Re)producing Social Class in
Aotearoa' in Eve Coxon et al.,
*The Politics of Learning and
Teaching in Aotearoa–New
Zealand*, p. 130.

70 Russell Bishop and Ted Glynn,
op. cit., p. 12.

71 Office of the Race Relations

Conciliator and the Ministry of Education, *In Tune: Students' Activities*.

72 Ruth Naumann, *Our Treaty: The Treaty of Waitangi 1840 to the Present*.

73 Ruth Naumann, Lyn Harrison and Te Kaponga Winiata, *Te Mana o Te Tiriti: The Living Treaty*, pp. 59–61.

74 Colin McGeorge, 'What Was "Our Nation's Story"', p. 46.

75 Department of Education, *Social Studies in the Primary School*, p. 2.

Chapter 7

1 James West Davidson et al., *Nation of Nations: A Narrative History of the American Republic Volume II: Since 1865*, p. 1172.

2 Ibid.

3 Jeremiah Creedon, 'To Hell and Back' in *Utne Reader*, No. 92, p. 56.

4 Frances Stonor Saunders, *The Cultural Cold War: The C.I.A. and the World of Arts and Letters*, p. 142.

5 Jorge Rosner, *Peeling the Onion: Gestalt Theory and Methodology*, p. 97.

6 Paul Kivel, *Uprooting Racism: How White People Can Work for Racial Justice*, p. 11.

7 Peggy McIntosh, 'Unpacking the Invisible Knapsack: White Privilege' in *Creation Spirituality*, pp. 33–35.

8 Paulo Freire, *Pedagogy of Hope: Reliving Pedagogy of the Oppressed*.

9 Nicola Hoffman and Wayne Scott, *Psychodrama Institute of New Zealand Inc. Handbook*, p. 99.

10 Gordon Dryden and Jeanette Vos, *The Learning Revolution*, p. 100.

11 Henry Reynolds, *Why Weren't We Told? A Personal Search for the Truth About Our History*, p. 251.

12 E. H. Carr, *What is History?*, p. 68.

13 Michael King, *Being Pakeha Now*, p. 69.

14 John O'Donohue, *Eternal Echoes: Exploring Our Hunger to Belong*, p. 163.

15 Deborah Wai Kapohe, *Borderless*.

16 Television One, *Face the Nation*, 27 July 2000.

17 Radio New Zealand, *Mana News*, 31 July 2000.

Chapter 8

1 Frank Delaney, *The Celts*, pp. 19–40.

2 Henry Reynolds, *Why Weren't We Told? A Personal Search For the Truth About Our History*, p. 247.

3 Michael King, *Being Pakeha*, p. 13.

4 Michelanne Forster, Story-writing Session, New Zealand Broadcasting School, Christchurch Polytechnic.

5 Carmel Bird (ed.), *The Stolen Children: Their Stories*.

6 Television One, *Holmes*, 29 May 1997.

7 Michelanne Forster, op. cit.

8 Television One, *Holmes*, 29 May 1997. For more information about the inquiry, see: *Bringing Them Home: Report of the National Inquiry into the Separation of Aboriginal and Torres Strait Islander Children from Their Families*, website.

9 Michael King (ed.), *Pakeha: The Quest for Identity in New Zealand*, p. 18.

10 Robert Kee, *The Most Distressful Country: The Green Flag, Volume One*, p. 19.

11 Ibid., p. 27.

12 M. J. Shiel (ed.), *A Forgotten Campaign: Aspects of the Heritage of South-east Galway*, A Word to the Reader, 1886–1986.

13 Ibid.

14 Ibid.

15 Ibid., p. 53.

16 Ibid., p. 54.

17 Peter Cuffley, *Family History Comes to Life*, p. 3.

18 Ibid.

19 Noel Ignatiev, *How the Irish Became White*, p. v.

20 Jorge Rosner, *Peeling the Onion: Gestalt Theory and Methodology*, p. 68.

21 Joseph Barndt, *Dismantling Racism: The Continuing Challenge to White America*, p. 78.

22 Moana Jackson, 'The Treaty and the Word: The Colonisation of Maori Philosophy' in Graham Oddie and Roy Perrett (eds), *Justice, Ethics, and New Zealand Society*, p. 10.

Chapter 9

1 Mason Durie, *Nga Matatini Maori: Diverse Maori Realities*, conference paper, Point 3.1.

2 Ibid., Point 6.4.

3 Ruth Millar, *An Investigation into Students' Perceptions of the Successful Aspects of 'Waitangi Workshops'*, Christchurch College of Education, p. 9. (Note: 49 Year 1 students in a pre-service teacher education course responded to the survey.)

4 Ibid., pp. xxvii, 10–12.

5 There are limits in comparing the research outcomes of the two different courses. The timeframe, setting and content of each course and the researchers' questions are obvious differences. However, Alison Jones's findings offer much insight into the difficulty many Pakeha have in separating out from their Maori and Pacific Island peers.

6 Alison Jones, 'The Limits of Cross-cultural Dialogue: Pedagogy, Desire and Absolution in the Classroom' in *Educational Theory*, p. 301.

7 Ibid., pp. 301–3.

8 Alison Jones, *Difference and Desire: Dividing Classrooms by Ethnicity*, p. 10.

9 Alison Jones, 'The Limits of Cross-cultural Dialogue', op. cit., p. 311.

10 Helen Clark, speech to Pacific Vision Conference, 28 July 1999.

Chapter 10

1 Waitangi Tribunal, *Wai 27: The Ngai Tahu Report*, Vol. 2, p. 527.

2 Irihapeti Ramsden, 'Cultural Safety and Nursing Education in Aotearoa and Te Waipounamu', thesis.

3 James Baldwin, *What is White Privilege?*, website.

4 Peggy McIntosh, 'Unpacking the Invisible Knapsack: White Privilege', in *Creation Spirituality*, p. 1.

5 Ibid., p. 1.

6 Theodore W. Allen, *The Invention of the White Race*, p. 35.

7 Ibid., p. 35.

8 Waitangi Tribunal, *Wai 27: The Ngai Tahu Report*, Vol. 2, p. 270.

9 Correspondence Relative to New Zealand No. 16, *From the Marquis of Normanby to Captain Hobson*; also Claudia Orange, *The Treaty Of Waitangi*, pp. 29–31.

10 Waitangi Tribunal Reports, website.

11 Waitangi Tribunal, *Wai 9: The Orakei Claim Report*, pp. 23–28.

12 Waitangi Tribunal, *Wai 27: The Ngai Tahu Report*, Vol. 1, p. xiv.

13 Jim McAloon, 'Resource Frontiers, Environment and Settler Capitalism 1769–1860' in Eric Pawson & Tom Brooking (eds), *Environmental Histories of New Zealand*, pp. 62–63.

14 Waitangi Tribunal, *Maori Land Councils and Maori Land Boards: A Historical Overview, 1900–1952*, pp. 75–76.

15 Claudia Orange, *The Treaty of Waitangi*, p. 86.

16 Andrew Alston et al. (eds), *Guide to New Zealand Land Law*, p. 200.

17 For a chronology of 'land taking laws' see David Williams, *'Te Kooti Tango Whenua': The Native Land Court 1864–1909*.

18 In addition to the $170 million, the Crown offered a public apology, first right of refusal to purchase land from the Crown's 'landbank' and detailed cultural redress. See Ngai Tahu website.

19 Radio New Zealand, *Insight*: Sir Tipene O'Regan, Treaty of Waitangi Settlements, 2 February 2003.

20 Waitangi Tribunal, *The Crown's Engagement with Customary Tenure in the Nineteenth Century*, p. 49.

21 I. H. Kawharu, *Maori Land Tenure: Studies of a Changing Institution*, p. 15.

22 Bryan Gilling, 'The Maori Land Court in New Zealand: An Historical Overview' in *The Canadian Journal of Native Studies*, p. 18.

23 Alan Ward, *An Unsettled History: Treaty Claims in New Zealand Today*, p. 128.

24 Gilling, op. cit., p. 20.

25 Alan Ward, *A Show of Justice: Racial 'Amalgamation' in Nineteenth Century New Zealand*, p. 187.

26 Williams, op. cit., p. 3.

27 Tom Bennion, review of *'Te Kooti Tango Whenua' The Native Land Court 1864–1909*, in *Maori Law Review*, July 1999.

28 Ward, *A Show of Justice*, op. cit., p. 36.

29 Edward W. Said, *Culture and Imperialism*, p. 202.

30 Gaynor Whyte, 'Beyond the Statute: Administration of Old-age Pensions to 1938' in Bronwyn Dalley and Margaret Tennant (eds), *Past Judgement: Social Policy in New Zealand History*, p. 134.

31 Ibid., p. 132.

32 Ibid., p. 132.

33 Margaret McClure, *A Civilized Community: A History of Social Security in New Zealand 1898–1998*, p. 79.

34 Whyte, op. cit., p. 134.

35 McClure, op. cit., p. 19.

36 Margaret McClure, 'A Badge of Poverty or a Symbol of Citzenship? Needs, Rights and Social Security, 1935–2000' in Bronwyn Dalley and Margaret Tennant (eds), op. cit., p. 145.

37 McClure, *A Civilised Community*, pp. 121–22.

38 McClure, 'A Badge of Poverty or a Symbol of Citizenship?', p. 145.

39 Ibid.

40 McClure, *A Civilised Community*, p. 79.

41 Ranginui Walker, *He Tipua: The Life and Times of Sir Apirana Ngata*, p. 190.

42 Ibid.

43 Claudia Orange, 'An Exercise in Maori Autonomy: The Rise and Demise of the Maori War Effort Organisation' in *New Zealand Journal of History*, p. 159.

44 McClure, *A Civilised Community*, p. 121.

45 Margaret Tennant, 'Mixed Economy or Moving Frontier' in Bronwyn Dalley and Margaret Tennant (eds), op. cit., p. 53.

46 Claudia Orange, 'An Exercise in Maori Autonomy', p. 162.

47 Ibid., p. 170.

48 Ibid.

49 Ibid.

50 See Waitangi Tribunal Reports, website, particularly Waitangi Tribunal, *National Overview* Vol. 1, by Alan Ward.

51 W. D. Borrie, *Immigration to New Zealand 1854–1938*, pp. 168–76.

52 For an overview of the period see Stuart W. Greif (ed.), *Immigration and National Identity in New Zealand* and Tony Simpson, *The Immigrants: The Great Migration from Britain to New Zealand 1830–1890*.

53 For an exploration of the policy of assimilation see Waitangi Tribunal, *Crown Policy Affecting Maori Knowledge Systems and Cultural Practices* by David Williams; also Andrew Armitage, *Comparing the Policy of Aboriginal Assimilation: Australia, Canada and New Zealand*.

54 For a full report see Waitangi Tribunal, *Public Works Takings of Maori Land, 1840–1981* by Cathy Marr.

55 TVNZ, *Bastion Point: The Untold Story*, Sir Douglas Graham.

56 Waitangi Tribunal, *Wai 45: Muriwhenua Land Report*, p. 1.

57 Ibid., p. 76.

58 For a full discussion on the 'European superiority thinking' see J. M. Blaut, *The Colonizers' Model of the World: Geographical Diffusionism and Eurocentric History*.

59 For an overview of racial prejudice among Europeans in the nineteenth and twentieth century see Angela Ballara, *Proud to Be White*.

60 Brendan Hokowhitu, *Maori as the Savage Other: Icons of Racial Representation*, p. 1.

61 Ibid., p. 1.

62 New Zealand government executive, *Closing the Gaps*, Budget 2000, website.

63 *NZ Herald*, 29 July 2004. Trevor Mallard, a Pakeha

Cabinet Minister, asserted that he is an indigenous New Zealander.

64 *The Press*, 19 August 2004.

65 TVNZ, *Bastion Point: The Untold Story*.

66 Hirini Matunga, 'Decolonising Planning: The Treaty of Waitangi, the Environment and a Dual Planning Tradition' in Ali Memon and Harvey Perkins (eds), *Environmental Planning and Management in New Zealand*, p. 38.

67 Ibid., p. 39.

68 Ibid., p. 40.

69 Ibid., p. 41.

70 Ibid., p. 45.

71 Ross Galbreath, 'Displacement, Conservation and Customary Use of Native Plants and Animals in New Zealand' in *New Zealand Journal of History*, p. 36.

72 Ibid., p. 36.

73 Ibid.

74 Ibid., pp. 37–38.

75 Ibid., p. 41.

76 Ibid., p. 43.

77 Ibid., p. 40.

78 Court of Appeal of New Zealand, *Ngati Apa, Ngati Koata and Ors v. Ki Te Tau Ihu Trust & Ors*, p. 26.

79 Ibid., p. 7.

80 Ibid.

81 Richard Boast, 'Constitutional Crisis over Foreshore and Seabed in Aotearoa' in *Pacific Ecologist*, p. 61.

82 Court of Appeal of New Zealand, op. cit., p. 8. For a legal overview we recommend also Nin Tomas & Kerensa Johnston, *Ask That Taniwha: Who Owns the Foreshore and Seabed of Aotearoa?*

83 The exception is the Green Party of Aotearoa New Zealand, which strongly opposes government legislation to put the foreshore and seabed in Crown ownership. Their position is 'that public access to the foreshore can be guaranteed in perpetuity, within a framework that recognises Maori customary title and Kaitiakitanga, which will also protect the environment. This can be achieved with simple changes to the Te Ture Whenua Maori Act.' 4 May 2004.

84 For a full report on the hikoi see *Mana* 58, June/July 2004.

85 Figures quoted by Bruce Ansley in the *New Zealand Listener*, 1 May 2004, p. 19. For a comprehensive overview of the foreshore and seabed debate see Tom Bennion et al., *Making Sense of the Foreshore and Seabed*.

86 *New Zealand Listener*, 1 May 2004, p. 19.

87 Ministry of Agriculture and Forestry, *Walking Access in New Zealand Outdoors: A Report by the Land Access Ministerial Reference Group*, p. 45.

88 Waitangi Tribunal, *Wai 1071: Report on the Crown's Foreshore and Seabed Policy*.

89 Ibid., p.129.

90 M. P. K. Sorrenson, 'A History of Maori Representation in Parliament' in *Report of the Royal Commission on the Electoral System: Towards a Better Democracy*, p. 26.

91 Ibid., pp. 23–26.

92 Neil Atkinson, *Adventures in Democracy: A History of the Vote in New Zealand*, p. 135.

93 Ibid., p. 137.

94 Neil Atkinson, op. cit., p. 136.

95 Ibid., p. 215.

96 *Mana* 59, August/September 2004, p. 47.

97 Department of Internal Affairs, *Local Authority Election Statistics*, 2003. (These statistics are based on 940 returns from 1083 elected.)

98 Ministry of Health, *Health and Independence Report, Director General's Report on the State of Public Health*, pp. 189–90.

99 Ibid., pp. 215–16.

100 *Mana* 56, February/March 2004, p. 42 .

101 Ministry of Health and University of Otago, *Decades of Disparity: Ethnic Mortality Trends in New Zealand 1980–1999*, pp. iii, ix.

102 Television One, *Breakfast*, 10 July 2003.

103 Ministry of Health and University of Otago, op. cit., p. iii.

104 Don Brash, *Nationhood - Don Brash Speech Orewa Rotary Club*, website.

105 E. T. Durie, *Will the Settlers Settle? Cultural Conciliation and Law*.

Chapter 11

1 *Nelson Evening Mail*, 27 November 1993, pp. 13–14.

2 Cate Brett, 'Death by Adventure' in *North and South*, March 1994, pp. 40–53.

3 Ibid., p. 50.

4 The statement read: 'The family of Trish and Robert Consedine have been involved in consultation and discussion with representatives of Outward Bound following the accidental death of their daughter Suzanne on 3 August 1993. No blame can or should be attached to Suzanne, any members of her group, or any staff member of Outward Bound for what happened. The family and Outward Bound are agreed that there was no history or reports to indicate that the type of group of which Suzanne was a member had entered the area of danger where the accident occurred. However, careful study of all relevant information shows how a combination of circumstances might, and in this case did, result in an accident, and measures now put in place address that issue. Outward Bound Trust has implemented safety measures and systems to prevent any recurrences and the family have made a positive contribution to the awareness and enquiry which has led to them.' (30 July 1994)

5 Stephanie Dowrick, 'The Art of Letting Go' in *Utne Reader*, p. 49.

6 John O'Donohue, *Eternal Echoes: Exploring Our Hunger to Belong*, p. 136.

7 Wole Soyinka, *The Burden of Memory: The Muse of Forgiveness*, p. 35.

8 *London Review of Books*, 14 October 1999.

9 For an overview of the debate, see David J. Rothman, 'The Shame of Medical Research' in

New York Review, 20 November 2000, pp. 60–64.

10 Robert S. McNamara, *In Retrospect: The Tragedy and Lessons of Vietnam*, p. 333.

11 Randall N. Robinson, *The Debt: What America Owes to Blacks*; Roy L. Brooks (ed.), *When Sorry Isn't Enough: The Controversy Over Apologies and Reparations for Human Injustice* (Critical America Series).

12 William Blum, *Killing Hope: US Military and CIA Interventions Since World War II*. In Guatemala the popular government wanted land reform in a country where 2.2 per cent of the landowners owned 70 per cent of the arable land. Much of the land was to be purchased from the American-owned United Fruit Company, which also owned a significant amount of the infrastructure of the country. The company wanted $16 million for the land. The government was offering $525,000—United Fruit's own declared valuation for taxation purposes. The American government and United Fruit used various actions to overthrow the Guatemalan government, including bribing the Guatemalan army, supplying arms, bombs, infiltration, leaflets, disinformation through the media, psychological warfare, assassination and gaining the support of the institutional Catholic Church. The result was nearly 50 years of civil war during which the government was overthrown and all policies to benefit the poor were cancelled.

13 Ibid. Since World War II the United States has interfered with and in some cases overthrown a number of democratically elected governments. The main crime of these governments was in wanting to run their own economies for the benefit of their own peoples. In the Cold War context any hint of socialism triggered American retaliation. Former American State Department official William Blum lists 55 thoroughly documented country case studies of American involvement in countries that were developing economic policies perceived to be unfriendly to US capital.

14 *Independent on Sunday*, 23 May 2004, p. 8.

15 William Blum, op. cit., p. 1.

16 Robert Elias, *Terrorism & American Foreign Policy*, p. 45.

17 Mark Curtis, *Web of Deceit: Britain's Real Role in the World*, pp. 414–15.

18 Arundhati Roy, *Power Politics*, p. 122.

19 Kathy Kelly, 'Raising Voices: The Children of Iraq, 1990–1999', in Anthony Arnove (ed.), *Iraq Under Siege: The Deadly Impact of Sanctions and War*, p. 111.

20 Anthony Arnove (ed.), op. cit., p. 10.

21 There are many books detailing interventions and killings by the US and Britain, among them Mark Curtis, *Web of Deceit:*

Britain's Real Role in the World; Noam Chomsky, The Culture of Terrorism; Noam Chomsky, Rogue States: The Rule of Force in World Affairs.

22 Helen Clark, Address to Chinese New Year Celebration, website.

23 Helen Clark, Speech at Samoa's 40th Anniversary of Independence, website.

24 Helen Clark, Clark Says Sorry to Gays, website.

25 Jeremiah Creedon, 'To Hell and Back' in Utne Reader, p. 59.

26 Mark Solomon, Collaboration for Economic Growth, Regional Development Conference, website.

27 Richard H. Bartlett, The Mabo Decision, p. vi.

28 Ibid., p. ix.

29 Economist, 19 April 1997.

30 Aboriginal and Torres Strait Islander Commission, website.

31 Henry Reynolds, Why Weren't We Told?, p. 221.

32 Robert Hughes, Beyond the Fatal Shore, BBC Television, 2000.

33 A. Dirk Moses, 'Revisionism and Denial', in Robert Manne (ed.), Whitewash: On Keith Windschuttle's Fabrication of Aboriginal History, p. 356.

34 Stuart Macintyre and Anna Clark, The History Wars, p. 3.

35 Robert Manne, 'Introduction', in Robert Manne (ed.), Whitewash, op. cit., p. 4; Human Rights and Equal Opportunity Commission, Bringing Them Home: Report of the National Inquiry into the Separation of Aboriginal and Torres Strait Islander Children from Their Families.

36 Manne, op. cit., p. 1.

37 A. Dirk Moses, op. cit., p. 350.

38 Deborah Lipstadt, Denying the Holocaust: The Growing Assault on Truth and Memory, p. iii; see also Peter Novick, The Holocaust and Collective Memory.

39 Rouben Paul Adalian, Armenian Genocide, website, pp. 1–3.

40 Richard T. Price, Legacy: Indian Treaty Relationships, p. 102.

41 Aboriginal and Torres Strait Islander Commission; Delgamuukw v. British Columbia, website.

42 Dave Kennedy Consulting, The British Columbia Treaty Process: A Road Map for Further Progress, p. 10.

43 Will Horter, Native Anger About to Catch Fire, website, p. 1.

44 Murray Angus, 'And the Last Shall be First': Native Policy in an Era of Cutbacks, p. 1.

45 Taiaiake Alfred, Peace, Power, Righteousness: An Indigenous Manifesto, p. 120.

46 BC Treaty Commission Costs and Benefits, website.

47 F. M. Brookfield, Waitangi and Indigenous Rights: Revolution, Law and Legitimation, p. 129.

48 Alan Ward, An Unsettled History: Treaty Claims in New Zealand Today, p. 46.

49 Waitangi Tribunal, Wai 307: The Fisheries Settlement Report.

50 Mason Durie, Te Mana, Te Kawanatanga: The Politics of Maori Self-Determination, pp. 169–70.

51 Ibid. Although this did not stop colonial governments from reducing Maori fishing rights to small-scale subsistence rights

from 1866 until 1986. This book has a full description on Maori fishing issues, pp. 149–74.

52 Paul Moon, 'The Creation of the Sealord Deal' in *Journal of the Polynesian Society*, p. 146.

53 Timeline, Te Ohu Kai Moana website.

54 *Te Reo o Te Tini a Tangaroa*, p. 3.

55 Johann Christoph Arnold, *The Lost Art of Forgiving: Stories of Healing from the Cancer of Bitterness*, p. 44.

Chapter 12

1 Don Oberdorfer, *The Two Koreas: A Contemporary History*, p. 2.

2 Kathleen Doherty, 'Reporting with Integrity' in *Tui Motu InterIslands*, December 2000.

3 For an overview of the changes, see P. G. McHugh, 'From Sovereignty Talk to Settlement Time: The Constitutional Setting of Maori Claims in the 1990s' in Paul Havemann (ed.), *Indigenous People's Rights in Australia, Canada and New Zealand*, pp. 447–467.

4 Ranginui Walker, *Ka Whawhai Tonu Matou: Struggle Without End*, p. 93.

5 Ranginui Walker, 'Immigration Policy and the Political Economy of New Zealand' in Stuart W. Grief (ed.), *Immigration and National Identity in New Zealand*, p. 282.

6 Ranginui Walker, *Ka Whawhai Tonu Matou*, op. cit., p. 93.

7 Richard Boast, 'Maori Land and the Treaty of Waitangi', in Richard Boast et al., *Maori Land Law*, p. 271.

8 Moana Jackson, *Treaty 2000 Conference*, Auckland, 7 July 2000.

9 F. M. Brookfield, *Waitangi and Indigenous Rights: Revolution, Law and Legitimation*, offers a full discussion on the constiutional issues relating to the Treaty.

10 *Dominion*, 1 May 1995, quoted in Jane Kelsey, *The New Zealand Experiment: A World Model for Structural Adjustment?*, p. 343.

11 Doug Graham, speech to the Waikanae/Kapiti Rotary Clubs, 3 May 1995, in Jane Kelsey, *The New Zealand Experiment*, p. 344.

12 F. M. Brookfield, op. cit., pp. 136–62.

13 E. Taihakurei Durie, *Treaties and the Common Law as Sources of Indigenous Rights*, Commonwealth Law Conference, Auckland, 1990.

14 Michel Chossudovsky, *The Globalisation of Poverty: Impacts of IMF and World Bank Reforms*, p. 15.

15 *Globalisation and Maori*, documentary video.

16 For a critique, see John Gray, *False Dawn: The Delusions of Global Capitalism*.

17 Paul Dalziel, *Changing Economic Realities*, Conference of the New Zealand Association of Counsellors, September 2000.

18 New Zealand Planning Council, *The Economy in Transition*, p. 166.

19 Brian Gaynor, 'We Now Know Who Owns New Zealand', *NZ Herald*, 2 October 1999, website.

20 Ibid.

21 Ibid.

22 Whatarangi Winiata, *Reducing the Socio-economic Disparities in Housing, Employment, Health and Education*, website, p. 2.

23 Francis Till, *New Zealand: Easiest Place in the World to Do Business*, website.

24 Susan Buckland, 'Children of the Poor', *NZ Listener*, 7 August 2004. Note: Susan Buckland was quoting Professor Innes Asher, Head of the Paediatrics Department, Faculty of Medical and Health Sciences, University of Auckland.

25 *Quality of Life Project: 2001 Report*, website. Figures have been averaged and rounded off by the authors.

26 'Well-heeled Need Platforms to Make Rich List', *NZ Herald*, 2 July 2004.

27 Jon Stokes, 'Summit to Refocus Energy of Maori Revival', *NZ Herald*, 18 September 2004.

28 'Pakeha Couples Top of the Wealth Heap', *NZ Herald*, 8 September 2002.

29 *Employment New Zealand*, June 2004, website.

30 Jon Stokes, op. cit.

31 'Racism Shock in Survey of Psychiatrists', *NZ Herald*, 7 March 2000.

32 Study Shows Ethnic Wage Gaps, Television One, *News*, 9 October 2000.

33 Maori Access to Health Questioned, Television One, *News*, 17 August 2001.

34 'Bashings, Lies by Police Claimed', *NZ Herald*, 22 March 2004.

35 Winiata, op. cit., p. 1.

36 Ibid.

37 Ibid., p. 2.

38 Mason Durie, 'Tino Rangatiratanga: Maori Self-determination' in *He Pukenga Korero, A Journal of Maori Studies*, pp. 50–51.

39 'Tino Rangitiratanga' in *20 Yrs of Protest Action 1979–1999, Te Kawariki*, p. 65.

40 Mason Durie, 'Tino Rangitiratanga', p. 52.

41 Donald A. Grinde, 'Iroquois Political Theory and the Roots of American Democracy' in Oren Lyons et al., *Exiled in the Land of the Free*, p. 231.

42 Ibid. For a full description of the Iroquois Confederacy, see Chapter 6.

43 Building the Constitution Conference, Wellington, 7–8 April 2000, website.

44 Patricia Grace, *The Treaty of Waitangi and the Expression of Culture in Aotearoa* in Proceedings of the Treaty Conference 2000, pp. 26–27.

BIBLIOGRAPHY

Books

Adams, James L. (1986), *Conceptual Blockbusting: A Guide to Better Ideas*, 3rd edn, Perseus Books, Reading.

Adams, Peter (1977), *Fatal Necessity: British Intervention in New Zealand 1830–1847*, Auckland University Press, Auckland.

Ahdar, Rex and John Stenhouse (eds) (2000), *God and Government*, University of Otago Press, Dunedin.

Alfred, Taiaiake (1999), *Peace, Power, Righteousness: An Indigenous Manifesto*, Oxford University Press, Ontario.

Alston, Andrew, Tom Bennion, Michele Slatter, Rod Thomas and Elizabeth Toomey (eds) (1997), *Guide to New Zealand Land Law*, Brooker's Ltd, Wellington.

Akenson, Donald Harman (1996), *The Irish Diaspora: A Primer*, P. D. Meany Company Inc. Publishers, Toronto.

Alinsky, Saul D. (1972), *Rules for Radicals*, Random House, New York.

Allen, Theodore W. (1995), *The Invention of the White Race: Racial Oppression and Social Control*, Vol. 1, Verso, London.

Angelou, Maya (1993), *On the Pulse of Morning*, Random House, New York.

Angus, Murray (1990), *'And the Last Shall Be First': Native Policy in an Era of Cutbacks*, Aboriginal Rights Coalition (Project North), Ottawa.

Arbuckle, Gerald A. (1990), *Earthing the Gospel*, Orbis Books, New York.

Arbuckle, Gerald A. (1993), *Refounding the Church: Dissent for Leadership*, Orbis Books, Maryknoll, New York.

Ardagh, John (1995), *Ireland and the Irish Portrait of a Changing Society*, Penguin Books, London.

Armitage, Andrew (1995), *Comparing the Policy of Aboriginal Assimilation: Australia, Canada and New Zealand*, University of British Columbia Press, Vancouver.

Arnold, Johann Christoph (1998), *The Lost Art of Forgiving: Stories of Healing from the Cancer of Bitterness*, The Plough Publishing House of the Bruderhof Foundation, Sussex.

Arnove, Anthony (ed.) (2000), *Iraq Under Siege: The Deadly Impact of Sanctions and War*, South End Press, Cambridge, Massachusetts.

Atkinson, Neill (2003), *Adventures in Democracy: A History of the Vote in New Zealand*, University of Otago Press, Dunedin.

Ballara, Angela (1986), *Proud to Be White*, Heinemann, Auckland.

Ballara, Angela (1998), *Iwi: The Dynamics of Maori Tribal Organisation from c.1769 to c.1945*, Victoria University Press, Wellington.

Barkan, Elazar (2000), *The Guilt of Nations: Restitution and Negotiating Historical Injustices*, W. W. Norton & Co., New York/London.

Barndt, Joseph (1991), *Dismantling Racism: The Continuing Challenge to White America*, Augsburg Fortress, Minneapolis.

Bartlett, Richard H. (1993), *The Mabo Decision*, Butterworths, Sydney.

Belich, James (1996), *Making Peoples: A History of the New Zealanders*, Allen Lane/Penguin Books, Auckland.

Bird, Carmel (ed.) (1998), *The Stolen Children: Their Stories*, Random House, Sydney.

Bishop, Russell and Ted Glynn (1999), *Culture Counts: Changing Power Relations in Education*, Dunmore Press, Palmerston North.

Blaut, J. M. (1993), *The Colonizers' Model of the World: Geographical Diffusionism and Eurocentric History*, Guilford Press, New York.

Blum, William (1995), *Killing Hope: US Military and CIA Interventions Since World War II*, Common Courage Press, Monroe.

Boast, Richard, Andrew Erueti, Doug McPhail and Norman F. Smith (1999), *Maori Land Law*, Butterworths, Wellington.

Borrie, W. D. (1991), *Immigration to New Zealand 1854–1938*, Highland Press, Canberra.

Brookfield, F. M. (1999), *Waitangi and Indigenous Rights: Revolution, Law and Legitimation*, Auckland University Press, Auckland.

Brooks, Roy L. (ed.) (1999), *When Sorry Isn't Enough: The Controversy Over Apologies and Reparations for Human Injustice* (Critical American Series), New York University Press, New York.

Broome, Richard (1992), *The Australian Experience: Aboriginal Australians*, Allen & Unwin, Sydney.

Burger, Julian (1990), *The Gaia Atlas of First Peoples*, Doubleday, Auckland.

Butt, Peter and Robert Eagleson (1996), *Mabo: What the High Court Said*, 2nd edn, The Federation Press, Sydney.

Byrnes, Giselle (2004), *The Waitangi Tribunal and New Zealand History*, Oxford University Press, Victoria.

Carr, E. H. (1987), *What is History?*, 2nd edn, R. W. Davies (ed.), Penguin Books, London.

Carroll, James (2000), *Constantine's Sword: The Church and the Jews: A History*, Horton Mifflin, Oxfordshire.

Carty, Anthony (1996), *Was Ireland Conquered? International Law and the Irish Question*, Pluto Press, London/Chicago.

Chittister, Joan (2004), *Called to Question: A Spiritual Memoir*, Sheed & Ward, Oxford.

Chomsky, Noam (1988), *The Culture of Terrorism*, South End Press, Boston, Massachusetts.

Chomsky, Noam (2000), *Rogue States: The Rule of Force in World Affairs*, South End Press, Cambridge, Massachusetts.

Chossudovsky, Michel (1997), *The Globalisation of Poverty: Impacts of IMF and World Bank Reforms*, Zed Books, London.

Coates, Ken (ed.) (1992), *Aboriginal Land Claims in Canada: A Regional Perspective*, Copp Clark Pitman, Ontario.

Collins School Series (circa 1900), *The New Zealand Graphic Reader Sixth Book*, Collins, Auckland/Wellington.

Consedine, Bob (1984), *New Zealand (1984) Ltd*, Four Star Books, Auckland.

Consedine, Jim (1999), *Restorative Justice: Healing the Effects of Crime*, Ploughshares Publications, Christchurch.

Consedine, Jim and Helen Bowen (1999), *Restorative Justice: Contemporary Themes and Practice*, Ploughshares Publications, Christchurch.

Coogan, Tim Pat (1995), *The I.R.A.*, HarperCollins, London.

Coogan, Tim Pat (1996), *The Troubles: Ireland's Ordeal 1966–1996 and the Search for Peace*, Arrow Books, London.

Cornwell, John (1999), *Hitler's Pope: The Secret History of Pius XII*, Viking, New York.

Coull, Cheryl (1996), *A Traveller's Guide to Aboriginal B.C.*, Whitecap Books, Vancouver/Toronto.

Cox, Lindsay (1993), *Kotahitanga: The Search for Maori Political Unity*, Oxford University Press, Auckland.

Coxon, Eve, Kuni Jenkins, James Marshall and Lauran Massey (eds) (1994), *The Politics of Learning and Teaching in Aotearoa–New Zealand*, Dunmore Press, Palmerston North.

Crosby, R. D. (1999), *The Musket Wars: A History of Inter-Iwi Conflict 1806–45*, Reed Publishing, Auckland.

Crossan, John Dominic (1996), *Who Killed Jesus?: Exposing the Roots of Anti-Semitism in the Gospel Story of the Death of Jesus*, Harper, San Francisco.

Cuffley, Peter (1999), *Family History Comes to Life*, Lothian Books, Melbourne.

Curtis, Mark (2003), *Web of Deceit: Britain's Real Role in the World*, Vintage, London.

Dacker, Bill (1994), *Te Mamae me te Aroha, The Pain and the Love: A History of Kai Tahu Whanui in Otago, 1844–1994*, University of Otago Press/Dunedin City Council, Dunedin.

Dalley, Bronwyn and Jock Phillips (eds) (2001), *Going Public: The Changing Face of New Zealand History*, Auckland University Press, Auckland.

Dalley, Bronwyn and Margaret Tennant (eds) (2004), *Past Judgement: Social*

Policy in New Zealand History, University of Otago Press, Dunedin.

Davis, Richard P. (1974), Irish Issues in New Zealand Politics 1868–1922, University of Otago Press, Dunedin.

Davidson, James West, William E. Gienapp, Christine Leigh Heyrman, Mark H. Lytle and Michael B. Stoff (1990), Nation of Nations: A Narrative History of the American Republic, Volume II: Since 1865, McGraw-Hill, New York.

De Bono, Edward (1992), Handbook for the Positive Revolution, Penguin Books, London.

de Ishtar, Zohl (ed.) (1998), Pacific Women Speak Out for Independence and Denuclearisation, Women's International League for Peace and Freedom, Aotearoa; the Disarmament and Security Centre, Aotearoa; Pacific Connections, Australia.

de Las Casas, Bartolomé (1992), In Defense of the Indians, Stafford Poole C. M. (ed.) (trans.), Northern Illinois University Press, Illinois.

Delaney, Frank (1989), The Celts, HarperCollins, London.

Delgamuukw (1998), The Supreme Court of Canada Decision on Aboriginal Title, Greystone Books/David Suzuki Foundation, Vancouver.

Deloria, Vine Jr (1990), Behind the Trail of Broken Treaties: An Indian Declaration of Independence, University of Texas Press, Texas.

de Lubac, Henri (1990), Christian Resistance to Anti-Semitism: Memories from 1940–1944, Ignatius Press, San Francisco.

Dickason, Olive Patricia (1992), Canada's First Nations: A History of Founding Peoples from Earliest Times, McClelland & Stewart, Toronto.

Donovan, Vincent J. (1982), Christianity Rediscovered: An Epistle from the Masai, 2nd edn, Orbis Books, Maryknoll, New York.

Donovan, Vincent J. (1997), The Church in the Midst of Creation, Orbis Books, Maryknoll, New York.

Dryden, Gordon and Jeannette Vos, (1997), The Learning Revolution: Your 21st Century Passport: for Families, Students, Teachers, Managers, Trainers, The Learning Web Ltd, Auckland.

Duff, Wilson (1992), The Indian History of British Columbia, Vol. 1: The Impact of the White Man, Royal British Columbia Museum, Victoria, British Columbia.

Dulles, S. J., Avery and Rabbi Leon Klenicki (2001), The Holocaust, Never to be Forgotten: Reflections on the Holy See's Document We Remember, (commentaries), Paulist Press, New Jersey.

Durie, Mason (1998), Te Mana, Te Kawanatanga: The Politics of Maori Self-Determination, Oxford University Press, Auckland.

Durie, Mason (1999), Whaiora: Maori Health Development, 2nd edn, Oxford University Press, Auckland.

Durie, Mason (2003), Nga Kahui Pou: Launching Maori Futures, Huia Publishers, Wellington.

Evison, Harry C. (1997), The Long Dispute: Maori Land Rights and European Colonisation in Southern New Zealand, Canterbury University Press, Christchurch.

Ewing, John L. (1970), *The Development of the New Zealand Primary School Curriculum 1877–1970*, New Zealand Council for Educational Research, Wellington.

Fiedler, Maureen and Linda Rabben (eds) (1998), *Rome Has Spoken: A Guide to Forgotten Papal Statements and How They Have Changed Through the Centuries*, Crossroad Publishing, New York.

Fisher, Robin (1992), *Indian–European Relations in British Columbia 1774–1890: Conflict and Contact*, University of British Columbia Press, Vancouver.

Fleras, Augie and Paul Spoonley (1999), *Recalling Aotearoa: Indigenous Politics and Ethnic Relations in New Zealand*, Oxford University Press, Auckland.

Fraser, Lyndon (1997), *To Tara via Holyhead*, Auckland University Press, Auckland.

Freire, Paulo (1972), *Pedagogy of the Oppressed*, Penguin Books, London.

Freire, Paulo (1992), *Pedagogy of Hope: Reliving Pedagogy of the Oppressed*, Continuum Publishing Company, New York.

Frideres, James S. (1993), *Native Peoples in Canada: Contemporary Conflicts*, 4th edn, Prentice Hall Canada, Scarborough (On.)

Gamez, George (1996), *Creativity: How to Catch Lightning in a Bottle*, Peak Publications, Los Angeles.

Gardiner, Wira (1996), *Return to Sender: What Really Happened at the Fiscal Envelope Hui*, Reed Publishing, Auckland.

Glen, Robert (ed.) (1992), *Mission and Moko: The Church Missionary Society in New Zealand 1814–1882*, Latimer Fellowship, Christchurch.

gkisedtanamoogk and Frances Hancock (1993), *Anoqcou: Ceremony is Life Itself*, Astarte Shell Press, Portland.

Goldhagen, Daniel Jonah (2002), *A Moral Reckoning: The Role of the Catholic Church in the Holocaust and Its Unfulfilled Duty of Repair*, Little, Brown, London.

Grace, Patricia (1992), *Cousins*, Penguin Books, Auckland.

Gray, John (1998), *False Dawn: The Delusions of Global Capitalism*, The New Press, New York.

Grief, Stuart W. (ed.) (1995), *Immigration and National Identity in New Zealand*, Dunmore Press, Palmerston North.

Harbison, Peter (1994), *Pre-Christian Ireland: From the First Settlers to the Early Celts*, Thames & Hudson, London.

Havemann, Paul (ed.) (1999), *Indigenous People's Rights in Australia, Canada and New Zealand*, Oxford University Press, Auckland.

Hayward, Janine (ed.) (2003), *Local Government and the Treaty of Waitangi*, Oxford University Press, Melbourne.

Hilberg, Raul (1985), *The Destruction of the European Jews*, Holmes & Meier Publishers, New York.

Hoffman, Nicola and Wayne Scott (1984), *Psychodrama Institute of New Zealand (Inc.) Handbook*, PINZ, Auckland.

Houghton, Philip (1980), *The First New Zealanders*, Hodder & Stoughton, Auckland.

Howitt, Richard and John Connell (eds) (1991), *Mining and Indigenous Peoples in Australasia*, Sydney University Press, Sydney.

Hunter, Dale, Anne Bailey and Bill Taylor (1992), *The Zen of Groups: A Handbook for People Meeting with a Purpose*, Tandem Press, Auckland.

Ignatiev, Noel (1995), *How the Irish Became White*, Routledge, New York.

Illich, Ivan (1970), *The Church: Change and Development*, Urban Training Center Press, Herder and Herder, New York.

Imai, Shin (1996), *The 1997 Annotated Indian Act*, Carswell Thompson Professional Publishing, Toronto.

Jaimes, M. Annette (1992), *The State of Native America: Genocide, Colonization and Resistance*, South End Press, Boston, Massachusetts.

Jesson, Bruce (1999), *Only Their Purpose is Mad: The Money Men Take Over New Zealand*, Dunmore Press, Palmerston North.

Joseph, Philip A. (1993), *Constitutional and Administrative Law in New Zealand*, The Law Book Company, Sydney.

Kawharu, I. H. (1977), *Maori Land Tenure: Studies of a Changing Institution*, Oxford University Press, Oxford.

Kawharu, I. H. (ed.) (1989), *Waitangi: Maori & Pakeha Perspectives of the Treaty of Waitangi*, Oxford University Press, Auckland.

Kee, Robert (1976), *The Most Distressful Country: The Green Flag*, Vol. 1, Quartet Books, London.

Kee, Robert (1994), *The Laurel and the Ivy: The Story of Charles Stewart Parnell and Irish Nationalism*, Penguin Books, London.

Kelsey, Jane (1990), *A Question of Honour? Labour and the Treaty 1984–1989*, Allen & Unwin New Zealand in association with Port Nicholson Press, Wellington.

Kelsey, Jane (1995), *The New Zealand Experiment: A World Model for Structural Adjustment?*, Auckland University Press with Bridget Williams Books, Auckland.

Kertzer, David I. (2001), *The Popes Against the Jews: The Vatican's Role in the Rise of Modern Anti-Semitism*, Alfred A. Knopf, New York.

Kinealy, Christine (1995), *This Great Calamity: The Irish Famine 1845–1852*, Robert Rinehart Publishers, Colorado.

King, Michael (1985), *Being Pakeha*, Hodder and Stoughton, Auckland.

King, Michael (ed.) (1991), *Pakeha: The Quest for Identity in New Zealand*, Penguin Books, Auckland.

King, Michael (1997), *God's Farthest Outpost: A History of Catholics in New Zealand*, Penguin Books, Auckland.

King, Michael (1999), *Being Pakeha Now*, Penguin Books, Auckland.

King, Michael (2000), *Moriori: A People Rediscovered*, revised edition, Penguin Books, Auckland.

Kivel, Paul (1996), *Uprooting Racism: How White People Can Work for Racial Justice*, New Society Publishers, Philadelphia and Gabriola Island, British Columbia.

Lange, Raeburn (1999), *May the People Live: A History of Maori Health Development 1900–1920*, Auckland University Press, Auckland.

Lipstadt, Deborah (1993), *Denying the Holocaust: The Growing Assault on Truth and Memory*, The Free Press, New York.

Lyons, Oren, John Mohawk, Vine Deloria Jr, Laurence Hauptman, Howard Berman, Donald Grinde Jr, Curtis Berkey and Robert Venables (eds) (1992), *Exiled in the Land of the Free*, Clear Light Publishers, Sante Fe.

MacEoin, Gary (ed.) (1998), *The Papacy and the People of God*, Orbis Books, Maryknoll, New York.

Macintyre, Stuart and Anna Clark (2003), *The History Wars*, Melbourne University Press, Victoria.

McClory, Robert (1995), *Turning Point*, Crossroad, New York.

McClure, Margaret (1998), *A Civilised Community: A History of Social Security in New Zealand 1898–1998*, Auckland University Press, Auckland.

McDonald, K. C. (compiler) (1927; 1960 13th printing), *Our Country: A Brief Survey of New Zealand History and Civics*, Whitcombe and Tombs, Wellington.

McGibbon, Ian (1991), *The Path to Gallipoli: Defending New Zealand 1840–1915*, GP Books, Wellington.

McHugh, Paul (1991), *The Maori Magna Carta: New Zealand Law and the Treaty of Waitangi*, Oxford University Press, Auckland.

McNamara, Robert S. (1996), *In Retrospect: The Tragedy and Lessons of Vietnam*, Vintage Books, New York.

McNeil, Kent (1989), *Common Law Aboriginal Title*, Clarendon Press, Oxford.

Mangan, J. A. (ed.) (1993), *The Imperial Curriculum: Racial Images and Education in the British Colonial Experience*, Routledge, London.

Manne, Robert (ed.) (2003), *Whitewash: On Keith Windshuttle's Fabrication of Aboriginal History*, Black Inc. Agenda, an imprint of Schwartz Publishing, Melbourne.

Maxwell, John Francis (1975), *Slavery and the Catholic Church: The History of Catholic Teaching Concerning the Moral Legitimacy of the Institution of Slavery*, Barry Rose Publishers, Chichester and London.

Memmi, Albert (1991), *The Colonizer and the Colonized*, Beacon Press, Boston.

Memon, Ali and Harvey Perkins (eds) (2000), *Environmental Planning and Management in New Zealand*, Dunmore Press, Palmerston North.

Miller, Harold (1954), *The Maori and the Missionary*, School Publications Branch, Department of Education, Wellington.

Miller, J. R. (1996), *Shingwauk's Vision: A History of Native Residential Schools*, University of Toronto Press, Toronto.

Monin, Paul (2001), *This Is My Place: Hauraki Contested 1769–1875*, Bridget Williams Books, Wellington.

Moon, Paul (1994), *The Origins of the Treaty of Waitangi*, Birdwood Publishing, Auckland.

Moon, Paul (1998), *Hobson: Governor of New Zealand 1840–1842*, David Ling Publishing, Auckland.

Moon, Paul (2000), *FitzRoy: Governor in Crisis 1843–1845*, David Ling Publishing, Auckland.

Moon, Paul (2002), *Te Ara Ki Te Tiriti, The Path to the Treaty of Waitangi*, David Ling Publishing, Auckland.

Mitchell, Hilary Anne and Maui John Mitchell (1993), *Maori Teachers Who Leave the Classroom*, New Zealand Council for Educational Research, Wellington.

Muldoon, James (1979), *Popes, Lawyers and Infidels*, University of Pennsylvania Press, Philadelphia.

Naumann, Ruth (2002), *Our Treaty: The Treaty of Waitangi 1840 to the Present*, New House Publishers, Auckland.

Naumann, Ruth, Lyn Harrison and Te Kaponga Winiata (1990), *Te Mana o Te Tiriti: The Living Treaty*, New House Publications, Auckland.

Neillands, Robin (1997), *A Fighting Retreat: The British Empire 1947–1997*, Hodder & Stoughton, London.

Nelson-Pallmeyer, Jack (1997), *School of Assassins*, Orbis Books, Maryknoll, New York.

Novick, Peter (2001), *The Holocaust and Collective Memory*, Bloomsbury, London.

Novitz, David and Bill Willmott (eds) (1989), *Culture and Identity in New Zealand*, GP Books, Wellington.

Oberdorfer, Don (1999), *The Two Koreas: A Contemporary History*, Little, Brown, London.

Oddie, Graham and Roy Perrett (eds) (1992), *Justice, Ethics, and New Zealand Society*, Oxford University Press, Auckland.

O'Brien, Maire and Conor Cruise (1994), *Ireland: A Concise History*, Thames & Hudson, London.

O'Donohue, John (1998), *Eternal Echoes: Exploring Our Hunger to Belong*, Bantam Press, London.

O'Malley, Vincent (1998), *Agents of Autonomy: Maori Committees in the Nineteenth Century*, Huia Publishers, Wellington.

Oliver, W. H. (ed.) (1981), *The Oxford History of New Zealand*, Clarendon Press, Oxford/Oxford University Press, Wellington.

Openshaw, Roger (ed.) (1992), *New Zealand Social Studies: Past, Present and Future*, Academic Monograph No. 12, Dunmore Press, Palmerston North.

Orange, Claudia (1987), *The Treaty of Waitangi*, Allen & Unwin, Wellington.

Orange, Claudia (1990), *An Illustrated History of The Treaty of Waitangi*, Allen & Unwin, Wellington.

Palmer, Alison (2000), *Colonial Genocide*, Crawford House Publishing, Hindmarsh, South Australia.

Pattel-Gray, Anne (1991), *Through Aboriginal Eyes: The Cry from the Wilderness*, WCC Publications, Geneva.

Pawson, Eric and Tom Brooking (2002), *Environmental Histories of New Zealand*, Oxford University Press, Auckland.

Peters, Michael (ed.) (1997), *Cultural Politics and the University in Aotearoa/New Zealand*, Dunmore Press, Palmerston North.

Peters, M. (ed.) (1999), *After the Disciplines: The Emergence of Cultural Studies*, Bergin & Garvey, Westport, Connecticut.

Phayer, Michael (2000), *The Catholic Church and the Holocaust: 1930–1965*, Indiana University Press, Bloomington, Indiana.

Pool, Ian (1991), *Te Iwi Maori: A New Zealand Population Past, Present and Projected*, Auckland University Press, Auckland.

Price, Richard T. (1991), *Legacy: Indian Treaty Relationships*, Plains Publishing Inc., Edmonton.

Prucha, Francis Paul (1984), *The Great Father: The United States Government and the American Indians, Vol. 1: Lincoln*, University of Nebraska Press, Omaha, Nebraska.

Read, Peter (1999), *A Rape of the Soul So Profound*, Allen & Unwin, St Leonards, New South Wales.

Redmond, Michael L. (1994), *A Nation's Holocaust and Betrayal: Ireland 1172–1992*, Pentland Press, Durham.

Renwick, William (ed.) (1991), *Sovereignty and Indigenous Rights: The Treaty of Waitangi in International Contexts*, Victoria University Press, Wellington.

Reynolds, Henry (1992), *The Law of the Land*, 2nd edn, Penguin Books, Victoria.

Reynolds, Henry (1996), *Frontier: Reports from the Edge of White Settlement*, Allen & Unwin, St Leonards, New South Wales.

Reynolds, Henry (1999), *Why Weren't We Told? A Personal Search for the Truth About Our History*, Viking, Penguin Books, Victoria.

Riseborough, Hazel (1989), *Days of Darkness: Taranaki 1878–1884*, Allen & Unwin, Wellington.

Robinson, Randall N. (2000), *The Debt: What America Owes to Blacks*, Dutton and Plume, New York.

Roesdahl, Else (1992), *The Vikings*, Penguin Books, London.

Rosner, Jorge (1987), *Peeling the Onion: Gestalt Theory and Methodology*, Gestalt Institute of Toronto, Toronto.

Roy, Arundhati (2001), *Power Politics*, South End Press, Cambridge, Massachusetts.

Said, Edward W. (1993), *Culture and Imperialism*, Vintage, London.

Salmond, Anne (1993), *Two Worlds: First Meetings Between Maori and Europeans 1642–1772*, Viking, Auckland.

Salmond, Anne (1997), *Between Worlds: Early Exchanges Between Maori and Europeans 1773–1815*, Viking, Auckland.

Saunders, Frances Stonor (1999), *The Cultural Cold War: The C.I.A. and the World of Arts and Letters*, New Press, New York.

Scott, Dick (1975), *Ask That Mountain: The Story of Parihaka*, Heinemann/ Southern Cross, Auckland.

Shiel, M.J. (ed.) (1986), *A Forgotten Campaign: Aspects of the Heritage of Southeast Galway*, Woodford Heritage Group, Woodford.

Shirres, Michael P. (1997), *Te Tangata: The Human Person*, Accent Publications, Auckland.

Simon, Judith (ed.) (1998), *Nga Kura Maori: The Native Schools System 1867–1969*, Auckland University Press, Auckland.

Simpson, Tony (1997), *The Immigrants: The Great Migration from Britain to New Zealand, 1830–1890*, Godwit Publishing, Auckland.

Sinclair, Keith (1986), *A Destiny Apart: New Zealand's Search for National Identity*, Allen & Unwin in association with Port Nicholson Press, Wellington.

Slack, David (2004), *Bullshit, Backlash and Bleeding Hearts: A Confused Person's Guide to the Great Race Row*, Penguin Books, Auckland.

Smith, Linda Tuhiwai (1999), *Decolonizing Methodologies: Research and Indigenous Peoples*, Zed Books, New York. University of Otago Press, Dunedin.

Soyinka, Wole (1999), *The Burden of Memory: The Muse of Forgiveness*, Oxford University Press, New York.

Spiller, Peter, Jeremy Finn and Richard Boast (1995), *A New Zealand Legal History*, Brookers, Wellington.

Spoonley, Paul and Cluny Macpherson, David Pearson and C. Sedgwick (eds) (1984), *Tauiwi: Racism and Ethnicity in New Zealand*, Dunmore Press, Palmerston North.

Spoonley, Paul and Walter Hirsh (eds) (1990), *Between the Lines: Racism and the New Zealand Media*, Heinemann Reed, Auckland.

Spoonley, Paul, David Pearson and Cluny Macpherson (eds) (1996), *Nga Patai: Racism and Ethnic Relations in Aotearoa/New Zealand*, Dunmore Press, Palmerston North.

Stenson, Marcia and Tu Williams (1991), *The Treaty of Waitangi*, Longman Paul, Auckland.

Stenson, Marcia (2004), *The Treaty: Every New Zealander's Guide to the Treaty of Waitangi*, Random House, Auckland.

Sternberg, Patricia and Antonina Garcia (1989), *Sociodrama: Who's in Your Shoes?*, Praeger Publishers, New York.

Stock Whitaker, Dorothy (1989), *Using Groups to Help People*, Tavistock/Routledge, London/New York.

Stogre, Michael (1992), *That the World May Believe: The Development of Papal Social Thought on Aboriginal Rights*, Editions Paulines, Quebec.

Sweetman, Rory (1997), *Bishop in the Dock: The Sedition Trial of James Liston*, Auckland University Press, Auckland.

Tatz, Colin (2003), *With Intent to Destroy: Reflecting on Genocide*, Verso, London.

Temm, Paul (1990), *The Waitangi Tribunal: The Conscience of the Nation*, Random Century, Auckland.

Tennant, Paul (1990), *Aboriginal Peoples and Politics: The Indian Land Question in British Columbia 1849–1989*, University of British Columbia Press, Vancouver.

Tinker, George E. (1993), *Missionary Conquest: The Gospel and Native Cultural Genocide*, Fortress Press, Minneapolis.

Trompenaars, Fons (1993), *Riding the Waves of Culture: Understanding Cultural Diversity in Business*, Nicholas Brealey Publishing, London.

Tutu, Desmond (1999), *No Future Without Forgiveness*, Rider, London.

Tyson, Trevor (1989), *Working with Groups*, MacMillian Education Australia, Melbourne.

Vaggioli, Dom Felice (trans. by John Crockett) (2000), *History of New Zealand and Its Inhabitants*, University of Otago Press, Dunedin.

Vaillancourt, Jean-Guy (1980), *Papal Power: A Study of Vatican Control over Lay Catholic Elites*, University of California Press, Berkeley and Los Angeles.

Walker, Ranginui (1990), *Ka Whawhai Tonu Matou: Struggle Without End*, Penguin Books, Auckland.

Walker, Ranginui (2002), *He Tipua, The Life and Times of Sir Apirana Ngata*, Penguin Books, Auckland.

Ward, Alan (1995), *A Show of Justice: Racial 'Amalgamation' in Nineteenth Century New Zealand*, Auckland University Press, Auckland.

Ward, Alan (1999), *An Unsettled History: Treaty Claims in New Zealand Today*, Bridget Williams Books, Wellington.

Whitcombe's Primary History Series (circa 1929), *Our Nation's Story: A Course of British History*, Whitcombe and Tombs, Wellington.

Williams, David V. (1999), *'Te Kooti Tango Whenua', The Native Land Court 1864–1909*, Huia Publishers, Wellington.

Wills, Garry (2000), *Papal Sin: Structures of Deceit*, Doubleday/Random House, New York.

Wilson, Desmond (1997), *Democracy Denied*, Mercier Press, Cork/Dublin.

Woodham-Smith, Cecil (1979), *The Great Hunger*, New English Library, London.

Zucotti, Susan (2000), *Under His Very Windows: The Vatican and the Holocaust in Italy*, Yale University Press, New Haven and London.

Reports and Government Publications

Bennion, Tom, Malcolm Birdling and Rebecca Paton (2004), *Making Sense of the Foreshore & Seabed*, Maori Law Review, Wellington.

British Columbia Treaty Commission, *1995–96 Annual Report*, Vancouver.

Correspondence Relative to New Zealand, No. 16, *From the Marquis of Normanby to Captain Hobson*, R.N., Downing Street, August 14th, 1839.

Dave Kennedy Consulting (May 2004), *The British Columbia Treaty Process: A Road Map for Further Progress*, prepared for the Business Council of British Columbia, Victoria, British Columbia.

Department of Education (1961), *Social Studies in the Primary School*, Primary School Syllabuses, Wellington.

Department of Education (1967), *Suggestions for Teaching Social Studies in the Primary School Index Parts 1, 2, 3, 4*, Wellington.

Department of Education (1977), *Social Studies Syllabus Guidelines Forms 1–4*, Wellington.

Department of Education (1986), *The Curriculum Review: A Draft Report Prepared by the Committee to Review the Curriculum for Schools*, Wellington.

Department of Education (1987), *Report on the Social Studies Subjects Survey 1981–1982*, Wellington.

Department of Internal Affairs–Te Tari Taiwhenua (2003), *Local Authority Election Statistics 2001: Maori in Local Government*, Wellington.

Department of Maori Affairs (1960), *Report on Department of Maori Affairs with Statistical Supplement*, by J. K. Hunn, Wellington.

Department of the Prime Minister and Cabinet (September 2003), *The Foreshore and Seabed of New Zealand, Protecting Public Access and Customary Rights: Government Proposals for Consultation*, Wellington.

Department of Social Welfare (1986), *Puao-Te-Ata-Tu (Daybreak)*, report of the Ministerial Advisory Committee on a Maori Perspective, Wellington.

Dunedin Community Law Centre (1995), *An Introduction to the Waitangi Tribunal with Reference to the Ngai Tahu Land Claim*.

Education Act 1877, reprinted 1878, Government Printer, Wellington.

Education Department (1937), *Syllabus of Instruction for Public Schools*, Wellington.

Government Review Team (September 1988), *Government Review of Te Kohanga Reo: Language is the Life Force of the People: Report of the Review of Kohanga Reo*, Wellington.

Human Rights Commission (1979), *Racial Harmony in New Zealand: A Statement of Issues*, Wellington.

Human Rights Commission (1982), *Race Against Time*, Race Relations Conciliator, Wellington.

Human Rights and Equal Opportunity Commission, Commonwealth of Australia (April 1997), *Bringing Them Home: Report of the National Inquiry into the Separation of Aboriginal and Torres Strait Islander Children from Their Families*, Sydney.

Maori Synod of the Presbyterian Church of New Zealand (1961), *A Maori View of the Hunn Report*, Christchurch.

Ministry of Agriculture and Forestry (August 2003), *Walking Access in the New Zealand Outdoors: A Report by the Land Access Ministerial Reference Group*, Wellington.

Ministry of Education (1991), *Social Studies Forms 3 & 4: A Handbook for Teachers*, Learning Media, Wellington.

Ministry of Education (1993), *Social Studies 14 Years On: An Evaluation of the Handbook for Teachers of Forms 3 & 4 Social Studies*, Report Series No. 1, Wellington.

Ministry of Education (1997), *Social Studies in the New Zealand Curriculum*, Learning Media, Wellington.

Ministry of Education (December 2003), *New Zealand's Tertiary Education Sector Report – Profile and Trends 2002*, Wellington.

Ministry of Education (June 2004), *Review of Regulation of Early Childhood*

Education, Implementing Pathways to the Future: Nga Huarahi Arataki, Wellington.

Ministry of Education and Office of the Race Relations Conciliator (1997), *In Tune: Students' Activities*, Learning Media, Wellington.

Ministry of Health (December 2003), *Health and Independence Report: Director General's Report on the State of Public Health*, Wellington.

Ministry of Health and University of Otago (July 2003), *Decades of Disparity: Ethnic Mortality Trends in New Zealand 1980–1999* by S. Ajwani, T. Blakely, B. Robson, M. Tobias and M. Bonne, Wellington.

New Zealand Education Department (1948), *The Primary School Curriculum Revised Syllabus*, School Publications Branch, Wellington.

New Zealand Educational Institute (1971), *A Teachers' Index of Core Materials for Social Studies*, Wellington.

New Zealand Institute of Economic Research (2000), *Allocating Fisheries Assets: Economic Costs of Delay, Report to Treaty Tribes Coalition*, Wellington.

New Zealand Planning Council (1999), *The Economy in Transition*, New Zealand Planning Council, Wellington.

New Zealand Public Health and Disability Act (2000).

Office of the Parliamentary Commissioner for the Environment Te Kaitiaki a Te Whare Paremata (1994), *Indigenous Claims and the Process of Negotiation and Settlements in Countries with Jurisdictions and Populations Similar to New Zealand's*, by Caren Wickliffe, Wellington.

Office of Treaty Settlements, Te Tari Whakatau Take e pa ana ki te Tiriti o Waitangi (2001), *Deed of Settlement of the Historical Claims of Ngaati Ruanui*, Wellington.

Office of Treaty Settlements, Te Tari Whakatau Take e pa ana ki te Tiriti o Waitangi (2002), *Ka tika a muri, ka tika a mua, He Tohutohu Whakamarama I nga Whakataunga Kereme e pa ana ki te Tiriti o Waitangi me nga Whakaritenga ki te Karauna, Healing the Past, Building a Future: A Guide to Treaty of Waitangi Claims and Negotiations with the Crown*, Wellington.

Office of Treaty Settlements, Te Tari Whakatau Take e pa ana ki te Tiriti o Waitangi (2004), *Ka tika a muri, ka tika a mua, He Tohutohu Whakamarama I nga Whakataunga Kereme e pa ana ki te Tiriti o Waitangi me nga Whakaritenga ki te Karauna, Healing the Past, Building a Future, A Guide to Treaty of Waitangi Claims and Negotiations with the Crown* (Summary Edition), Wellington.

Office of Treaty Settlements, Te Tari Whakatau Take e pa ana ki te Tiriti o Waitangi (2004), *Quarterly Report to 30 June 2004*, Wellington.

Primary School Bulletin (1958), *Te Tiriti o Waitangi*, by R. M. Ross, Wellington.

Regulations for Inspection and Examination of Schools, supplement to *New Zealand Gazette*, 14 April 1904, *Parliamentary Papers*, Wellington.

Report of The Royal Commission on the Electoral System: Towards a Better Democracy (1986), *A History of Maori Representation in Parliament* by M. P. K. Sorrenson, Wellington.

Royal Commission on Social Policy (1988), *The Treaty of Waitangi and Social Policy*, Discussion Booklet No. 1., Wellington.

Statistics Canada (2003), *2001 Census: Analysis Series, Aboriginal peoples of Canada: A Demographic Profile*, Canada.

Statistics New Zealand, Te Tari Tatau, *2001 Census: Snapshot 4*, Wellington.

Te Puni Kokiri (1999), *Strategic Overview*, post-election brief to incoming Minister of Maori Affairs, Wellington.

Te Puni Kokiri (2001), *He Tirohangao o Kawa Ke te Tiriti o Waitangi: A Guide to the Principles of the Treaty of Waitangi as Expressed by the Courts and the Waitangi Tribunal*, Wellington.

Tertiary Education Commission, Te Amorangi Matauranga Matua (2003), *Collaborating for Efficiency: Report of the Responsiveness to Maori Sub-group*, Sarah-Jane Tiakiwai and Lani Teddy (eds), Wellington.

The Post-Primary School Curriculum (1944) report of the committee appointed by the Minister of Education in 1942, Wellington.

Treaty of Waitangi Fisheries Commission (August 2002), *Ahu Whakamua: The Treaty of Waitangi Fisheries Settlement, What It Means for You, Summarising the Report for Agreement on the Allocation of Assets and Distribution of Benefits of the Treaty of Waitangi Fisheries Settlement*, Wellington.

Treaty of Waitangi Fisheries Commission (April 2003), *He Kawai Amokura: This report represents the 'Full Particulars' of a model for allocation of the Fisheries Settlement Assets*, Wellington.

Treaty of Waitangi Fisheries Commission (December 2003), *Te Reo o te Tini A Tangaroa*, Issue No. 70, Wellington.

Waitangi Tribunal (1985), *Wai 8: The Manukau Claim Report*, Department of Justice, Wellington.

Waitangi Tribunal (1986), *Wai 11: Te Reo Maori Report*, Department of Justice, Wellington.

Waitangi Tribunal (1987), *Wai 9: The Orakei Claim Report*, Department of Justice, Wellington.

Waitangi Tribunal (1988), *Wai 22: Muriwhenua Fishing Report*, Department of Justice, Wellington.

Waitangi Tribunal (1991), *Wai 27: The Ngai Tahu Report*, Vol. 1., Department of Justice, Wellington.

Waitangi Tribunal (1991), *Wai 27: The Ngai Tahu Report*, Vol. 2., Brooker and Friend, Wellington.

Waitangi Tribunal (1992), *Wai 307: The Fisheries Settlement Report*, Department of Justice, Wellington.

Waitangi Tribunal (1996), *Maori Land Councils and Maori Land Boards: A Historical Overview, 1900–1952*, Donald M. Loveridge, Rangahaua Whanui National Theme K, Wellington.

Waitangi Tribunal (1997), *The Crown's Engagement with Customary Tenure in the Nineteenth Century*, Hazel Riseborough and John Hutton, Rangahaua Whanui National Theme C, Wellington.

Waitangi Tribunal (1997), *Wai 45: Muriwhenua Land Report*, GP Publications, Wellington.

Waitangi Tribunal (1997), *National Overview Vol. 1*, by Alan Ward, Rangahaua

Whanui Series, GP Publications, Wellington.

Waitangi Tribunal (1997), *Public Works Takings of Maori Land, 1840–1981*, Cathy Marr, Rangahaua Whanui National Theme G, Wellington.

Waitangi Tribunal (2001), *Crown Policy Affecting Maori Knowledge Systems and Cultural Practices*, David Williams, Wellington.

Waitangi Tribunal (2004), *Wai 1071: Report on the Crown's Foreshore and Seabed Policy*, Legislation Direct, Wellington.

Waitangi Tribunal (Haratua/May 2004), *Te Manutukutuku*, Wellington.

World Council of Churches (1983), *Racism in Children's and School Textbooks*, Programme to Combat Racism, Office of Education, Geneva.

Articles

Black, Rose (October 2000), 'Political Implications of the Name "Pakeha"', in *Living Justly in Aotearoa*, Justice and Peace Office and the Bicultural Desk of the Auckland Catholic Diocese and Pax Christi Aotearoa.

Boast, Richard (Autumn/Winter 2004), 'Constitutional Crisis Over Foreshore & Seabed in Aotearoa' in *Pacific Ecologist*, double issue 7/8.

Brett, Cate (March 1994), 'Death by Adventure' in *North and South*.

Brooking, Tom (1992), '"Busting Up" the Greatest Estate of All: Liberal Maori Land Policy 1891–1911' in *New Zealand Journal of History*, Vol. 26, No. 1.

Buckland, Susan (7 August 2004), 'Children of the Poor' in *New Zealand Listener*.

Creedon, Jeremiah (April 1999), 'To Hell and Back' in *Utne Reader*, No. 92.

Doherty, Kathleen (December 2000), 'Reporting with Integrity' in *Tui Motu InterIslands*.

Dowrick, Stephanie (April 1999), 'The Art of Letting Go' in *Utne Reader*, No. 92.

Durie, Mason (1995), 'Tino Rangatiratanga: Maori Self-Determination' in *He Pukenga Korero: A Journal of Maori Studies*, Vol. 1, No. 1.

Economist, 19 April 1997.

Elias, Robert (summer 2002/2003), 'Terrorism & American Foreign Policy' in *Pacific Ecologist*, issue 4.

Ferguson, Philip (December/January 1996), 'Ireland: The End of National Liberation' in *New Zealand Monthly Review*, No. 353.

Galbraith, Ross (2002), 'Displacement, Conservation and Customary Use of Native Plants and Animals in New Zealand' in *New Zealand Journal of History*, Vol. 36, No. 1.

Gilling, Bryan D. (1993), 'The Maori Land Court in New Zealand: An Historical Overview' in *The Canadian Journal of Native Studies*, Vol. 13, No.1.

Johnson, Elizabeth A. (19 November 1999), 'Galileo's Daughters' in *Commonweal*.

Jones, Alison (1999), 'The Limits of Cross-cultural Dialogue: Pedagogy, Desire and Absolution in the Classroom' in *Educational Theory*, Summer, Vol. 49, No. 3.

The Journal of the Polynesian Society, Vol. 113, No. 1, March 2004.

London Review of Books, 14 October 1999.

Malone, E. P. (1973), 'The New Zealand School Journal and the Imperial Ideology' in *New Zealand Journal of History*, Vol. 7, No. 1.

Mana, issue 56, February/March 2004.

Mana, issue 58, June/July 2004.

Mana, issue 59, August/September 2004.

McGeorge, Colin (1999), 'What Was "Our Nation's Story"? New Zealand Primary School History Textbooks Between the Wars' in *History of Education Review*, Vol. 28, No. 2.

McIntosh, Peggy (1992), 'Unpacking the Invisible Knapsack: White Privilege' in *Creation Spirituality*, Vol. VIII, No. 1.

McIntosh, Peggy (1992), *White Privilege: Unpacking the Invisible Knapsack*, from Working Paper 189, 'White Privilege and Male Privilege: A Personal Account of Coming to See Correspondences through Work in Women's Studies' (1988), Wellesley College Center for Research on Women, Wellesley, Massachusetts.

Moon, Paul (1998), 'The Creation of the Sealord Deal' in *Journal of the Polynesian Society*, Vol. 107, No. 2.

Moon, Paul (1999), 'Three Historical Interpretations of the Treaty of Waitangi (1840)' in *Electronic Journal of Australian and New Zealand History*.

Mutch, Carol (1996), 'New Zealand Social Studies 1961–1995: A View of Curriculum Change' in *Children's Social and Economics Education*, Vol. 1, No. 1.

Mutch, Carol (1998), 'Current Perceptions of the New Social Studies Curriculum in New Zealand' in *Children's Social and Economics Education*, Vol. 3, No. 0.

National Catholic Reporter, 22 October 1993, 2 June 2000, 27 October 2000.

Evening Mail, 27 November 1993.

New York Review, 25 May 2000.

New Zealand Herald, 2 October 1999; 7 March 2000; 8 September 2002; 22 March 2004; 2 July 2004; 18 September 2004.

New Zealand Institute of Economic Research (2003), *Maori Economic Development: Te Ohanga Whanaketanga Maori*, Wellington.

New Zealand Listener, 1 May 2004.

O'Toole, Fintan (5 October 2000), 'Are the Troubles Over?' in *New York Review*.

Orange, Claudia (April 1987), 'An Exercise in Maori Autonomy: The Rise and Demise of the Maori War Effort Organization' in *New Zealand Journal of History*, Vol. 22, No. 2.

Owens, J. M. R. (1968), 'Christianity and the Maoris to 1840' in *New Zealand Journal of History*, Vol. 2, No. 1.

Pablo, Richard (19 December 1997), 'Inculturation Defends Human, Cosmic Life' in *National Catholic Reporter*.

Ross, John O. (1980), 'Busby and the Declaration of Independence' in *New Zealand Journal of History*, Vol. 14, No. 1.

Rothman, David J. (30 November 2000), 'The Shame of Medical Research' in *New York Review*.

Stenhouse, John (1996), 'A Disappearing Race Before We Came Here: Doctor Alfred Kindome Newman, the Dying Maori, and Victorian Scientific Racism' in *New Zealand Journal of History* Vol. 30, No. 2.

Stenson, Marcia (1990), 'History in New Zealand Schools' in *New Zealand Journal of History*, Vol. 24, No. 2.

Synod of Catholic Bishops (1971), *Justice in the World*, Typis Polyglottis Vaticanis, Rome.

Taonui, Rawiri (2004), 'Truly People of the Land' in *The Press*, 19 August 2004.

Te Kawariki (1999), *20 Yrs of Protest Action 1979–1999*, Te Kawariki, Box 546, Kaitaia.

The Age, Melbourne, 17 December 1995.

Tremewan, Peter (1992), 'The French Alternative to the Treaty of Waitangi' in *New Zealand Journal of History*, Vol. 26, No. 1.

Waters, Hazel (1995), 'The Great Famine and the Rise of Anti-Irish Racism' in *Journal of Race and Class*.

Whitaker, Raymond and Justin Huggler (23 May 2004), *The Independent*.

Yarwood, A.T. (1970), 'The Missionary Marsden—An Australian View' in *New Zealand Journal of History*, Vol. 4, No. 1.

Conference Papers

Black, Titoki, Philip Marshall and Kathie Irwin (2003), *Maori Language Nests in NZ: Te Kohanga Reo, 1982–2003*, United Nations Permanent Forum on Indigenous Issues, 12–22 May 2003, New York.

Consedine, Robert (1997), 'Keynote address: Journeying Together: The Contemporary New Zealand Treaty Experience. A Pakeha/European Perspective'. Aboriginal Education Conference, Gathering of Nations. 5–8 February, Victoria, British Columbia.

Dalziel, Paul (2000), *Changing Economic Realities*, Conference of the New Zealand Association of Counsellors, Christchurch.

Durie, E. Taihakurei (1990), *Treaties and Common Law Rights as Sources of Indigenous Rights*, Commonwealth Law Conference, Auckland.

Durie, Mason, *Nga Matatini Maori: Diverse Maori Realities* (1995), Wananga Purongo Korerorero Ngaruawahia—Maori Health Framework Seminar, 14–17 February, Turangawaewae Marae.

Durie, Mason (24 February 2001), *A Framework for Considering Maori Educational Advancement*, Hui Taumata Matauranga, Turangi, Taupo.

Grace, Patricia (2000), *The Treaty of Waitangi and the Expression of Culture in Aotearoa* in Proceedings of the Treaty Conference 2000, Auckland.

Hokowhitu, Brendan (2001), *Maori as the Savage Other: Icons of Racial Representation*, paper accepted for presentation at the Tokyo Foundation International Forum on Social Inequality, 31 October to 2 November, Howard University, Washington DC.

Philips, Jock (2000), *The Constitution and Independent Nationhood*, Building the Constitution Conference, 7–8 April, Wellington.

Ross, Ruth (1972), *The Treaty on the Ground* in *The Treaty of Waitangi: Its Origins and Significance*, papers presented at a seminar at Victoria University, Wellington.

Sanders, Douglas (1993), *State Practice and the United Nations Draft Declaration on the Rights of Indigenous Peoples*, Conference on Becoming Visible: Indigenous Politics and Self-government, Tromso, Norway.

Wootten, Hal (1994), *Eddie Mabo's Case and its Implications for Australia*, Native Title and Trans Tasman Experience Conference (Mabo) Papers, Trans Tasman Consultants, Christchurch.

Broadcast Media and Music

Bastion Point: The Untold Story, Television New Zealand, 23 June 1999.

Breakfast, Television One, 10 July 2003.

Face the Nation, Television New Zealand, 27 July 2000.

Globalisation and Maori (1998), documentary video, TKM Productions, Auckland.

Holmes, Television New Zealand, 29 May 1997.

Hughes, Robert (2000), *Beyond the Fatal Shore*, BBC Television.

Insight, Radio New Zealand, Sir Tipene O'Regan, Treaty of Waitangi Settlements, 2 February 2003.

Mana News, Radio New Zealand, 31 July 2000.

O'Connor, Sinead (1994), 'Famine', Universal Mother, Ensign Records, Ireland.

Radio New Zealand, Brian Gaynor interview with John Campbell, 7 October 2000.

Television One News, Maori Access to Health Questioned, 17 August 2001.

Television One News, report by Mihingarangi Forbes (source: Ministry of Education/Wellington East Girls' College), 31 August 2000.

Television One News, Study Shows Ethnic Wage Gaps, 9 October 2000.

Te Matakite o Aotearoa: The Maori Land March (1975), co-ordinated by New Perspectives on Race, Seehear Productions Ltd in co-production with Television Two, Auckland.

Wai Kapohe, Deborah (Waitangi Day 2004), *Borderless*, at The World Premiere of Timeless Land, Dunedin.

Unpublished Papers

Consedine, Robert (1992), 'Diary of Churchill Fellowship Study Tour'.

Consedine, Robert (1992), 'Exiled in the Land of the Free: A journey through North America, England and Ireland to study anti-racism programmes and treaties on a Churchill Fellowship'.

Consedine, Robert (1995), 'Parallel Treaty Workshops'. (This paper was prepared in consultation with Irihapeti Ramsden, Ngai Tahu/Rangitane.)

Consedine, Robert (1997), Canada/Scotland Diary.

Theses and Other Publications

Court of Appeal of New Zealand (2003), *Ngati Apa, Ngati Koata, & Ors v. Ki Te Tau Ihu Trust & Ors [2003] NZCA 117* (19 June 2003) CA 173/01.

Cowie, Dean (1994), *To Do All The Good I Can: Robert FitzRoy, Governor of New Zealand 1843–1845*, Auckland University.

Department of Maori Studies, Massey University (1997), *Te Kawenata o Waitangi: The Treaty of Waitangi in New Zealand Society*, Study Guide One, Palmerston North.

Durie, E.T. (1996), *Will the Settlers Settle? Cultural Conciliation and Law*, F W Guest Memorial Lecture, Otago Law Review, Dunedin.

Jones, Alison (1999), *Difference and Desire: Dividing Classrooms by Ethnicity*, Auckland University.

Millar, Ruth (1995), *An Investigation into Students' Perceptions of the Successful Aspects of 'Waitangi Workshops'*, Christchurch College of Education, Christchurch.

Murphy, Nigel (2002), *The Poll-tax in New Zealand*, A Research Paper Commissioned by the New Zealand Chinese Association, Office of Ethnic Affairs, Wellington.

Ramsden, Irihapeti Merenia (2002), *Cultural Safety and Nursing Education in Aotearoa and Te Waipounamu*, Victoria University of Wellington.

Tomas, Nin and Kerensa Johnston (2003), *Ask That Taniwha, Who Owns the Foreshore and Seabed of Aotearoa?*, Faculty of Law, University of Auckland.

Websites

www.aaf.gov.bc.ca/aaf/treaty/treaty Ministry of Aboriginal Affairs, Province of British Columbia: *Treaty Negotiations in British Columbia* and *The Nisga'a Final Agreement in Brief* (1998).

www.aboriginalcanaca.com/firstnation/dirfunb.htm Lee Cohen *Miingignoti-Keteaoag Legal Issues* (1997).

www.aiatsis.gov.au/research/dp8/genocide.htm Colin Tatz, *Genocide in Australia*, AIATSIS Research Discussion Paper No. 8, Australian Institute of Aboriginal and Torres Strait Islander Studies, GPO Box 553, Canberra (2000).

www.armenian-genocide.org/genocide.html Rouben Paul Adalian, *Armenian Genocide*, Armenian National Institute, Washington DC, (1999).

www.atsic.gov.au Aboriginal and Torres Strait Islander Commission (ATSIC) Council for Aboriginal Reconciliation, Australia (2000).

www.atsic.gov.ac Aboriginal and Torres Strait Islander Commission (ATSIC) Council for Aboriginal Reconciliation, *Delgamuukw* v. *British Columbia* (1997).

www.austlii.edu.au/au/spec *Bringing Them Home: Report of the National Inquiry into the Separation of Aboriginal and Torres Strait Islander Children from Their Families* (1997).

www.bctreaty.net *Negotiation Update*, BC Treaty Commission, Vancouver.

www.bctreaty.net/miscellany/trbk=issues.html (Aboriginal Rights and Title/Self-government 2000).

www.bigcities.govt.nz/2001report A. C. Neilson, *Quality of Life Project – 2001 Report*. Accessed 5 October 2004.

http://bullsburning.itgo.com/essays/NCPCR2001.htm Tony Castanha, *Address* on the Revocation of the Papal Bull "Inter Cetera", National Conference on Peacemaking and Conflict Resolution 2001, George Mason University, Fairfax, Virginia (2001). Accessed 8 August 2004.

www.cstc.bc.ca/treaty/delgmkwsmry.html *Delgamuukw* v. *British Columbia* (2000).

http://dogwoodinitiative.org/in_the_news/archives/00540.html Will Horter, Paper, *Native Anger about to Catch Fire*, 18 June 2004. Accessed 25 August 2004.

www.emigratenz.org/unemployment-june-2004.html *Employment New Zealand*, Statistics New Zealand, June 2004. Accessed 4 October 2004.

www.ero.govt.nz/Publications/pubs2002/Kura.htm Education Review Office, Te Tari Arotake Matauranga, *The Performance of Kura Kaupapa Maori*, June 2002, Wellington.

www.ethnicaffairs.govt.nz Rt Hon Helen Clark Prime Minister, *Address to Chinese New Year Celebration*, 12 February 2002. Accessed 27 September 2004.

www.executive.govt.nz/budget2000/gaps-table NZ Government Executive, *Closing the Gaps*, Budget 2000. Accessed 7 November 2000.

www.freerepublic.com/focus/f-news/1211696/posts Francis Till, *New Zealand: Easiest Place in the World to do Business*, National Business Review (10 September 2004). Accessed 4 October 2004.

www.greens.org.nz/searchdocs/PR7414.html (4 May 2004), Jeanette Fitzsimons MP, *Green MPs to greet Hikoi at Parliament*. Accessed 10 August 2004.

http://ili.nativeweb.org/dovision.html *Declaration of Vision: Toward The Next 500 Years*, From The Gathering of the 1003 United Indigenous Peoples at the Parliament of the World's Religions, Chicago, Illinois (1994). Accessed 22 March 2004.

http://ili.nativeweb.org/ricb.html Valerie Taliman, *Revoke the Inter Cetera Bull*, (1994). Accessed 7 March 2004.

www.kohanga.ac.nz Te Kohanga Reo National Trust website.

www.labour.org.nz He Putahitanga Hou—Labour on Maori Development (1999).

www.labour.org.nz/labour_team/mps/mps/trevor_mallard/speeches Trevor Mallard, speech, *We Are All New Zealanders*, Stout Research Centre, Victoria University, 28 July 2004. Accessed 30 September 2004.

www.minedu.govt.nz/web/document/document_page.cfm Briefing for the incoming Minister of Education (1999).

www.minedu.govt.nz/index Ministry of Education, Kohanga Reo Statistics, 1 July 2003.

www.minedu.govt.nz/goto/tertiaryanalysis Ministry of Education, *Maori in Tertiary Education*, April 2004.

www.minpac.govt.nz/publications/newsletters Rt Hon Helen Clark Prime Minister, *Speech at Samoa's 40th Anniversary of Independence*, 3 June 2002. Accessed 2 October 2004.

www.mtholyoke.edu/org/wsar/intro.htm James Baldwin, *What is White Privilege?*, 2002. Accessed 15 March 2004.

www.national.org.nz/speech Don Brash, *Nationhood – Don Brash Speech Orewa Rotary Club* (27 January 2004). Accessed 30 January 2004.

www.nationalcatholicreporter.org, *National Catholic Reporter*, 19 December 1997, 2 June 2000, 27 October 2000.

www.ngaitahu.iwi.nz/office-claims-settlement.html Te Runanga o Ngai Tahu, The Deed of Settlement. Accessed 15 August 2004.

www.ngaitahuproperty.co.nz Ngai Tahu Property Ltd website.

www.nzherald.co.nz Rt Hon Helen Clark Prime Minister, *Clark Says Sorry to Gays* 6 June 2002. Accessed 2 October 2004. Waitangi Day: Next Year will be different, 7 February 2004.

www.ots.govt.nz Office of Treaty Settlements, NZ Government, Wellington.

www.regdev.govt.nz/conferences/2003/solomon/ Mark Solomon, *Collaboration for Economic Growth*, Speech to Regional Development Conference 24-26 September 2003. Accessed 25 August 2004.

www.sgc.gc.ca/epub/abocor/e199214/e199614.htm Carol LaPrairie, *Examining Aboriginal Corrections in Canada* (1999).

www.thetyee.ca/thindex.htm The Tyee website.

www.tokm.co.nz/allocation/history-timeline.htm Timeline, Te Ohu Kai Moana. Accessed 27 September 2004.

www.tokm.co.nz Te Ohu Kai Moana, Treaty of Waitangi Fisheries Commission, Wellington.

www.tpk.govt.nz/publications/subject/default.asp#gov Te Puni Kokiri, New Zealand Government, Wellington.

www.transalliancesociety.org/advocacy/individual.html *Aboriginal Poverty Law Manual* (2002). Accessed 29 September 2004.

www.treatyofwaitangi.govt.nz *The Treaty of Waitangi* (2004). Accessed on 13 September 2004.

http://twm.co.nz/nzprivn.htm Brian Gaynor, *We Now Know Who Owns New Zealand*, 2 October 1999. Accessed on 4 October 2004.

http://twm.co.nz/Msoln Win.html Professor Whatarangi Winiata, *Reducing the Socio-Economic Disparities in Housing, Employment, Health & Education*, 8 December 1998. Accessed on 4 October 2004.

www.vuw.ac.nz/inst-policy-studies Building the Constitution Conference, Wellington (2000).

www.waitangi-tribunal.govt.nz/news/temanutukutuku Waitangi Tribunal, *Te Manutukutuku* newsletters, Wellington.

www.ualberta.ca/~pimohte/suicide.html Glen Coulthard, *Colonization, Indian Policy, Suicide, and Aboriginal Peoples* (1999). Accessed 29 September 2004.

www.vatican.va/roman curia/congregations/cfaith/documents/ rc con cfaith doc 20000307 memory-reconc-itc-en.html Joseph Cardinal Ratzinger, International Theological Association, Vatican (1999).

INDEX